THE CEREMONY OF THE GRAIL

About the Author

One of the most respected writers and teachers in the occult field today, John Michael Greer has written more than fifty books on esoteric traditions, nature spirituality, and the future of industrial society. An initiate in Druidic, Hermetic, and Masonic lineages, he served for twelve years as Grand Archdruid of the Ancient Order of Druids in America (AODA). He lives in Rhode Island with his wife Sara. He can be found online at www.EcoSophia.net.

JOHN MICHAEL GREER

THE CEREMONY OF THE GRAIL

LLEWELLYN PUBLICATIONS
WOODBURY, MINNESOTA

ANCIENT MYSTERIES, GNOSTIC HERESIES, AND THE LOST RITUALS OF FREEMASONRY

FIRST EDITION
First Printing, 2022

Book design by Samantha Peterson
Cover design by Shannon McKuhen
Interior art by Llewellyn Art Department

Llewellyn Publications is a registered trademark of Llewellyn Worldwide Ltd.

Library of Congress Cataloging-in-Publication Data (Pending)
ISBN: 978-0-7387-5950-0

Llewellyn Publications
A Division of Llewellyn Worldwide Ltd.
2143 Wooddale Drive
Woodbury, MN 55125-2989
www.llewellyn.com

Printed in the United States of America

Other Books by John Michael Greer

Atlantis

The Celtic Golden Dawn

Circles of Power

The Coelbren Alphabet

Earth Divination: Earth Magic

Elementary Treatise of Occult Science

Encyclopedia of Natural Magic

The Golden Dawn

Inside a Magical Lodge

Monsters

Natural Magic

The New Encyclopedia of the Occult

Paths of Wisdom

The Secret of the Temple

Secrets of the Lost Symbol

The UFO Phenomenon

CONTENTS

CONTENTS

INTRODUCTION

I began writing this book several months after the publication of *The Secret of the Temple: Earth Energies, Sacred Geometry, and the Lost Keys of Freemasonry.* Its genesis, however, began well before the prolonged course of research and reflection that led to that earlier book. I first read of the Holy Grail in retellings of the Arthurian legend meant for children, which abounded in public libraries when I was young. Already in those earliest encounters I wondered about the motif of the Waste Land, the region of ecological devastation that surrounded the Grail Castle in the legends, which could only be healed if a wandering knight reached the castle, saw the Grail, and asked the right question.

Growing up in the 1960s and 1970s, when the state of the environment was a constant theme of news stories and popular media alike, that imagery seemed relevant. As I grew up and began to revisit the old legends with eyes increasingly attuned to the lessons of ecology and history, I began to wonder whether the Waste Land of legend had been an actual place, the devastation it suffered a real event—or series of events—located somewhere in the history or prehistory of our species. By the late 1980s those questions led me to the writings of Jessie Weston, whose groundbreaking studies of the origins of the Grail legend gave me crucial clues. By that time, however, my own research had taken me in a different direction, toward glimpses of a forgotten archaic technology embodied in ancient temples and medieval churches that boosted agricultural productivity using natural energies.

That research eventually led to the writing of *The Secret of the Temple*. While I worked on that book, however, it became clear to me that the old legends of the Waste Land and the Holy Grail had profound connections to the temple technology, on the one hand, and to a broader and equally fascinating range of archaic beliefs and practices on the other. I included some of what I found in that earlier book, but there turned out to be much more—and Jessie Weston, once again, proved to be the most useful guide into the ancient secrets and tangled historical events that surrounded the Grail legend.

At the heart of Weston's own understanding of the Grail was the recognition that the accounts of that mysterious object in the earliest medieval romances on the subject were more or less garbled descriptions of a ceremony of initiation. That ceremony, she argued, had parallels all over the world, but its specific form traced its descent from the rituals of the ancient Greek Mysteries, which spread across the Roman world in the heyday of the Empire and survived in isolated corners of western Europe long after Rome fell. In her earlier writings on the subject, she traced the ceremony of the Grail to the mountains of Wales where, she believed, it had lingered into the Middle Ages before going extinct. In her last book on the subject, *From Ritual to Romance*, her views had shifted dramatically: she traced the hiding place of the Grail ceremony to the isolated region where England and Scotland border each other, and she stated that the ceremony had not gone extinct at all, but was still being practiced in her time.

Weston's theory about the origins of the Grail legend were widely accepted in her own time. After the Second World War, however, as academic prejudices against occult traditions hardened, it was roundly ignored, and it remains largely ignored today. Nonetheless, the evidence that Weston unearthed remains just as important and relevant as it ever was, and following her trail in the light of another century of historical research looked like a worthwhile project. It ended up leading me in plenty of unexpected directions because the Grail legends—and especially the *Elucidation*, the enigmatic Grail narrative that was central to Weston's own research—turned out to offer an unexpected window back thousands of years into the lost world of megalithic Europe, and they cast a great deal of light on a number of strange customs surviving from ancient times, including some of the roots of the temple technology discussed in *The Secret of the Temple*.

Readers should be aware, however, that the investigation chronicled in this book is highly speculative in places. That cannot be avoided. I have tried to tease out, from fragmentary traces in history, legend, and myth, all that can be known today of a ritual that was guarded for generations by small groups of people whose lives would have been forfeit if their secret was discovered. That ritual in its long-lost original form was linked to archaic teachings in which the old temple technology mingled with daring speculations about the shape of history and ancient techniques that attempted to conquer death itself.

Later, in Greek and Roman times, this tradition gave rise to the rites of the ancient Mysteries. After the rise of Christianity and the coming of the Middle Ages, it endured in simplified forms as folk customs in isolated regions, while a more complete version was put into practice by medieval heretics. With the coming of the early modern period, it played a role in the rise of Freemasonry, and in the early twentieth century it flourished again briefly as the secret inner circle of one of the most vibrant occult movements of the time. The ritual itself may still exist. Certainly, though, enough can be known of it from the varied traces it has left through time to enable it to be reconstructed in outline.

In the course of this investigation I have received a great deal of help from certain institutions and individuals, which I am glad to acknowledge here. Much of the research that made this book possible took place in Masonic libraries, especially those of the United Grand Lodge of England in London and the Grand Lodge of Rhode Island in East Providence; in the archives of the Order of Bards Ovates and Druids in Lewes, England; in Weaver Library of the East Providence public library system; and in the International Archive for the Preservation of Spiritualist and Occult Periodicals, online at www.iapsop.com. The staff of all these institutions have been unfailingly helpful. I would also like to thank Carl Hood Jr. and Robert Mathiesen for helpful suggestions and unexpected bits of data, and my wife Sara for her interest and enthusiasm all through the quest. My thanks go with all.

PROLOGUE IN ANTIQUITY

Pale stars wink into being overhead as you follow your guide through the village to the hall at its center. The rising wind carries the salty tang of ocean and the harsh, clean scent of winter's first snow on its way. Off past the homes and barns of your people, you glimpse fields left bare and brown by the harvest, forest rising dark beyond them, an edge of light beyond the wall of trees heralding the rising moon. Cattle, sheep, and swine have been driven indoors for the night, and for good reason: the howl of a wolf sounds long and lonely in the distance, raising the small hairs on your neck.

It is not the wolf's cry that has your heart thudding, though.

Outside the great western door of the hall, others wait: boys and girls of the village, each guided by an elder of their kin. Like you, they wear plain homespun garments. The tunics and trousers of the boys are plain brown wool; the dresses of the girls show the muted colors of woodland dyes. Like you, they are hushed, excited, expectant.

Time passes, and you wait. The wolf howls again, further off. The moon rises.

The sound of the doors being unbarred comes so suddenly that it makes you jump. A moment later, the doors open. Inside, you see the golden light of flames in the open central hearth. Silhouetted against the glow, the figure of the old priestess is pure darkness. She gestures, welcoming you in. You draw in a shaken breath and go forward with the others.

Others wait in the hall: village elders in robes of white wool, the old men on one side of the hall, the old women on the other. Their faces look unhuman in the flickering light and the wood smoke, like the carved wooden faces of the gods in the grove where your people make their offerings. It seems impossible that this one is your grandmother and that one taught you how to follow tracks in the forest. Have they not always been here, seated in silence?

Your guide leads you around the central hearth: boys going to the men's side and girls to the women's. The old priestess waits until all the children are in place, then walks to the hall's eastern end, where a carved wooden chair has been set. She sits and gestures, inviting you to sit as well. You settle on the familiar packed-earth floor. Already, young as you are, you have been in the hall more times than you can count. Feasts, ceremonies, discussions and debates among the village folk—all have taken place around this hearth, beneath those great oaken rafters. Even so, a strangeness gathers along with the smoke.

You know what brings the strangeness. Like the other children, like all the children of your people for years beyond counting, you have come to hear a story.

Growing up in the village, you have watched the dances at midsummer, the whirling circle of young men with their flashing swords, the green-clad figure falling to the ground as though dead, only to be revived with a drink from a brightly painted bowl. You have taken such small parts as children are permitted in the rituals in the grove and the fields, and you have watched in awe as processions went to the green mound on the hill where the greatest and most secret ceremonies are worked. All of it has to do with a story—not one of the little stories you learned at your grandmother's knee when you were smaller, or the middle stories that traveling bards bring from distant villages, but a great story, the greatest of all stories, which came over the sea long ages ago and which contains the highest and deepest wisdom your people know.

It is a story about life and death: you already know that much. Your own life and death are part of it, and so are the lives and deaths of those people in your village, one in each generation, who are chosen to go into the green mound and remain there, passing beyond life and death in some sense that is hidden from you. Yet it also embraces the life and death of the grain in the fields that sustains your life, and the life and death of your village and your people, and the lives and deaths of whole ages of the world. You have heard hints and whispers about what else it might teach, and your heart thuds within you as you face the old priestess in her wooden chair, expectant.

Once you hear the story, and then learn it by heart, you will be part of the village and part of your people in a way that not even being born there can accomplish. Once you hear it, and then learn it by heart, you will be able to join in the dances, take other parts in the rituals in the grove and the fields, go with the processions to the mound, and be prepared to learn the highest and deepest wisdom, the wisdom that came across the sea. Maybe someday you will be an elder, too, and will sit in silence as grandchildren of your own gather in hushed expectancy.

First, though, you must hear the story.

We don't know the story that was told there, and in countless other villages across the Old World in those ancient times. All we have are fragments of it, and piecing together those fragments is a task that has kept scholars busy for more than two centuries.

Oral tradition is far more effective as a means of preserving information than most people nowadays realize. Poetry and narrative, which we use today for entertainment, were originally sophisticated technologies of information storage and retrieval. Think of the nursery rhymes and children's songs you grew up with. Most people, given the opening words of one of these they learned early on, instantly remember the rest of it, and often have to make an effort not to repeat it in the singsong tones they used in childhood. Now imagine what you could do if you had trained your mind since infancy to make use of that same ability, and your entire education consisted of memorizing long narratives in verse.

Storytelling was an important form of information storage and transmission in the days before writing was invented, and it remained important even after the first scribes learned to make marks on clay tablets or papyrus sheets to represent words. Like every other human technology, from axes and temples to computers and spacecraft, the technology of storytelling went through periods of innovation and stagnation. By the time those first scribes took the time to write down stories, however, storytelling was a mature technology, and skilled practitioners could store impressive amounts of data by creating and remembering stories.

The secret to using storytelling as a means of information storage and transfer is that it is a two-step process. First, preferably in childhood, you learn the stories word for word, taking advantage of the keen memory for detail and the love of repetition most children have. Then, later on, you learn the meaning—or, rather, the meanings.[1] It is quite common for stories to encode multiple meanings. Jewish mystical lore, for example, holds that every verse of the Old Testament contains four distinct meanings, of which the literal meaning is the least important.

A very simple example of the way a story can convey unexpected meaning is found in "The Strange Musician," one of the many German folktales collected by Jacob and Wilhelm Grimm. At first glance it's a very odd story. A fiddler goes walking through the woods, playing as he goes. He meets a wolf, a fox, and a hare, all of whom want to learn music from him, and he traps each of them in a bizarre way—he wedges the wolf's paws in a split tree trunk, stretches the fox between two saplings, and gets the hare to run around a tree with a cord tied to him until the cord binds the hare to the trunk. The animals get loose and come after the fiddler, but in the meantime he meets a woodcutter, who defends him from the animals with his axe, so the animals go away disappointed.[2]

What does this strange tale communicate? The right way to string a fiddle with old-fashioned gut strings, of the sort that musicians used in earlier times. Gut strings didn't come cut to length as modern strings do, so they required a different way of handling. First of all, you wedge one end of the string in the fiddle's tailpiece. Next, you stretch the string gently out toward the head. Then you wrap it around the key and tighten it, and only after that do you cut the string. Doubtless, generations of children learned this tale as part of their early musical education in medieval Germany.

---

1. This mode of learning was still standard among African tribal peoples well into the twentieth century; see de Santillana and von Dechend, *Hamlet's Mill*, 53–55.

2. I am indebted to Lambert, *The Gnostic Notebook*, for my introduction to this charming folktale.

Effective though it is, however, oral tradition has a weakness, and it's visible in the story just discussed. By the time the story got to the Brothers Grimm, musicians had purchased pre-cut strings for a long time; the habits needed to handle old-fashioned gut strings had dropped out of use, and the meaning of the tale was lost. Break the chain of transmission so that no one passes on the inner meaning of those colorful verses: that's how you end an oral tradition. The stories themselves will be saved here and there, but once the meanings are lost, the stories themselves begin to drift. Details are forgotten or replaced by similar details from other stories; sometimes entire stories are reduced to little fragments, preserved like flies in amber in other tales. Time passes and stories go from land to land; poets and playwrights take up ancient tales and rewrite them to fit their own creative visions, and even when the results are great literature—and they often are—the lost tradition behind it all fades further and further from sight, hidden like the castle in the fairy tale behind a great wild hedge of thorns.

Sometimes, however, it becomes possible to see past the thorns to the castle inside it—to glimpse the shape of the original narrative and to be able to make a first guess at the secrets it once concealed. That happens most often when someone notices that the fragments of an ancient tale preserved in some later setting match up in unexpected ways with fragments from another source. Our age of specialization makes that harder than it has to be, but there's another side to that coin, for the labors of specialist scholars very often turn up exactly those details that can be assembled, like pieces in a jigsaw puzzle, by those who are prepared to take a broader view.

This book attempts to fit together pieces of an ancient tradition in exactly this way. Those pieces come from what will seem, at first glance, like a wild gallimaufry of sources. At first glance, certainly, there's no obvious reason to link together the origins of Freemasonry with the medieval stories surrounding Merlin, the archetypal enchanter of Arthurian legend, much less to connect any of these to the Holy Grail, a forgotten Gnostic heresy, the precession of the equinoxes, the labors of nineteenth-century philologists, the ancient Greek Mysteries, the rise and fall of megalithic societies in prehistory, or the invention of modern fantasy fiction. Yet the pieces fit together, and not in a random way. In each case, furthermore, a little careful research is enough to uncover connections in space and time that make sense of the emerging picture and fit it into its broader historical context.

Much of the picture that this book sets out to reassemble was first pieced together in modern times by a pioneering independent scholar named Jessie Weston, who was active in the early decades of the twentieth century. Working on her own, without the help of a university or any other institution, she published a series of books on the Arthurian legends, beginning with a translation of the Grail romance *Parzival* in 1897 and ending with a radical reinterpretation of the Grail legend, *From Ritual to Romance*, in 1920. With the help of another century of specialist research, it is possible to go even further than she did, to connect the Grail legend backward into the mists of megalithic prehistory and forward into the secretive underground of esoteric traditions in the early modern era and the modern era.

To make sense of the results, it is necessary to start where she did: with the legends surrounding the figure of King Arthur and that mysterious object, the Grail. Like the children waiting expectantly in that ancient longhouse, we begin with a story.

PART ONE
THE GRAIL RIDDLE

FROM RITUAL
TO ROMANCE

The rise of the Arthurian legends is among the most remarkable events in the history of world literature. All through the chaotic years of the Dark Ages, folktales about a war leader from the last days of Roman Britain were remembered and retold among the peoples of Wales and Brittany, two closely related Celtic countries later incorporated in the modern nations of Great Britain and France, respectively. Beginning around 1050, as the waves of chaos finally ebbed and a new feudal aristocracy rose to power across western Europe, Welsh and Breton storytellers found new audiences for their ancient tales. In the halls of knights and barons, eager listeners gathered around to hear colorful narratives of war, adventure, and love. Over the years that followed, the tough and ruthless Roman-British general Artorius was reworked into the noble King Arthur, the cavalrymen whose charges shattered the Saxon lines at the battle of Mount Badon got decked out in the trappings of medieval knights, and one of the world's great cycles of legend and literature came into being.

During that first bright springtime of Arthurian legend, dozens of old stories that originally had nothing to do with Artorius and his battles against the Saxon invaders got swept up in the excitement and turned into raw material for more stories about King Arthur and his knights. As far as anyone knows, for example, Merlin originally had nothing to do with King Arthur. The most important of the several historical figures behind the legend of Merlin, Myrddin Wyllt, lived in southern Scotland a century after Artorius and was present at a famous battle there, which we will discuss later on. Sir Tristram, to give another example, was apparently a historical figure of a generation or two after the time of Artorius; his original name was Drustans, and his grave in Cornwall has been found by archaeologists.

Yet there were other, deeper layers behind the stories of Artorius and their transmutations into the romances of King Arthur, as there are behind every great cycle of legend. Stories of this kind inevitably draw on archetypal patterns in the deep places of the mind, the raw material of religion and myth. The great English poet William Blake was among those who grasped this inner secret of the Arthurian legend. In an 1809 essay he wrote, "The giant Albion, was patriarch of the Atlantic; he is the Atlas of the Greeks, one of those the Greeks called Titans. The stories of Arthur are the acts of Albion, applied to a prince of the fifth century."[3] Go back far enough behind the story, in other words, and you encounter mythology, the doings of gods and titans. Merlin was among the figures who had a mythological dimension; behind the figure of Myrddin Wyllt, as I have pointed out elsewhere, was an ancient Celtic god whose myths and attributes contributed a great deal to the later figure of legend.[4]

The tale central to this book is another story that was not originally part of the story of King Arthur and has a potent mythological dimension behind its surface. It started out, as we will see, in the depths of antiquity, and in the usual way, drew on a galaxy of half-forgotten myths and deities. It swept up a range of historical figures in its current, and it finally found its way into the imaginary landscape of Arthurian legend in the same way as Merlin and Sir Tristram. This is the story of the Holy Grail.

That story has become so confused in recent centuries, and it will be so important to the investigation of this book, that a summary of the basic story in its original form is worth including here. In the oldest Grail stories, a knight on his way through wild and desolate country stops at a mysterious castle. The

---

3. Ashe, *Camelot and the Vision of Albion*, 14.

4. Greer, *The Mysteries of Merlin*.

lord of the castle, the Fisher King or Rich Fisherman, appears as an old man who is crippled by a wound in the genitals—euphemistically, the stories usually say he has been wounded in the thighs. He can take many shapes and many disguises, and he seems to be, in some sense, caught between life and death.

He and his servants welcome the knight and offer him hospitality. That evening at supper, in perfect silence, a procession of figures moves past: first, a squire carrying a spear upright, with three drops of blood trickling from the spear's point; after him, two more youths carrying candlesticks with lit candles in them; and finally, a maiden carrying the Grail. If the knight asks the Fisher King the right question at this point, the Fisher King will be healed of his wound, the land will be freed from the curse that makes it desolate, and the knight himself will become the next keeper of the Grail. If he fails to do so, he will go to sleep that night, and when he wakes the next morning, the castle will be empty, with no trace of the Fisher King or the Grail. When he leaves the castle, it will vanish behind him. It will take the knight years of searching to find it again, ask the question, and bring healing to the king and the land.

The oldest surviving version of this strange tale is *Perceval ou le Conte du Graal* (*Perceval, the Story of the Grail*) by Chrétien de Troyes, which was written sometime around 1180. Chrétien never finished his story, and most scholars today assume that he died before completing it. In the decades that followed, three other French authors wrote stories that pick up where Chrétien left off. These *Continuations* differ from Chrétien's version of the story, and from each other as well. Meanwhile, other writers got into the act with Grail stories of their own, and all these disagree with Chrétien, the *Continuations*, and one another. The one thing all of them have in common is the Grail.

What is the Grail? That very question is the one that has to be asked at the Fisher King's castle in some versions of the Grail legend. There is not a simple, straightforward answer. The word *grail* was originally spelled *gradal* or *grasal*, and in early medieval French it meant a large, flat serving dish, of the kind that was used to serve fish at banquets.[5] Before the Grail legend became famous, *gradal* was an unusual word, found only here and there in surviving medieval documents; it was much more common in the south of France than in the

---

5. Carey, *Ireland and the Grail*, 11.

north.[6] Once the legend made the word famous, it stopped being used for anything else but *the* Grail, though some regional dialects of French still use words descended from *gradal* for serving dishes of various kinds.[7]

In Chrétien's version of the Grail story, accordingly, the Grail is a platter, but it didn't stay that way for long. Twenty years after he wrote, the German poet-knight Wolfram von Eschenbach, whose *Parzival* is one of the finest of the Grail legends, made the Grail into a magical green stone, which he calls "the perfection of paradise...which surpasses all earthly perfection."[8] He gives the stone a strange name, Lapsit Exillas, which has a straightforward meaning in Latin—*lapsit ex illas* means "he, she, or it fell from among them"—but has also been interpreted in a variety of different ways: as *lapis ex caelis*, "a stone from heaven," and as *lapis exilis*, "stone of exile," among others.[9]

Robert de Boron's *Joseph d'Arimathie*, written just a few years after *Parzival*, describes the Grail as a platter—but in Robert's version it had become the platter from which Jesus and his apostles ate the Last Supper. Most of the later authors of Grail stories turn the Grail into a cup, usually the cup that Jesus drank from during the Last Supper, but one of the German Grail romances that follows in Wolfram's footsteps claims that the Grail is an emerald that fell from the crown of Lucifer when that former archangel was flung down out of heaven, while the Welsh Grail story *Peredur* replaces the Grail entirely with a platter bearing a human head! One of the French Grail stories memorably sums up the confusion by noting that the Grail has five forms, of which the fifth is secret—but the author fails to mention what any of those forms are.

Associated with the Grail in the early stories are a standard set of people and places. The Fisher King and the questing knight are two of the people. There are many others, including a frightfully ugly maiden who knows all the secrets of the Grail and can reveal them to the questing knight, and a beautiful maiden who carries the Grail in the ceremony. Among the places, two are more important than the others. The first is the Chapel Perilous, a chapel in

---

6. Carey, *Ireland and the Grail*, 12.

7. Barber, *The Holy Grail*, 95–96.

8. Von Eschenbach, *Parzival*, 129.

9. The first word should properly be *lapsavit*, but this was routinely contracted to *lapsit* in poetry.

the midst of a graveyard where a dead knight lies on a stone platform between candles. Here the questing knight must keep vigil before approaching the Grail. The second is the castle of the Fisher King itself, which has many names in the legends. In the French versions it is often called Carbonek, but the German legends call it Muntsalväsche, a bit of neatly garbled Germanified French that can mean both "the Wild Mountain" and the "Mountain of Salvation."

In all its forms, the Grail is seen as a source of abundance, and in many of them it miraculously causes food to appear. Most Grail romances place the castle of the Grail in the midst of the Waste Land, a realm that was once rich but is now stricken with a terrible curse and lies barren and desolate. In many of the legends, the landscape of the Waste Land bears signs that, to a modern eye, suggest ecological catastrophe. The *Elucidation*, which has one of the strangest and most detailed accounts of the Waste Land, describes it in this way:

> The kingdom was laid waste so that no tree bore leaves. The mead-
> ows and the flowers withered and the waters dried up.[10]

This curious relation to environmental abundance and devastation is far from the only strange and secret thing associated with the Grail. Beginning with the earliest surviving versions of the legend, in fact, the Grail is wrapped in secrets.[11] In Chrétien's *Perceval*, for example, the Grail seeker Perceval is counseled by a holy hermit, who teaches him a prayer that uses secret names of Christ which, he explains to the knight, should never be spoken aloud except at times of grave danger. (Of course, Chrétien is careful not to give these names himself.) In most of the other medieval Grail legends, similarly, there are constant references to the secrets of the Grail, "which no man can hear without shivering and trembling, changing color and going pale with fear."[12] Here is a typical passage from *Joseph d'Arimathie* by Robert de Boron:

---

10. See appendix 1: The *Elucidation*.

11. References to secrets of the Grail are helpfully summarized in Barber, *The Holy Grail*, 161–66. Ironically, Barber then attempts to insist that the Grail is not associated with secrets of any kind.

12. Barber, *The Holy Grail*, 163.

Then Jesus spoke some other words to Joseph which I dare not tell you—nor could I, even if I wanted to, if I did not have the high book in which they were written: and that is the creed of the great mystery of the Grail.[13]

Passages like this appear all through the Grail legends. The medieval sources claim over and over again that the Grail is said to embody a tremendous and terrifying secret, which can be passed on to others only under very specific conditions, and which exposes those who know it to considerable danger.

◇

Talk about hidden prayers and secret teachings was not a casual matter during the Middle Ages, and especially not during the period when the original Grail romances were written. In western Europe in those years, the Roman Catholic church was struggling to maintain its spiritual monopoly against a rising tide of religious dissidence. The most influential of the rival movements was the Cathars, or "Pure Ones." Their enemies called them the Albigensians, "those people from Albi," after the town in southern France where they established their first significant presence around 1030.

That first foundation was apparently followed by an influx of heretical ideas and inspirations from a different source. During the Crusades, which began in 1096, European knights conquered an area in the Middle East roughly where Israel is located today. Though it was founded in a frenzy of religious zealotry, the Crusader Kingdom of Jerusalem quickly became a portal through which the learning and technology of the much more literate and civilized Arab world found its way northwest to Europe. The Knights Templar, an order of warrior monks founded to help defend the Kingdom of Jerusalem, took a leading role in bringing Arab learning back to Europe. Later on, rumors spread that the Templars had brought back something more secret—the teachings of one of the forbidden Gnostic sects.

The Gnostics, as most people know nowadays, were heretical Christian groups active in ancient times that saw *gnosis*—direct personal experience of spiritual realities—as the key to salvation, instead of faith in the dogmas of an

---

13. Barber, *The Holy Grail*, 42.

established church. While the mainstream churches denounced the Gnostics in shrill language and executed as many of them as they could catch, the Gnostics themselves claimed that theirs was the original Christian faith and that the mainstream churches had veered away from the truths revealed by Jesus. (At least one influential modern scholar of Christian origins has argued that the Gnostics were right.[14]) Despite savage persecution, several Gnostic sects still existed in the Middle Ages, and the heyday of the Grail was the period in which they experienced their last flowering before modern times.

The Cathar faith was the largest of the medieval Gnostic sects. Like many other Gnostics, but not all, the Cathars believed that there are two gods in the cosmos, one good and one evil, and argued that the material world is the creation of the evil god, a prison of matter in which souls are trapped. In their theology, Jesus was an emissary of the good god, and he had descended from a world of light to reveal to human souls the way to escape the evil god's world and return to their true home. The Cathars had sacraments unknown to the Catholic church, including the *Consolamentum*, a ritual of purification and commitment that most believers received on their deathbeds, and they also had their own scriptures, of which one—*The Book of the Two Principles*—has survived to the present day.

While the Cathars began as wandering missionaries, they quickly won a widespread following in southern France, not least because they did a better job of living according to their beliefs than their Catholic rivals in that part of Europe. At first, Rome responded by flooding the area with missionaries of its own. When this did nothing to change the situation, the Catholic hierarchy panicked and turned to violence. In 1184 the Inquisition was founded to hunt down and execute Cathars—only later did it turn its attention to witches and Jews—and in 1209 the Pope proclaimed a crusade against the heretics and called on all good Catholic warriors to kill them. Forty years later, half the population of southern France was dead.

The history of the Cathars and the history of the Grail legend have the same location in space: as already noted, the word that became "grail" was mostly used in southern France, the area in which the Cathars flourished. The timeline is also identical. The first Arthurian stories began to find listeners among

---

14. Davies, *The Gospel of Thomas and Christian Wisdom*.

the French nobility something like twenty years after the first known Cathar congregation appeared in France. In 1125, when the Cathar movement was spreading rapidly, the chronicler William of Malmesbury commented on the abundance of Arthurian romances in his time.[15] The Grail's first documented appearance is in Chrétien de Troyes's *Perceval*, which was written in or around 1180, right around the time the Cathar movement reached its zenith, though there are a few references from other French writers that may have been a little earlier.[16]

Thereafter, Grail romances appeared in profusion for sixty years: Wolfram von Eschenbach's *Parzival* around 1210, Robert de Boron's Grail romances by 1215, the Vulgate Cycle (the source of the Grail story in Sir Thomas Malory's *Le Morte d'Arthur*) by 1240. Then, not long after the last Cathars were hunted down and slaughtered, the Grail romances stopped. After the awkwardly named Post-Vulgate Cycle, which appeared around 1250, the next known Grail romances appeared in the late fifteenth century.

Some scholars have argued, on the basis of these shared dates, that the Grail romances must have some connection to the Cathar movement. It's a plausible suggestion, and not just because of the way that the Grail and the Cathars overlap in time and place. Literacy in medieval Europe was largely restricted to a small, intellectual elite. Outside that elite, the mechanisms of oral transmission through storytelling were still very much in use—that is why, for example, instructions on how to string a fiddle were encoded in a German folktale, as discussed in the Prologue to this book. Thus, creating a vivid and memorable story to encode, in symbolic form, a heretical religious belief would have been a reasonable strategy at the time.

Certain details of the legends also support this theory. To begin with, one of the distinctive features of the Grail legend in its early forms is that the Grail is always carried by a woman. In medieval Catholicism, having a woman carry a sacred object was unthinkable—only the all-male priesthood was permitted to handle holy things—but the Cathars and other Gnostic sects allowed women as well as men to exercise priestly functions. References to secret teachings, prayers, and names of Jesus in the Grail legends also find ample echoes in the

---

15. Lacy and Ashe, *The Arthurian Handbook*, 69.

16. Carey, *Ireland and the Grail*, 271–75.

Gnostic tradition, which traditionally kept some teachings secret for those of advanced spiritual standing, and in later times kept its very existence secret in an attempt to stave off persecution. Yet, attempts to find specific details of Cathar theology and teachings in the Grail legend have come up short.

In my previous book *The Secret of the Temple*, I argued that one important part of what was hidden behind the glittering screen of the Grail legends was not theology but technology: an archaic folk technology, developed by trial and error over thousands of years, that improved agricultural yields by using properly designed structures as resonating chambers for certain natural energies. It is an odd fact that over much of the world, certain specific kinds of religious architecture are traditionally associated with agricultural and ecological abundance.

The Temple of Solomon at Jerusalem is one of many examples. Many passages in the *Talmud*, commentaries on the Jewish scriptures compiled in the centuries immediately after the Temple's final destruction, describe the sharply improved harvests that followed the Temple's construction by Solomon and its rebuilding by Zerrubabel and Ezra after the captivity in Babylon, and they note the equally sharp decrease in the fertility of the land near Jerusalem after the destruction of these two temples by the Babylonians and the Romans.

Similar passages can be found in the sacred lore of many other countries. My research into the tradition suggests that this folklore reflects the set of practices I have called the temple technology, or a related practice—found in countries as widely dispersed as Central America, Mesopotamia, and China—that made use of stair-stepped pyramids or "earth altars" for similar purposes. Modern scholars like to dismiss these traditions as mere legends. As I discuss at length in *The Secret of the Temple*, however, scientists in other fields have found evidence that certain natural energies—terrestrial magnetism, on the one hand, and low-intensity electromagnetic fields on the border between infrared and microwaves on the other—can be concentrated and directed by the simple methods available in ancient times, and they have measurable effects on crop fertility.

My theory is that ancient peoples first stumbled across these effects by accident in megalithic times, refined the methods of using them by trial and error through the centuries, and passed on the temple technology as a religious secret until recent times, when it was finally lost. The Grail, that mysterious object that could restore a devastated land to fertility and prosperity, a focus of tremendous secrets, was one of the ways that the temple technology was at once concealed and symbolized when it was reintroduced to Europe from the Middle East by the Knights Templar around the middle of the twelfth century.

No one in the twelfth century had any way to measure terrestrial magnetism or low-intensity microwaves, however, nor did any of the priests and loremasters of earlier times have any clearer idea of the nature of the energies they were using. What they knew was that if you built a temple or a church according to certain traditional standards and did certain things with it, improved crop yields would follow. Though there was nothing supernatural about the temple technology, it came to be understood in religious and magical terms because that was the only context its creators and transmitters had.

That meant, inevitably, that it would be caught up in the struggles between orthodoxy and heresy that convulsed twelfth- and thirteenth-century Europe. The guardians of the temple technology seem to have been able to keep the secret alive in the wake of those difficult years by finding a home for it in certain monasteries, notably Glastonbury Abbey in Britain. They also succeeded in transmitting some elements of it to stonemasons' guilds, especially but not only in Scotland. The bitter religious struggles of the sixteenth and seventeenth centuries, however, turned out to be one challenge too much for the temple technology. The dissolution of the monasteries in Britain and other Protestant countries and the imposition of strict religious orthodoxy on monasteries in Catholic countries made it impossible for the tradition to survive. After that, only an assortment of legends, together with a few scraps of surviving lore in the rituals of Freemasonry, preserved any trace of the secret lore that once made the fields flourish.

The links between the temple technology and medieval heresy that gave rise to the Grail tradition had an unexpected effect later on, however. They inspired one of the most thoughtful scholars of the Grail legend to glimpse something else that had become linked to the temple technology and to the stories of the Grail: a ritual of initiation descended from the mystery cults of the ancient world.

Jessie Laidlay Weston was born in 1850, the daughter of a successful tea merchant and his second wife. She wrote poetry from childhood on and took art classes, but like so many other people in the Victorian era, she was fascinated by the legends of King Arthur, and she ended up pursuing a career as a scholar of Arthurian literature. Like many people of her time, she was a devoted fan of Richard Wagner's operas. *Parsifal*, Wagner's version of the Grail legend, inevitably became one of her favorites as soon as it premiered in 1882, and it may well have influenced her choice of a career.

Weston was a significant figure in her time. At a time when few women received university educations, she studied at the Sorbonne in Paris and the University of Hildesheim in Germany, then settled in Bournemouth, England, where she spent the rest of her life. Her first published work, appropriately enough, was a 1894 translation of Wolfram von Eschenbach's Grail romance *Parzival*. She continued to publish on Arthurian legends and other medieval traditions throughout her long and busy life. Her last and most famous work, *From Ritual to Romance*, was also on the Grail legends; it was published in 1920, and she died in 1928.

While she was exploring the Arthurian legends, one of the great revolutions of the history of ideas was taking place around her. Until the eighteenth century, most European scholars knew practically nothing about the history and culture of the world outside of Europe. With the exception of the Jewish history included in the Bible, history for them began in Greece, passed from there to Rome, and thereafter fixated on the doings of European countries, noticing the rest of the world only when it did something that affected Europe. During the eighteenth century, that narrow focus broadened somewhat as the civilizations of Egypt, India, and China became impossible to ignore. In the second half of the nineteenth century, however, as the new science of anthropology hit its stride, the Eurocentric illusion shattered forever as the art and literature of cultures around the world finally came to the attention of European scholars.

One of the leading figures in that intellectual revolution was Sir James Frazer. At a time and place when ancient Greece and Rome were still idealized as the summits of civilization while people of color around the world were dismissed by respectable British thinkers as savages, he set out to show that there was no difference worth noticing between the two. His method was ingenious. He started from a single puzzling custom from Roman times—the rites surrounding the priests of the sacred grove of Nemi, north of Rome.

The priest of Nemi, who was the guardian of the grove, got the job by killing the previous priest, and he could expect to someday be killed and replaced in turn. In Roman times this office was always held by a runaway slave, who could not be forced to return to his master once he took office, and who remained safe in the grove so long as he could defeat anyone else who came to take the position from him. Frazer showed, however, that the tradition of Nemi reached back far into antiquity, when the men who held similar positions were not slaves but kings. He unpacked the entire tradition of Nemi one detail at a time, showing how every part of it had exact parallels in African, Asian, Native American, and pre-Christian European traditions.

Frazer's work on the subject, *The Golden Bough*, eventually filled twelve hefty volumes, and it left the comfortable certainties of his readers in shreds. He showed that ancient religions had focused with laser intensity not on moral goodness, the stock in trade of Victorian religion, but on sheer biological fertility. Life, not morality, was the keynote of the myths, customs, and ceremonies he explored. The creators and practitioners' goal was to participate in the cycle of the seasons that brought life and plenty after the barren months of winter. Having shown this, Frazer proceeded to demonstrate that this same focus on abundant fertility ran through the myths and traditions of ancient Greek and Roman antiquity, and it had left substantial traces in the narratives and symbols of Christianity itself.

One of the many things Frazer explored in his gigantic work was the way that myths and rituals intertwined. Until his time, scholars had paid very little attention to rituals, but he showed over and over again how details in a ritual could only be understood if you knew the myth that governed it, and details of a myth could only be understood if you knew the ritual that enacted it. In the wake of *The Golden Bough*, scholars in dozens of fields woke up to the importance of rituals in their subjects—and one of those scholars was Jessie Weston.

The Arthurian legends were ripe for the kind of analysis that she and other researchers brought to them. Some Arthurian tales, for example, center on a tradition all but identical to the one Frazer described, in which a knight guarded a magic well and its lady and fought all comers. Whoever defeated and killed the knight became the guardian of the well and the lover of the lady of the well in his place; the romance *Ywain*, another product of Chrétien de Troyes's busy pen, is a classic example of the type. All those black knights who stood guard at river crossings in Arthurian stories and fought everyone who tried to cross are a simplified version of the same story motif. Yet the most richly symbolic and ritualistic of all the Arthurian stories, and the one that most closely echoed Frazer's findings, was the legend of the Holy Grail.

By the time Weston began her studies, other scholars had already noticed that the earliest Grail romances seemed to be describing a ritual much like the ones Frazer explored in *The Golden Bough*. What set it apart to some extent was that it was a ritual of initiation. The entire sequence of events at the Grail Castle made sense once it was treated as an initiation ceremony: the knight, who filled the role of the candidate for initiation, was brought into a mysterious place difficult to locate, witnessed a procession of sacred objects, and then had to ask a specific question before the ceremony could proceed. The ritual, moreover, had the same meaning as many of the ceremonies Frazer explored: it was about the return of life and fertility to the Waste Land, an echo of the seasonal cycle on the grand scale.

In the early versions of the story, the Grail had nothing to do with moral virtue. It was a talisman of abundant life, and it only gradually absorbed elements of Christian symbolism and moral teaching. In its earliest forms, in fact, it was called the Rich Grail, not the Holy Grail. Only in the final years of the original tradition, in the Grail stories written just after the extermination of the Cathars, did the theme of fertility and the healing of the Waste Land fade out completely, to be replaced by a more conventional fixation on the Christian virtues—especially on chastity.

The difference in theme is marked by the replacement of one protagonist by another. The oldest surviving versions of the story feature Sir Perceval, who begins his quest as a brash young idiot and gradually ripens into a brave and chivalrous knight; Wolfram von Eschenbach's version of the tale, *Parzival*, describes the theme of the tale with fine precision as "a brave man slowly wise."[17] Perceval does become wise in the end, but he never becomes a saint.

One of the things Jessie Weston discovered in the course of her studies, however, was that Sir Perceval was not the original Grail knight. Hints and

---

17. Von Eschenbach, *Parzival*, 5.

scraps in surviving sources show that before the romances that give Perceval the starring role, there was an earlier series of Grail stories, now lost, that assigned that role to Sir Gawain, Arthur's nephew. Gawain is even less of a saint than Perceval, and he spends much of his time in the romances tumbling into bed with a substantial number of ladies. It is in the Grail romances that feature Gawain that the ritual elements are most evident.

The replacement for Gawain and Perceval in the later versions of the legend is Galahad, who is best described as a plaster statue dressed up as a knight. Christian mystics adore him. Nearly everyone else finds him an insufferable prig. Galahad never has an impure thought; he vanquishes every opponent through sheer moral goodness; he achieves the Grail almost without trying, then dies on the spot, and his soul is carried by angels straight to heaven. In the stories in which Galahad features, the curious ritual of initiation that appears to be linked with the Grail is erased, and what is put in its place is the ordinary communion ceremony of mainstream Christianity. In the later versions, furthermore, much is made of the claim that the Grail no longer exists on Earth, having been wafted away to heaven by angels or otherwise put out of the picture—a detail that does not appear anywhere in the earlier (and less Christian) versions of the legend.

Jessie Weston duly read and commented on the later Christianized versions of the Grail legends, but her main interest was always the earlier versions. As she began to correlate the Grail stories with the immense body of evidence brought to light by Sir James Frazer and the speculations of other Arthurian scholars, her focus narrowed in on the question of the original form of the legend. That brought complexities of its own because the earliest Grail romances that have survived all have their own versions of the story, which differ in important ways. Even before Weston went to work on the subject, scholars had already concluded that the romances that had survived to modern times were only a fraction of the total, and the original version was lost long ago.

There were good reasons for that conclusion. Before the invention of the printing press, books were rare and expensive, since making a copy involved sitting down and writing the whole thing out word for word with pen and ink. The more settled conditions of the later Middle Ages allowed many manuscripts from that period to be preserved, but the further back you go into the waning years of the Dark Ages, the fewer writings survive, and plenty of references in old texts tell of manuscripts that have been lost. Various passages in early medieval writings, for example, make it clear that in England before the Norman invasion of 1066, there were at least a dozen epic poems in Old English about the doings of the heroes of the wars between the Danes and the Geats in the Dark Ages. Only one of those, *Beowulf*, still exists—and only a single copy of it survived.

In the same way, many earlier Grail stories must have existed before Chrétien de Troyes got to work on his version and then were lost at some point between the twelfth and nineteenth centuries. Chrétien himself wrote that he learned about the Grail from a book that was lent him by his patron Count Philip of Flanders. Wolfram von Eschenbach similarly wrote that his story was based on a French book by one Kyot of Provence, who got the story from the writings of a heathen named Flegetanis. Many scholars today, however, insist that these books were pure inventions of Chrétien and Wolfram, and the books were intended to give an air of spurious authenticity to their tales.

Jessie Weston disagreed. She argued that Chrétien and Wolfram should be taken seriously when they claimed to have gotten their story from other authors' books, and she suggested that the considerable differences between their versions of the story were best explained by the fact that they worked from different sources. Scholars in her time had learned how to trace back stray details and differing versions of a story to multiple originals, and she was able to use this same approach to tease out some of the history of the legend.[18] First, she argued, a century or more before Chrétien's time, stories began to circulate about a young hero who starts out foolish, becomes wise and brave, and meets and marries a faery woman. Forgotten minstrels blended these tales with other stories about a mysterious talisman of fertility, which was originally associated with a different Celtic hero, the one whose name comes down to us as Gawain. (In Welsh his name was Gwalchmai, the Hawk of May.)

Both those themes, variously combined, found their way into the book owned by Count Philip of Flanders, from which Chrétien learned the story, and which Wauchier de Demain, another associate of Count Philip and the author of the first of the *Continuations*, also seems to have read. Meanwhile, a different book based on the same stories found its way to Wolfram and inspired

---

18. Weston, *The Legend of Sir Perceval*, vol. 1, 319–25.

his version of the story. None of this is at all unusual in writings from the Middle Ages. It was standard in those days, in fact, for authors to piece together their own stories out of scraps of older writings, many of which no longer survive.

◻

All this was familiar ground to the scholars of Weston's time, and as already noted, her own research into the Grail built on the work of others who had already noticed the ritualistic side of the Grail romances. Toward the end of Weston's life, however, a new and unexpected note suddenly entered—a suggestion that the Grail ritual was not merely a dim memory of the medieval past. In the first of her two popular works on the Grail legend, *The Quest of the Holy Grail*, she presented the ritual elements of the tale as an echo of ancient traditions no longer understood by those who transmitted them. The Grail legend, in her view, was "the confused and fragmentary record of a special form of nature-worship, which, having been elevated to the dignity of a 'mystery,' survived in the form of a tradition."[19] She also had a very specific idea about the geographical location where it had been preserved: it was "secretly practiced in lonely and inaccessible districts in Wales; the mountain fastnesses of that country offering shelter to the worshippers of a dying faith."[20]

By the time her final word on the Grail legend, *From Ritual to Romance*, appeared in 1920, all this had changed. The Grail ritual had not vanished after all—in fact, it was still being practiced in her time, and she knew this because she was in contact with people involved in it. "No inconsiderable part of the information at my disposal," she wrote, "depended on personal testimony, the testimony of those who knew of the continued existence of such a ritual, and had actually been initiated into its mysteries."[21] Whether or not she herself participated in the ritual was not a point she discussed. As we will see, there is some reason to think that some of the personal testimony she described was based on her own experiences.

---

19. Weston, *The Quest of the Holy Grail*, 98.

20. Weston, *The Quest of the Holy Grail*, 109.

21. Weston, *From Ritual to Romance*, 4.

Her understanding of the origins of the Grail legend had changed as well. In *The Quest of the Holy Grail* and a number of earlier papers, she had traced the Grail ritual back to rites once performed in honor of Adonis, a deity of vegetation whose annual death and rebirth was celebrated in Greece and also across much of the Middle East. In *From Ritual to Romance*, by contrast, she traced the ritual back to the rites in honor of a different vegetation god, Attis, and linked them also with a particular Gnostic sect called the Naassenes, who are known to have assigned a special importance to the cult of Attis.

Weston's sense of the geographical focus of the legend had also shifted. She traced one of the central locations—the Chapel Perilous, the site of the terrifying vigil that formed the first great test of the questing knight—to a different part of Britain, near the little village of Blanchland in the rugged moors of Northumberland, in far northeastern England.[22] Following clues in an assortment of Grail romances and medieval documents, Weston came to see the town of Alston, on the high moors between Blanchland and the city of Carlisle, as the original site of the Chapel Perilous, where candidates for initiation into the secrets of the Grail proved their courage before proceeding to the next stage of the initiation. The remainder of the ritual, to judge by an essay of hers she cited in her book (reprinted here for the first time as appendix 2), took place at a temple somewhere on the coast of northern Britain, probably not too long a journey from Alston, at a site she does not name but describes in some detail.

All the way through *From Ritual to Romance*, Weston dropped hints about the Grail ceremony as a living tradition in her time. It is clear from these hints that not only did she know people who celebrated a ritual that she believed to be the original ceremony of the Grail, but that this same knowledge was widespread in at least some part of the British occult scene. "Without entering into indiscreet details," she noted, "I may say that students of the mysteries are well aware of the continued survival of this ritual under circumstances which correspond exactly with the indications of two of our Grail romances."[23] The names of the two romances, of course, were among the indiscreet details she chose to hide.

---

22. Weston, *From Ritual to Romance*, 183.

23. Weston, *From Ritual to Romance*, 171.

To judge from her book, Weston clearly was convinced that she had not merely discovered proof of her theories about the Grail, but that something woven into the Grail secret was of immense importance, and not just to scholars. What was more, the reading public by and large agreed with her. *From Ritual to Romance* has been in print continuously since the day of its original publication, not least because one of the great works of twentieth century poetry—T. S. Eliot's tremendous poem "The Waste Land," which used the Grail legend to explore the shattering of western society after the First World War—drew its structure and much of its imagery from Weston's book.[24]

When *From Ritual to Romance* was first published, many of the leading scholars in the field of Grail studies applauded it. Some, such as Roger Sherman Loomis, the most influential scholar in the field at that time, declared themselves convinced by her arguments. Of course, there were dissenting voices. Then as now, literary and historical research into the Grail romances is divided among many competing points of view, and those scholars who were firmly committed to some other theory of the origins of the Grail legend rejected the ritual theory and Weston's development of it out of hand.

Another dissenting voice came from a different direction. Arthur Edward Waite, the famous Christian occultist, devoted a lengthy chapter in his book *The Holy Grail* to denouncing the ritual theory root and branch.[25] His argument was quite simply that Weston must have been hoodwinked by unscrupulous occultists who fed her a fake origin story for their manufactured Grail ritual. He did not, as it happens, offer any evidence for this argument, other than his insistence that he knew it to be true. At the heart of his argument, and of his entire book, was an angry insistence that the Grail legend was and had to be exclusively Christian in origin, and strictly orthodox in its Christianity at that.

Waite's strident denunciation has a secret of its own to reveal, as we will see in chapter 13. Ironically, however, it was his viewpoint—trimmed of its Christian theology, to be sure—that won out in the end. Scholars in the relevant fields today dismiss everything Jessie Weston wrote, when they do not simply ignore her existence entirely, with a few noteworthy exceptions.[26] Her theory

---

24. Eliot stated as much in his notes to the poem; see Eliot, *The Waste Land*, 47.

25. Waite, *The Holy Grail*, 407–74.

26. The Irish scholar John Carey is among these; see Carey, *Ireland and the Grail*.

that the Grail romances described a once-secret ritual with its origins in the ancient Mysteries gets only the briefest and most dismissive mentions in most books about the Grail, when these discuss her work at all. As for her claim that the Grail ritual had survived to be celebrated in her time, it has been erased not only from the literature of the Grail, but from the memory of today's occult scene. These days there is plenty of talk about the Hermetic Order of the Golden Dawn, Aleister Crowley's Argenteum Astrum and Ordo Templi Orientis, Dion Fortune's Society of the Inner Light, and other British occult orders of the early twentieth century. Yet, the Grail ritual and the organization that celebrated it have apparently vanished without a trace—and so, apparently, has any remaining curiosity about the extraordinary discoveries Weston made.

Weston, her theory, and the ceremony of the Grail she discovered deserve better treatment than that. As I hope to show in this book, her quest for the origin and meaning of the Grail casts an unexpected light on some of the most puzzling corners of prehistory, and on some of the deepest secrets of the human spirit. She believed that the Grail legends enshrined a ritual that could trace its ancestry back to the ancient Mysteries of Greece, by way of a Gnostic sect known as the Naassenes. Before we go on to take a closer look at her sources, we need to examine the ancient Mysteries themselves, because these remarkable rituals and their survival in later centuries are central to the investigation of this book.

THE RITES
OF GENERATION

Across much of the ancient world in the centuries before the coming of Christianity, religious life followed a pattern that seems very strange to most people nowadays. Religion in those days had nothing to do with what people believed. It was a matter of practice, not of faith. Nobody worried about whether everyone had the same notions about the gods. What is more, people didn't gather together in congregations to sing hymns, recite prayers, and listen to sermons. If you wanted to know about ethics and morals, you went to a scribe or, later on, a philosopher, not to a priest or priestess. The ritual at the center of religious life was a family or community barbecue in honor of the gods. It was a very different world.

Religious life in ancient Greece and the Greek-speaking world at that time centered on three locations. The first was the home, where most ordinary rituals and religious practices took place. The second was the temple, which was a house for a god or goddess, not a place for congregations to meet—the altar where you sacrificed meat animals to the gods for the barbecues just mentioned was out in front of the temple, and few people went inside. The third is less easy to describe in modern terms. This third setting was the place set aside by the community for the celebration of the Mysteries.[27] Whether or not it had its own buildings, it was only active for a few days a year.

These days, the English word *mystery* means a novel about crime or, more broadly, anything that's hard to figure out. The Greek word *mysterion*, from which it derives, had a stranger and more specific meaning. A *mysterion* was a ritual of initiation descended from archaic agricultural ceremonies. It was meant to confer the blessings of a deity on the initiates. It reenacted a traditional story in which the acts of the founding deity were central. The story was not a vehicle for some kind of teaching, however. The Greek philosopher Aristotle, who had plenty of opportunities to find out, said that initiates of the Mysteries were not taught any particular set of doctrines. What happened instead was that they had an experience and were put into a certain state of mind.[28]

Each set of Mysteries was celebrated once a year at some traditional point in the seasonal cycle, and initiates were sworn to secrecy about what they experienced in the most important parts of the ritual. Those who passed through the ritual once were called *mystai*, "initiates," but the deeper levels of the mystery were reserved for *epoptai*, "those who have seen," those initiates who passed through the ritual again after they had been initiated. Many epoptai attended the Mysteries every year in the same spirit that devout Christians attend the annual celebration of Easter.

The most famous of all these rites of initiation were the Eleusinian Mysteries, which were celebrated every autumn in the town of Eleusis twenty miles away from Athens. Like most of the Mysteries, it was open to men and women alike irrespective of social standing; slaves, who made up a large share of the population of Athens as of most ancient cities, were just as eligible for initiation into the Mysteries of Eleusis as anyone else. The Eleusinian Mysteries, according to an ancient legend, were founded by the goddess Demeter herself, in gratitude to the people of Eleusis for the hospitality they gave her during her search for her daughter Persephone, who had been kidnapped by Pluto, the god of the underworld.

There were other Mysteries that claimed the same origin and told versions of the same story. The town of Amyklai near Athens had its own mystery rit-

---

27. See Meyer, *The Ancient Mysteries*, for a good general overview of the Greek Mysteries.

28. Meyer, *The Ancient Mysteries*, 12.

ual based on the same legend, and it became customary for people to receive the initiation of Amyklai, wait a year, and then receive the more important and prestigious initiation at Eleusis. Another set of Mysteries based on the same traditional story, the Andanian Mysteries, were celebrated outdoors in a sacred grove near the city of Messene.[29]

Many other Mysteries celebrated the doings of different gods and goddesses. During the heyday of classical Paganism, many cities had their own unique mystery celebrations each year, and even small towns might have a mystery performed each year. The little town of Phlya, which was not much more than a suburb of Athens, had its own Mystery rites, for example.[30] Some of these Mysteries were recent creations, but the more traditional ones were stunningly ancient—Walter Burkert, in his classic study of Greek religion, traces their origins back to the invention of agriculture in the late Stone Age—and most of them had deep, symbolic connections with agriculture and the fertility of the soil.[31]

Among the most widespread of these rites of generation in the later years of Greek and Roman Paganism were the Mysteries of Attis and the Great Mother Cybele. These were not originally Greek; they came from the city of Pessinus in what was then the country of Phrygia and is now central Turkey. These Mysteries spread outside of Phrygia into the Greek world early on, and they came to be practiced all through the ancient world in Roman times. They were among the most popular of the ancient Mysteries in the final golden summer of classical Pagan spirituality, and they were among the last of the ancient Mysteries to be celebrated publicly in the teeth of Christian persecution.[32] They were also, according to Jessie Weston, the Mysteries that evolved over time to give rise to the ceremony of the Grail.

Another set of Mysteries that spread widely were the Mysteries of Mithras, a Persian god whose rites became popular in the Roman Empire a few centuries before Christianity began to spread. The Mithraic Mysteries differed from most of the others in important ways. They had little to do with agriculture and the fertility of the land, and they had seven rituals of initiation rather than

---

29. Meyer, *The Ancient Mysteries*, 47–59.

30. Burkert, *Greek Religion*, 276–77.

31. Burkert, *Greek Religion*, 278.

32. Laing, *Survivals of Roman Religion*, 123.

the usual one. They were celebrated in distinctive underground temples, called *mithraea*, which has made them easy for archaeologists to find. They were especially popular among Roman officials and the officers and soldiers of the Imperial army. Some modern scholars have described Mithraism as the Roman equivalent of Freemasonry, and the comparison has much to recommend it.

One thing that makes the Mysteries of Mithras especially important in terms of our theme is the fact that they only admitted men. The gender politics of Roman society were considerably more complex than modern stereotypes would suggest, and Roman women had their own active religious lives and their own traditional rites. According to several ancient sources, in places where the Mysteries of Mithras were practiced, it became common for the Mysteries of Cybele to also be adopted so that the wives of Mithraic initiates could have their own mystery rituals to celebrate.[33] As we will see, this connection will offer an important clue in our search.

Exactly what took place in any of the ancient Mysteries remains a mystery, even in the modern sense of the word. Some details, however, are mentioned in writings by initiates from ancient times. We know that most Mystery rituals began with purification rites and sacrificial offerings to the gods and goddesses, followed by a period of fasting, mourning, and lamentation in darkness. Some writers hint at terrifying visions seen during this phase of the ritual. Then the initiates passed out of darkness and grief into regeneration and light. The sacred emblems of the mystery were shown to them, and a festive banquet followed. The Greek writer Plutarch describes the rites of the Mysteries in the following terms:

> At first there is wandering, and wearisome roaming, and fearful traveling through darkness with no end to be found. Then, just before the consummation, there is every sort of terror, shuddering and trembling and perspiring and being alarmed. But after this a marvelous light appears, and open places and meadows await, with voices and dances and the solemnities of sacred utterances and holy visions. In

---

33. Weston, *From Ritual to Romance*, 145.

that place one walks about at will, now perfect and initiated and free,
and wearing a crown, one celebrates religious rites, and joins with
pure and pious people.[34]

The pivotal moment of transition in each of the Mysteries was marked by two things. The first, as Plutarch points out, was a sudden change from darkness to light; the second was an important symbolic action accompanied by a set of traditional words. According to the Naassene document—a text we'll discuss later in this book—at the moment of transition in the Eleusinian Mysteries, light flooded the place of initiation, and the hierophant who conducted the initiation held up a single stalk of grain and announced, "The Lady has brought forth a holy Son, Brimo has given birth to Brimos." Other Mysteries had their own secret revelations and words, but the basic pattern seems to have been the same.

Initiates who had passed through a mystery were given a *symbolon*, a cryptic statement that they could use as a password to identify themselves as mystai to other mystai. The symbolon for the Eleusinian Mysteries was as follows:

I have fasted; I have drunk the kykeon [a sacred beverage of grain
and pennyroyal]; *I have taken something from the chest, and worked*
with it; I put it into the basket, and then moved it from the basket into
the chest.[35]

We know a little more about the Eleusinian Mysteries than this, for the heart of each of the ancient Mysteries was a story, and the story central to the Eleusinian Mysteries is known in quite some detail. It is the story of how the goddess Persephone, also known as Kore ("the Maiden"), was kidnapped by Pluto, god of the underworld, and taken down to Hades to be his bride. Her grieving mother Demeter went in search of her, and since Demeter was the goddess of agriculture, no plants grew while she grieved. Finally, after she had come to Eleusis, she learned what had happened and demanded that Zeus force Pluto to let her daughter return to her. Since Persephone had eaten a pomegranate seed in the underworld, she could not remain above the earth

---

34. Meyer, *The Ancient Mysteries*, 9.

35. Meyer, *The Ancient Mysteries*, 18.

indefinitely, but spent four months of each year as the queen of the under-world and the other eight months in Olympus with her mother.

Most scholars nowadays interpret this story as a straightforward allegory of the seasons, with Persephone's four-month stint belowground as winter and her eight months aboveground as the warmer seasons of Greece. Scholars in the nineteenth and early twentieth centuries more often thought of the story in agricultural terms, with Persephone as the seed that descends into the earth at sowing and rises again with the growth of the grain. It is entirely possible that both of these were among the ways that the Mysteries of Eleusis were interpreted in ancient times.

Compare this story to the Grail legends we have been discussing, and another aspect of the story stands out. Once again we have a story of environmental devastation and recovery. After Persephone was kidnapped, the world became a Waste Land like the one described in the Grail legends, in which no crops grew and no leaves sprouted. Once Persephone was restored to her mother, on the other hand, the land became green again, just as it did when Perceval asked the right question in the Grail Castle. The parallels are strong enough that one of Jessie Weston's fellow Grail scholars, William A. Nitze, argued that the Grail might preserve some traces of the ritual of the Eleusinian Mysteries.[36]

The Mysteries that Weston identified as the ultimate source of the Grail ritual were not, as already noted, the Mysteries of Demeter and Persephone, but those of Cybele and Attis. (Weston and Nitze, in fact, carried on a lively debate on the subject in the pages of scholarly journals.) Some fragments of the traditions that once surrounded the Mysteries of Cybele and Attis have also survived. The symbolon given to initiates is among them. It ran as follows:

> *I have eaten from the tambourine; I have drunk from the cymbal;*
> *I have carried the sacred dish; I have stolen into the inner shrine.*[37]

It is not hard to see a definite parallel to the Grail legend in one part of this symbolon, which also centers on a sacred dish. What the other elements of the symbolon mean, however, remains secret to this day.

---

36. See Nitze, "The Fisher King in the Grail Romances," and Nitze, "The Sister's Son and the Conte del Graal."

37. Meyer, *The Ancient Mysteries*, 115.

The story at the heart of the Mysteries of Cybele and Attis also survives, though the most complete version is found in a Christian source and, as usual, has been distorted for the sake of religious propaganda. In broad outline, however, the story of Attis involves the miraculous birth of two youths. The first, Acdestis, was born from a huge rock that was also in some sense the goddess Cybele, who was impregnated by Zeus. A hermaphrodite, Acdestis was wild and fierce and lived in the wilderness. To tame Acdestis, the gods cut off his male genitals so that he became a woman, and a pomegranate tree grew from the blood spilled on the ground from the wound. A virgin princess, seeing the tree, took one of its fruits and ate it and became pregnant. When she gave birth to a beautiful boy, her father ordered the child to be left in the wilderness to die, but goatherds found the infant, fed him on goat's milk, and named him Attis.

Attis grew up strong and handsome, and wild Acdestis fell in love with him, courting him with gifts of wild game. Attis kept his relationship with Acdestis secret, and he claimed that he himself hunted the game he brought back each day. The goatherds became suspicious, got him drunk, and found out the real source of the abundance of game. Word reached the local king, and he had Attis brought to the city of Pessinus so that the handsome youth could marry the king's daughter. Distraught, Acdestis followed her beloved, and with the help of Cybele she entered the city and caused all its people to be seized by madness. Attis, out of his wits, ran off to the woods, castrated himself beneath a pine tree, and bled to death. He was mourned by Acdestis and Cybele, and though Zeus refused to allow him to return to life, he entered into a state between life and death, where he remains.

Along with the symbolon and the story, we have a few scraps of information about the ritual itself because in this one case, the records of the Christian heresy-hunters are supplemented by the testimony of a faithful initiate. The Greek philosopher Sallust, a devout Pagan of a relatively ascetic sort who was an associate of the last Pagan emperor, Julian, included a careful discussion of the rites of Attis and Cybele in his book *On the Gods and the World*. Here is how he described the ceremonies:

> [W]e observe a festive day. And, in the first place, we ourselves falling from the celestial regions, and associating with a nymph, the symbol of generation, live immersed in sorrow, abstaining from

> *grain [...] afterwards, the incisions of a tree and fasting succeed, as*
> *if we would amputate from our nature all farther progress of gen-*
> *eration; at length we employ the nutriment of milk, as if passing*
> *by this means into a state of regeneration; and lastly, festivity and*
> *crowns, and a re-ascent, as it were, to the gods succeed.*[38]

Sallust's account does not fit the other accounts of the myth exactly, but this is typical in the world of ancient Pagan spirituality. Since the old nature religions had no scriptures and no concept of doctrinal orthodoxy, sacred stories varied from place to place and time to time, and even from believer to believer. Though Sallust clearly is not willing to betray his oath of secrecy, his words combine with other scraps of surviving knowledge about the rites to provide a glimpse into how these Mysteries were celebrated. Participants ate no grain for several days before the ceremony, perhaps eating wild game in commemoration of the gifts of Acdestis to Attis. They began the day of the ceremony itself fasting and first decorated a pine tree, then cut branches from it in a symbolic castration and mourned the death of Attis. Later, they broke their fast by drinking milk, possibly from a cymbal. Later still, the new mystai were crowned and took part in a festive banquet. Doubtless there were other events over the course of the day that did not find their way into the fragmentary evidence.

Of all the old Mystery initiations, the two we have just discussed—the Eleusinian Mysteries and the Mysteries of Cybele and Attis—turned out to have the most staying power. Even before Christianity seized control of the ancient world, a long sequence of severe economic and political crises made it difficult for many forms of Pagan worship to continue in their original forms, which often involved considerable expense. Many Mystery celebrations simply stopped once they could no longer be funded on the grand scale.[39] The initiates of the Mysteries of Demeter and Cybele, on the other hand, adapted the rituals so they could be celebrated on a smaller scale in the homes of senior initiates. For centuries thereafter, even under the Christian yoke, Pagan families in Greece and elsewhere celebrated the Mysteries of Cybele every spring and the

---

38. Sallust, *On the Gods and the World*, 21–22.

39. See, for example, Rogers, *The Mysteries of Artemis of Ephesos*.

Mysteries of Eleusis every autumn. Not until Emperor Justinian abolished the last Pagan institutions and stripped Pagans of civil rights were these Mysteries no longer celebrated in public.

The same legal penalties that stopped public celebrations of the Mysteries were applied with equal savagery to dissident Christians, including a variety of Gnostic sects. Despite waves of persecution, history shows the Gnostics survived and found new adherents for many centuries. The Cathars were the last public Gnostic movement in western Europe until modern times, but other corners of the world proved to be less inhospitable. Some Gnostic groups, such as the Mandeans, have continued to survive in various corners of the Middle East to this day. Thus, it's by no means impossible that one of the ancient Greek Mysteries might have survived as well, especially if it was one of those that had been reworked so that it could be celebrated in private by circles of initiates.

$$\diamondsuit$$

It was Jessie Weston's conviction that at least one of the old Mysteries had survived, and that its ritual had gradually mutated over time into the strange rite that is acted out in the oldest of the Grail romances. She did not claim, however, that it had survived by itself. Her argument, as already mentioned, was that a Gnostic sect, the Naassenes, had preserved one set of Mysteries as part of its own traditional rituals. She proposed that this Gnostic tradition, like the tradition that gave rise to the Cathars, had endured the centuries of persecution and flourished again, however briefly, in the Middle Ages, giving rise to the Grail legends as we know them.

To understand this aspect of her theory, it's crucial to realize that Gnosticism was not a single monolithic phenomenon. There was no Gnostic orthodoxy, no one set of beliefs that every Gnostic was expected to accept. Rather, Gnosticism was a very broad and diverse movement united solely by the conviction that personal spiritual experience, rather than blind faith in doctrine, was the key to salvation.

The Cathars belonged to the largest and best-known branch of the Gnostic movement, the faction that argued that the world of matter was a prison in which our souls were confined—a prison that was created and ruled by a wicked god. That branch of the Gnostic movement embraced an ascetic attitude to the world, rejecting sexuality and biological existence itself as evil. The older Grail romances, by contrast, delight in biological realities, glorifying sexual love as well as the flourishing of vegetation and the cycles of nature. They are closer to the Naassene end of the Gnostic movement, the branch that had a less ascetic sense of the way to personal knowledge of spiritual realities.

This is not to say that the Naassenes were a fertility cult pure and simple. They taught a rich and complex system of spiritual development, which has been sketched out in a thoughtful book by scholar of religions Mark Gaffney.[40] Central to their faith, in contrast to the belief of dualist Gnostics such as the Cathars, was the doctrine of divine immanence: the concept that God is not "out there" in some heavenly otherworld, gazing down at sinful humanity from a distance, but present in everything in the cosmos, even in the densest form of matter. That was why the Naassenes valued the ancient Mysteries so highly: these ancient rites focused on divine powers manifested in fertility and so revealed the presence of God in the material world.

Like most Gnostic sects, and many other mystical sects of the same era, the Naassenes expected senior initiates to practice celibacy so the energies of sex could be redirected to spiritual purposes—"the waters of the Jordan flowing upstream," in the classic Gnostic metaphor. (Since the Jordan in Gnostic writings was identified with the spinal canal, the fluid-filled tube that surrounds the spinal cord, this was apparently their term for what Hindu and Buddhist Tantric teachers call "raising kundalini.") However, the Naassenes had a far less negative attitude toward fertility, and toward rituals that focused on fertility, than many other Gnostic groups did.

Whether the Naassenes themselves, or some other Gnostic group with similar ideas, were active in southern France at the same time as the Cathars is anyone's guess. Very little documentary evidence survived the crusade against the Cathars. Certainly, however, there were Gnostic sects other than the Cathars active in southern France in those years. One of them passed on certain teachings to the Jewish community in Narbonne in the twelfth century and gave rise to the Kabbalah, one of the core mystical traditions within Judaism.[41] The elements of Gnostic teaching within the Grail legends suggests that there was at

---

40. See Gaffney, *Gnostic Secrets of the Naassenes*.

41. See Scholem, *The Origins of the Kabbalah*, for thorough documentation of this point.

least one other Gnostic sect that found new adherents during the brief, doomed heyday of the Cathars. Thus, a closer look at the Naassenes is in order.

As with most of the Gnostic sects, most of what we know about the Naassenes comes from their enemies. The richest source among the writings of the orthodox is *The Refutation of All Heresies* by Bishop Hippolytus of Pontus, who lived in the early years of the third century CE. When Hippolytus wrote, Christianity did not yet have the grip on political power it gained later, and so he was forced to argue with heretics instead of simply having them rounded up and murdered. His thundering critiques of the Gnostic sects are thus extremely detailed, and the Naassenes come in for a particularly extensive rant, including substantial quotations from one of their teaching documents. They were, in fact, the first of the Gnostic heresies Hippolytus denounced in his volume, and he treats them as the source of all the others.

The outline of Naassene teachings that emerges from all this is startling.[42] Unlike most of the Christian or quasi-Christian sects of their time, the Naassenes accepted the spiritual validity of older Pagan traditions. They saw the revelation of Christ as the natural completion of the Pagan faiths, not as a rejection of the older traditions. They paid especially close attention to the Mystery initiations and the traditions that surrounded them. Hippolytus remarks sourly that the Naassenes were particularly eager to participate in the Mysteries of Attis and Cybele.

To the Naassenes, the quest for gnosis required the seeker to pass through three gates. The first of these gates, as recorded by Hippolytus, comprised "the little Mysteries, those of the Fleshly Generation."[43] In less ornate language, these were the Pagan Mysteries, which celebrated the life cycle of vegetation and the process of human sexuality and reproduction. The link between the Mysteries and the Naassene path is easy to understand, because what the mystai and epoptai received in the Mysteries was gnosis—a direct, personal experience of spiritual realities. Thus, it makes perfect sense that the Naassenes, with their inclusive attitude toward spirituality, would recognize the Mysteries as a valid stage in their own quest for enlightenment and would encourage members of

---

42. Weston, *From Ritual to Romance*, 149–63.

43. Weston, *From Ritual to Romance*, 155.

their sect to receive Mystery initiations as a first, preparatory step toward the Naassene gnosis.

The second gate, according to the Naassenes, consisted of the rites of Christianity, which they called the greater or heavenly Mysteries: "For this is the Gate of Heaven, and this is the House of God, where the Good God dwells alone, into which house no impure man shall come."[44] The third gate, the final step in the quest, was the attainment of gnosis, the great mystery of spiritual awakening that Jesus came to bring to humankind. "And of all men," said the Naassene document Hippolytus cites, "we alone are Christians, accomplishing the Mystery at the third gate."

Many Christian sects through the years have thought of themselves as the only "real" Christians, and so it's not surprising to see the Naassenes claiming this title. It's fascinating to note, however, that some scholars think the Naassenes may have been right—that they may have preserved the original teachings of Jesus of Nazareth from before the days when they were reworked to fit the needs of a dogmatic and hierarchical church. Mark Gaffney is one of these scholars. In *The Gospel of Thomas and Christian Wisdom*, Stevan L. Davies similarly pointed out that the Gnostic Gospel of Thomas, when judged by scholarly methods of form criticism, appears to be older and more authentic than any of the officially accepted Gospels.[45] The Naassenes used the Gospel of Thomas as one of their sacred scriptures.[46]

If the earliest of the Grail legends do contain fragmentary traces of the teachings of a Gnostic sect with links to the earliest forms of Christianity, this would explain the way that the older versions of the Grail legend so consistently combine Christian symbolism with hints of secrets not known to the official church. Yet, one of the old Grail romances, the puzzling document called the *Elucidation*, contains the echoes of even older and stranger secrets. It is to this account of the Grail that we now turn.

---

44. This and the following quote are from Weston, *From Ritual to Romance*, 155.

45. Davies, *The Gospel of Thomas and Christian Wisdom*. Form criticism is a method of comparing different versions of a story or a text to work out which is the original and which are copied from it. It is widely used in many branches of scholarship.

46. Gaffney, *Gnostic Mysteries of the Naassenes*, 66.

THE VOICES OF
THE HILLS

The *Elucidation* survives as a prologue to two French copies of Chrétien de Troyes's *Perceval* and to one German translation of the same story. It has been available to scholars since the nineteenth century, but translations were hard for the general public to access until the last decade or so, when several translations appeared online.[47] More recently still, Caitlin and John Matthews have discussed it in detail in a thoughtful work, *The Lost Book of the Grail*, which contains a capable new translation of the text.[48] (I have included my own translation of the *Elucidation* in this volume as appendix 1.) The *Elucidation* is not a Grail romance in the usual sense—that is, it is not a tale that follows a knight of King Arthur's court on his quest for the Grail. Instead, it is a framing narrative that purports to explain the whole story of how the Grail was lost and the Waste Land devastated, and what happened afterward.

After the usual warning about the dangerous secret of the Grail—a "secret no man should tell in prose or rhyme"—the text plunges straight into an unfamiliar

---

47. See Evans, *The Elucidation*, and Kibler, *The Elucidation*.

48. See Matthews and Matthews, *The Lost Book of the Grail*.

story. Long ago in the kingdom of Logres, enchanted maidens dwelt in the *puis* and offered hospitality to travelers. (In medieval French, *puis* can mean "hills" or "wells," and scholars have been debating for many years which meaning the authors had in mind. For reasons I will explain later, I favor "hills," but as we will see, both may have been involved.) Those who wandered the roads in those days needed only to find one of the hills and ask, and at once a maiden would appear with a golden cup and serve the traveler whatever food he desired.

Then Amangons, the king of the land who was supposed to guard and protect the maidens, raped one of them instead, stole her golden cup, and had all his meals served in it from then on. His vassals followed his lead and assaulted the other maidens of the hills in the same way. At once the custom ceased, the kingdom of Logres suffered ecological devastation, and the court of the Rich Fisherman, the source of the kingdom's wealth, could no longer be found. Thus, the voices of the hills were lost and the land was plunged into desolation and misery.

A long and bitter age passed. Then Arthur became king of the Britons, and the best knights in all the world came to join his Fellowship of the Round Table. They swore a mighty oath to restore the wells, defend the damsels, recover the golden cups, and destroy the heirs of Amangons and his vassals. As Arthur's knights pursued their quest, they had many adventures, for they found damsels roaming the forests of Logres, each of them protected by a knight in armor. In the usual fashion of Arthurian legend, these knights challenged all comers and had to be defeated in a fair fight before they would reveal anything to their challengers. (The connections linking this part of the *Elucidation*'s story to the legends of knights guarding wells and river crossings, on the one hand, and the priesthood of Nemi as discussed by Sir George Frazer on the other, were not lost on Weston.)

The first of these wandering knights to be vanquished was named Bleheris. Sir Gawain, who defeated him, sent him in the usual way as a hostage to Arthur's court, where his talents as a storyteller charmed everyone. He explained to his hosts that the damsels and knights in the forest were descended from the maidens who had been raped by Amangons and his vassals. Only when Arthur's knights found the court of the Rich Fisherman again, he explained to the knights and ladies of the court, would the land of Logres be healed.

Thereafter, after many more adventures, seven knights of the Round Table succeeded in finding the court of the Rich Fisherman. Sir Perceval was the first to accomplish the quest, and he asked certain questions and partly healed the land, but he neglected to ask certain other questions. After him, Sir Gawain found the court, asked the remaining questions, and completed the work of restoring the land to fertility and life. But the adventures were not yet over, for once the seven knights had reached the court of the Rich Fisherman, a people full of malice came out of the hills and built castles, cities, and strongholds, from which they warred on King Arthur. There were 7,686 of them—366 lords who each had twenty knights—and Arthur and the knights of the Round Table fought against them for four years before finally defeating them all and restoring peace to the land of Logres.

While unfolding this narrative, the *Elucidation* also speaks of the seven guardians of the world, who are also seven cloaks and the seven natural stories that proceed from the Grail. These passages are extremely cryptic, and so far they have largely resisted scholarly attempts at explanation. While the text promises to name the seven guardians, it never does so. When it lists the seven natural stories, its descriptions are so vague that only three of them can be identified clearly: the story of the Holy Spear, which wounded the side of Jesus when he was crucified; the story of the great sorrows and how Lancelot du Lac came to the place where he lost his virtue, which is the story of the Knight in the Cart, a famous Arthurian tale about Lancelot; and the adventure of the shield, which refers to events in the legend of Joseph of Arimathea. The others are the story of "the great content of the labor" (*del grant content de la travalle*); the story of wrath and the loss of Huden; the story of Heaven and of the dead knight in the boat that came first to Glamorgan; and the story of the warrior who frightened Castrars and how Pecorin, the son of Amangons, was wounded. Attempts to identify these with anything in the surviving Grail romances have had only the most equivocal results.

In the middle of all these Mysteries, the *Elucidation* gives one of the most detailed descriptions of the ceremony of the Grail—a description that would give Weston crucial clues in her quest, and which will provide us with equally important guidance as we follow her trail. This is what the text says:

For three hours at a time, three times a day, there was lamentation so great that no man, no matter how brave, could hear it without being stricken with fear. Then they hung four censers on four rich candlesticks that were at the corners of the bier. When they had done the service, straightway the cries continued again, and every man vanished away. The hall, great and wide, remained empty and terrible, and the stream of blood ran from the vessel the held the Lance through the rich channel of silver.

Then the palace filled with folk and knights, and the fairest feast in all the world was made ready. Then the unknown King came forth in all his apparel. From a chamber he came forth robed. [...] As soon as the King was seated, then you would see all the knights seated at the other high tables. Then the bread was quickly served and the wine put before them in great cups of gold and silver. After that you would see the Graal come through the chamber door without servant or bearer and serve in a worthy fashion onto dishes of gold that were worth a great fortune. The first serving it put before the King, and then it served all the others around him, and the food it brought to them was no less than a wonder. And then came the great wonder to which no other can be compared.[49]

What that "great wonder" was, the *Elucidation* does not say. Even so, we have a first detailed sketch of the Grail ritual. First comes a period of lamentation and solitude in darkness, which takes place beside a richly decorated bier on which a corpse is laid. The bier is lit by candles in candlesticks, and after a certain period, censers burning incense were brought in and hung from the candlesticks. Meanwhile, the spear that accompanies the Grail stands nearby, dripping blood through a silver channel. To judge by the evidence given in other Grail romances, the knight seeking the Grail kept a vigil by the bier for several hours, surrounded by weeping and wailing voices, before the ritual proceeded.

---

49. See appendix 1: The *Elucidation*.

Jessie Weston was far from the only person in her time to notice the similarities between this description and the first stage of the old Greek Mysteries.

The next stage of the ritual is more celebratory. Here tables are laid for a feast and the Rich Fisherman is present in royal garb. Once bread and wine—the elements of the Christian communion ritual—were set out, the Grail came and miraculously provided other food for the gathering. It was at this point, as explained in all the early versions of the story, that the knight who sought the Grail had to ask the question that would heal the Rich Fisherman and the Waste Land. And then—but what happened next, the final stage in the Grail ritual, is not discussed in the *Elucidation*.

Of all the fascinating details of the *Elucidation*, perhaps the most intriguing is the storyteller knight Bleheris. He was not simply an invention of the unknown author of the *Elucidation*, for his name appears in several other Arthurian sources, variously spelled but with an impressive consistency of detail.[50] Wauchier de Denain, who took up Chrétien's unfinished poem and wrote the first of the *Continuations*, also called him Bleheris and said that he was born and raised in Wales. An early French version of the story of Tristan and Iseult called him Bréri and said that he knew every story of all the kings and lords of Britain. There is also the figure of Bleis or Bleys, who was said by some writers to have written a book containing all that was known about the Grail.[51] Entirely apart from the realm of Arthurian stories, finally, the medieval author Gerald of Wales (Giraldus Cambrensis), who lived from 1146 to 1223 and wrote several important works about the medieval Celtic countries, mentioned a man named Bledhericus, "that famous storyteller who lived a little before our time."[52]

As Jessie Weston pointed out, there was a historical figure who corresponded precisely to all these scraps of data.[53] His name was Bleddri ap Cydifor, and he was born in southern Wales sometime in the early twelfth century. The earliest reference to him in the fragmentary Welsh records of that time dates

50. Carey, *Ireland and the Grail*, 269–96.

51. Loomis, "Onomastic Riddles in Malory's 'Book of Arthur and His Knights,'" 184–85.

52. Gerald of Wales, *The Journey through Wales and the Description of Wales*, 252.

53. Weston, *From Ritual to Romance*, 189–209.

from 1113 and the last dates from 1131—a little before the time of Gerald of Wales, in other words. The Welsh and Norman records give his name in Latin as Bledericus, and one mentions that he was literate in Latin, a rare achievement among aristocrats in that era. These references also make it clear that he allied with the Norman rulers of England against his own people, to the extent of joining with other pro-Norman Welsh aristocrats to defend the Norman stronghold at Carmarthen against Welsh assaults. Jessie Weston and other scholars of her era thus argued that Bleddri ap Cydifor was the person who brought the Grail legend out of Wales and introduced it to the medieval world.

We know very little about Bleddri's biography, but his connection with the Normans offers a fascinating parallel with the *Elucidation*. In that text, Bleheris was sent to Arthur's court as a captive and became a storyteller who "knew such good stories that no one ever grew weary of listening to his words." Bleddri ap Cydifor could well have become a hostage or prisoner of the Normans— that happened to a great many Welsh chieftains and nobles in his time—and he would not have been the only Welsh aristocrat, in the course of the tangled and bitter politics of the time, to have moved from that status to become an ally of his former captors. In the story of Bleheris in the *Elucidation*, in other words, we have what appears to be a precise description of Bleddri's own role in the society of his time, and if Gerald of Wales's comments about Bledhericus "the famous storyteller" refer to Bleddri, the identification is complete.[54]

That identification offers another startling insight into the legend. According to Wauchier de Demain, Bleheris went to France and told the story of the Grail to the court of the Count of Poitiers there.[55] According to the *Elucidation*, Bleheris went to the court of King Arthur and told the story of the Grail to the assembled knights and ladies there. If these references are to the same person, as the evidence suggests, then a further implication cannot be avoided: the comments about "the court of King Arthur" in the *Elucidation* may not be meant literally. Someone else is concealed behind the mask of Arthur.

---

54. That identification has been rejected by a great many recent scholars, but as John Carey points out, their rejection is oddly disconnected from the evidence; it is simply a matter of flat assertions and question-begging. See Carey, *Ireland and the Grail*, 276–78.

55. Loomis, "Bleheris and the Tristram Story," 322–23.

More precisely, as we have already noted, the figure of Arthur conceals several different layers of meaning. Some of those layers reach back into an astonishing antiquity, but others have to do with the place and time when the Arthurian legends were written down. Just as pundits and pop-culture figures in the 1960s labeled John F. Kennedy's presidency "Camelot" and mapped assorted bits of Arthurian legend onto the grubby realities of mid-twentieth century American politics, the author of the *Elucidation* clearly had some of his own contemporaries in mind when he wrote of Arthur and his court.

Can we identify the figures behind the Arthurian disguise of the *Elucidation*? Wauchier de Denain gives us a crucial clue. If he is correct, as already noted, Bleddri traveled to France and told the story of the Grail to the Count of Poitiers. There is nothing improbable about this claim. The Norman barons with whom Bleddri associated spent as much time in France as in England, and Bleddri himself would have been as fluent in French as in Welsh and Latin due to his long association with the French-speaking Normans. A close look at the counts of Poitiers in Bleddri's time is in order, since they and their court, or some other group of aristocrats connected to them and to the early stages of the Grail legend, might have been the model for the *Elucidation*'s Round Table.

During most of the period we are discussing, the Counts of Poitiers were among the great aristocrats of medieval Europe. They ruled the provinces of Poitou and Aquitaine in western and southwestern France until 1137, when the heiress Eleanor of Aquitaine married first King Louis VI of France and then, after divorcing him, King Henry II of England, taking her landholdings with her to each monarch in turn. Either of the last two counts of Poitiers, William VII (reigned 1086–1126) and William VIII (reigned 1126–1137), could have been the one Wauchier had in mind. William VII was himself a famous poet, and both he and his son William VIII were notable patrons of minstrels and storytellers, the kind of aristocrats who would have welcomed a French-speaking Welshman like Bleddri ap Cadifor who knew plenty of lively Celtic stories.

The counts of Poitiers had an ambiguous relationship to the thriving Cathar movement that was spreading across southern France in their time. The counts of Poitiers intermarried, conspired, and occasionally fought with their near neighbors, the counts of Toulouse, who were deeply enmeshed in the Cathar movement—Count Raymond of Toulouse was the chief military leader of the Cathar side once the Pope proclaimed a crusade and fighting began. The counts of Poitiers did not side with the Cathars, but they also seem to have done nothing to stop them from making converts in the Poitevin domains. It is possible—though for the moment this can only be a speculation—that this moderate policy concealed an involvement with, or at least a toleration for, a different branch of Gnosticism, the one commemorated in the legends of the Grail.

So there may be a contemporary political context hidden behind the Grail legend as the *Elucidation* and the other early texts present them. Yet the historical indications hidden within the *Elucidation* are not the only layer of meaning that can be found in this enigmatic text. Another deeper layer connects the *Elucidation* directly to the Gnostic heresies that flourished when the Grail legend was born and were destroyed or driven into hiding just before the Grail legend dropped out of sight.

As already noted, scholars before Jessie Weston's time had already noticed that the Grail legends and the Cathar movement in France appeared and disappeared around the same time, and the theory of a Cathar connection to the Grail has been advanced more than once. The great difficulty faced by that theory is that there is no obvious connection between the Grail narratives and what is known of Gnostic teaching, Cathar or otherwise. As already noted, the later versions of the legend that make Galahad the central figure are solidly rooted in orthodox Christian theology, but attempts to find something recognizably Gnostic even in the early versions of the legend have turned up very little so far.

There is, in fact, a Gnostic clue in the Grail legends, and it has been hiding in plain sight all along in the pages of the *Elucidation*. The Gnostics, like many other mystical groups, made use of the curious fact that in most ancient alphabets, letters are also numbers. Each word in many ancient languages thus adds up to a number, and an entire system of mathematical symbolism, called *gematria* in Hebrew, evolved around interpreting the symbolic numbers of names. Hebrew was only one of several languages used this way. Gnosticism arose in the eastern Mediterranean at a time when Greek was the common language of scholarship and trade, and the Gnostics accordingly used the Greek alphabet as the basis for their gematria.

The basic rule of gematria is that words that add up to the same number represent the same thing in symbolic terms. It was traditional to allow any large number to have the number one added to it or subtracted from it without changing the meaning; this unit is called *colel* in Hebrew. All this may seem very strange to modern eyes, but it was used constantly in Gnostic writings. The Naassene interest in the Mysteries of Attis, for example, becomes much clearer when the key of gematria is applied: the name of Attis, Ἀττις in Greek, adds up to 811, the same number as the most famous Gnostic name of God, ΙΑΩ or Iao.

Apply the same key to the *Elucidation* and this mysterious story suddenly becomes much less mysterious. One of the two most important names in the text is that of Bleheris, the minstrel knight descended from the maidens of the wells who was vanquished by Gawain and brought stories with him to the court of King Arthur. His name in Greek letters is Βλεέρις, which adds to 352, a number extraordinarily rich in meaning. 352 is the number of ἡ οδος, *he hodos*, "the Way," and ὁ βιος, *ho bios*, "the Life"—two of the three titles Jesus gives himself in a famous passage from the Bible. Subtract colel from the number of the name of Bleheris and you have 351, the number of ὁ γοης, *ho goes*, "the wizard"; add colel to the same name and you have 353, the number of Ἑρμης, Hermes, the god of knowledge and magic, who as Hermes Trismegistus was credited with the authorship of books treasured by the old Gnostics. Bleheris is given another name in the *Elucidation*, Blihos; in Greek this is βλιός and works out to 312, which is the number of αγγελος, *angelos*, "messenger"—another pointer to Hermes, the messenger of the gods.

The choice of this number suggests that the author of the *Elucidation* may have meant to identify Jesus with Hermes—a connection that has been made in many esoteric teachings down to the present day. The link with Hermes has something else to communicate, too, because Hermes has another connection to the Grail. One of the ancient treatises attributed to Hermes Trismegistus is titled *The Krater*—that is, "the cup"—and uses the image of a wondrous, holy cup as a symbol for the spiritual experience of gnosis that the Gnostics sought. The possibility of a direct connection between this treatise and the Grail has been explored by scholars Henry and Renée Kahane—and as we'll see in chapter 11, it was also discussed by a figure closely associated with Jessie Weston.[56]

Another of the treatises attributed to Hermes, the most influential and widely read of them all, may offer another glimpse at the secrets hidden within the *Elucidation*. The *Poemandres*—this word means "shepherd of men"—appears first in the *Corpus Hermeticum*, the traditional collection of the works of Hermes Trismegistus. It describes, among many other things, how the human soul descended at the beginning of time through the spheres of the seven planets known to ancient astronomers and astrologers, submitting itself to the rulership of the planets. In the attainment of gnosis, the *Poemandres* teaches, the soul rises up through the spheres of the planets and liberates itself from their power. The seven veils of the *Elucidation* thus can be identified as the seven spheres of the planets in Gnostic and Hermetic thought, and the seven guardians are the seven planetary archons, who rule over the world of matter and who must be overcome by the Gnostic in order to rise beyond them to the eternal world of light from which the human soul originally came.

And the other important name in the story, the name of Amangons, the wicked king? In Greek letters it is spelled Αμανγωνς and adds to 1145. 1145 by gematria works out to two different Greek phrases. The first is 'η καθεδρα τες βασιλειας Γαιης, *he kathedra tes basileias Gaies*, "the throne of the kingdom of Earth." The second and more important is ληστις Κορες, *lestis Kores*, "despoiler of Kore"—and Kore, remember, is the Maiden, the alternative title of the Greek goddess Persephone.[57] Here we have the clue that Jessie Weston searched for, but it points along the road she did not take, toward the Eleusinian Mysteries instead of the Mysteries of Cybele. The "despoiler of Kore" is, of course, the god Pluto or Hades, the underworld god whose kidnapping of Persephone set the great drama of Eleusis in motion.

The word *grail* itself—*graal* in the *Elucidation* and the other medieval French romances—has a similar if more straightforward message to pass on. In Greek letters, *graal* is spelled γρααλ, which adds to 135, the number of δοξα, *doxa*, which means "splendor" and "glory" but also "teaching." (The orthodox were those who believed they had the correct teaching, *orthos* + *doxa* in Greek.) This

---

56. See Kahane and Kahane, *The Krater and the Grail*.

57. This works out to 1144, but colel can, as usual, be added without changing the meaning.

suggests that all those hints about secrets of the Grail were not empty air; there was a teaching associated with the legend.

Subtract colel from the number of *doxa*, in turn, and you have 134, the number of ἅγιον, *hagion*, "holy thing." "Holy things" played a central role in the Eleusinian Mysteries, as we have seen; concealed in a sacred basket, they were carried from Eleusis to Athens every year just before the celebration of the Mysteries, and carried back with the candidates for initiation on the day of the ceremony. That was the original Grail procession. In the later form of the Eleusinian Mysteries, as practiced in private homes to avoid the threat of Christian persecution, it would have been reenacted in brief form, and the procession of the Grail witnessed by Perceval in Chrétien's tale is a very plausible image of how that was done.

There is at least one more numerical clue woven into the *Elucidation*, though I have not yet been able to decipher it. This has to do with the people full of malice who came out of the hills after Arthur's knights found the court of the Rich Fisherman again. The author of the *Elucidation* goes out of his way to stress that there were exactly 7,686 of them. In all probability this number is equal to the value of some specific sentence, but trying to identify which sentence equals so large a number is a difficult process. My guess, though this is only a guess, is that the sentence in question relates in some way to mainstream Christianity, but certainty will have to wait until someone succeeds in cracking this part of the *Elucidation*'s code.

It was a common practice among all the mystical traditions that made use of gematria to choose words and change the common spellings of names in order to make them fit some preexisting numerical symbolism. Thus, it's typical that the Welsh name Bleddri (or its Latin equivalent, Bledericus) was deliberately misspelled as Bleheris to make it communicate what the anonymous author of the *Elucidation* wanted it to communicate: the key that allows the Grail legends to be read as a Gnostic allegory and identifies the Grail as the Krater of Hermes. Equally, the obscure word *grail* was doubtless chosen by the creators of the original Grail legend because it added up to the right number and could thus communicate the secret to those who knew how to read the message.

The presence of gematria in the *Elucidation* is thus a significant clue pointing to Gnosticism, and to a particular kind of Gnosticism, in the background of the Grail legend. As far as anyone knows, the Cathars had no interest in the ancient Greek Mysteries and did not make use of the writings attributed to Hermes Trismegistus. The Naassenes, on the other hand, had a much more tolerant attitude toward the old Pagan Mysteries, and to judge by the comments of Hippolytus, incorporated at least one set of Mysteries—those of Attis and Cybele—in their system of spiritual development. The fragmentary references to Naassene teachings make it impossible to say for certain whether they included the Hermetic writings among the texts they had their initiates study, but some Gnostics certainly did: writings attributed to Hermes were included in the Nag Hammadi collection, the famous library of ancient Gnostic texts discovered in Egypt.

Of all the Gnostic sects whose traces survive today, certainly, the Naassenes have the most in common with the Grail legend. They embraced the ancient Mysteries, with their rites of "fleshly generation," and included ordinary Christian rites as the second stage in their way of ascent to gnosis.[58] They had an ascetic dimension to their teachings, as all the Gnostics did, and expected serious practitioners to practice celibacy in order to redirect the sexual energies away from generation, but their attitude toward the world of life and sexuality is far less hostile than that of many other Gnostic sects.

This same balance between asceticism and tolerance can be found in the early, pre-Galahad Grail legends as well. Arthur's knights are not monks. What brings about the destruction of Logres in the *Elucidation* is King Amangons's violent abuse of sexuality, not sexuality as such, and when the Waste Land is finally healed the knights and damsels celebrate by hunting, hawking, and making love in the woods until the arrival of summer. This is not the kind of allegory you can expect from an ascetic, world-hating creed. It is, however, the kind that might be expected from the Naassenes.

Finally, as though to complete making Jessie Weston's case for her, the Naassene document quoted by Hippolytus identifies gnosis with a cup, repeating the identification five times in a handful of pages. Here is the most important of these passages:

> This is the drinking-vessel—the Cup in which "the king drinketh and divineth." This was found hidden in the "fair seed" of

58. Weston, *From Ritual to Romance*, 155.

Benjamin. The Greeks also speak of it with inspired tongue, as follows:

"Bring water, bring wine, boy!
Give me to drink, and sink me in slumber!
My Cup tells me of what race I must be born,
Speaking with silence unspeaking."

This would be sufficient alone if men would understand—the Cup of Anacreon speaking forth speechlessly the ineffable mystery. For Anacreon's Cup is speechless—in as much as it tells him (says Anacreon) with speechless sound of what race he must be born—that is, spiritual, not carnal—if he hear the hidden mystery in silence.[59]

The poem quoted in this passage is part of a bawdy drinking song by the ancient Greek poet Anacreon, and it is typical of the Naassene sense of humor that they took it and redefined it as a revelation of spiritual wisdom. The "race" discussed in this passage, by the way, was not a biological race. To the Gnostics, all human beings irrespective of ethnicity belonged to one of three categories, which were termed "races": the material, the mental, and the spiritual categories of humanity. These correspond precisely to the three gates mentioned earlier. The *hylikoi*, or material people, can only pass through the first gate of the Pagan Mysteries. The *psychikoi*, or mental people, can pass through that and the second gate of ordinary Christianity, while the *pneumatikoi*, or spiritual people, alone can go on beyond these two to "accomplish the Mystery at the third gate." Anacreon's cup, by speaking the hidden mystery in silence, is telling the poet that he belongs to the third, spiritual category of people—those whom the Grail serves.

Remarkably, however, Jessie Weston did not mention this passage from Hippolytus in her books on the Grail. She knew about it—the version of the Naassene document she used in her writings, the one edited by her friend and associate G. R. S. Mead, includes it—and it provides an additional piece of evidence connecting the Naassene tradition with legends about a sacred cup, and thus

---

59. Gaffney, *Gnostic Secrets of the Naassenes*, 134.

potentially with the Grail. Why did she leave it unmentioned? The answer to that question will be discussed in part IV of our exploration.

Yet the *Elucidation* provides the seeker with many other doors, and these will need to be opened in order to make sense of the tradition we are exploring. The maidens in the hills who provided food for all, the devastation of Logres in response to Amangons's brutal act, the vision of a land restored by the asking of a question, the seven cloaks and stories and guardians of the world, and the detailed account of a ritual that seems to echo the ceremonies of the ancient Mysteries in some of its crucial details: all these point back to traditions of immense antiquity. To understand these traditions is to reach back through time to touch the legacy of the megalithic era, when standing stones and earthen barrows embodied a forgotten technology that helped create the temple tradition I have explored elsewhere. It is also an attempt to grasp some of the issues that were in play when the Grail romances were written—and were in play once again when Jessie Weston wrote.

PART TWO
THE ANCIENT
WISDOM

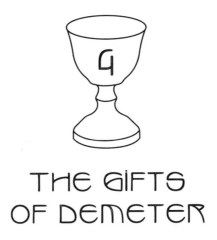

THE GIFTS
OF DEMETER

They call it Dodoni now, but twenty-five centuries ago the small town in the mountains of northwestern Greece was called Dodona. Even today, oak trees grow in the green valley between Mount Tomaros and Mount Manoliassa, and the wind off the Ionian Sea thirty miles to the west whispers in their branches. Sometime in the third millennium BCE, maybe earlier, priestesses of an ancient goddess learned to listen to the wind in the leaves, and they found answers in the wind's voice to questions that local folk brought to them.

Times changed, gods changed, but the voice of the wind remained. When ancient Greece was in its golden age, Dodona ranked among the greatest of Greek oracles. Embassies from the Greek city-states usually took their questions to Apollo's oracle at Delphi, but ordinary Greeks who needed the gods' advice more often journeyed to Dodona. Pilgrims came there throughout the year from every corner of the Greek world, up the mountain roads from Phocis or by ship to the harbor across from the island of Corcyra. The goddess of the oaks was called Dione by then, and the sacred oaks were claimed by her divine husband Zeus, king of the gods, but priestesses still tended the oracle. By a custom so old the Greeks themselves considered it ancient, they went barefoot, never washed their feet, and slept on the bare ground beneath the sacred oaks.

Like any important religious center, the oak grove at Dodona became the center of a social ecosystem of fair complexity, and visitors today often have a hard time seeing past the traces of that structure to the natural presence at its core. Dodona had its own amphitheater, one of the largest in Greece, where athletes competed in the Naian Games every four years. The *bouleterion*, or office building, close by was the administrative center of the oracle, where priests and temple servants managed the business affairs of an enterprise that drew tens of thousands of seekers every year. Marble temples to Heracles and Dione attracted their share of attention. In the midst of it all, a stone wall surrounded the old sacred grove, its entrance flanked with stone urns full of water that pilgrims used to purify themselves before entering the oracle.

At the center of the whole complex, hard by a small temple dedicated to Zeus, stood a single oak tree. Bronze cauldrons on tripods clustered around it, catching and amplifying the voice of the wind, and doves sacred to Dione gathered in its branches. When the oracle at Dodona was at its height, pilgrims filed into the grove, made their offerings at the temple, and then approached the priestesses one at a time to ask their questions. The sound of the wind, shaped into a low unearthly keening by the cauldrons, and the movements and calls of the doves answered, and the priestesses translated those answers into terms the pilgrims could understand.

A common cliché nowadays among the ecologically aware suggests that nature offers answers to some of the most pressing questions human beings ask themselves about their lives and the fate of their societies. The memory of Dodona, and of the many other oracles scattered across ancient Greece, serves as a reminder that people of an older time took this idea much more seriously than we do. The thousands of pilgrims who came to Dodona each year in ancient times placed the perplexities of their lives in the hands of a deity who spoke in the language of the Dodonese ecosystem, a language of winds and birds—and many of those pilgrims went their way satisfied by the answers they received.

It might be tempting to dismiss Dodona and everything it represents as an example of primitive superstition, except that the same ancient Greek culture that sought answers from the wind in Dodona's oaks also invented logic and gave philosophy to the Western world. Other aspects of ancient Greek culture show the same intertwining of spirituality and nature as Dodona, and many of these reveal a core of ecological wisdom hard to square with modern ideas about the nature and purpose of religion. As we explore the hidden ecological subtext within these traditions of archaic spirituality, in fact, quite a few common modern assumptions about so-called "primitive superstitions" may turn out to be in need of a second look.

▱

What does it mean to follow a religion of nature, to worship gods who are part of nature and reveal themselves in the wind among the leaves? The place of ancient Greece at the fountainhead of Western civilization, and the rich documentation that survives from its Pagan past, make it a good place to begin asking these questions.

Travelers to Greece nowadays see the white marble ruins of temples standing alone on bare hilltops beneath the fierce Mediterranean sun. Two millennia ago, when the temples stood intact and served the religious needs of millions of people, visitors encountered a very different sight. In those days the temples were brightly painted, and they rose out of lush greenery. Nearly every Greek temple stood in the middle of a *temenos*, a sacred area that was left to natural vegetation. Dodona's huge oaks stood out because of their age and the oracle tradition that surrounded them, but most temples of any size had at least one sacred tree near the sanctuary, and many had sizeable groves close by.

Demeter, the goddess of agriculture, was especially famous for her sacred groves.[60] In Athens, the ancient Greek city we know most about today, Demeter had at least three splendid temples inside the city itself, but most of her sanctuaries lay well outside the city walls. The small town of Eleusis west of Athens had the most important of those, where crowds went to celebrate the Eleusinian Mysteries every autumn, and it had an area of wild land scaled to match, called the *hiera orgas*, which ran west from Eleusis to the border of the neighboring city-state of Megara. Scores of smaller patches of Athenian territory belonged to Demeter as well, and most of them were given over to

---

60. Birge, "Sacred Groves in the Ancient Greek World," is a fine survey of the data.

natural vegetation, holy nature sanctuaries in the midst of the bustling life of ancient Greece's human population.

From a modern perspective, three things about these patches of sacred wilderness call for attention. First, veneration of sacred groves wasn't simply a pious wish. It had hefty legal penalties backing it up. In Athens, any livestock that strayed onto sacred ground became the property of the adjoining temple and was usually offered up as a sacrifice at once. Even gathering fallen wood from a sacred grove was so serious a crime in Athens that charges involving it had to be filed with the *basileus*, the highest religious official in the city, and cutting down an olive tree—*any* olive tree, anywhere in Athenian territory—was an act of sacrilege that carried the death penalty. In Arcadia, the rugged heartland of southern Greece, the sacred precinct of Zeus atop Mount Lykaion was surrounded by equally harsh laws: those who deliberately entered the precinct faced death by stoning, while those who strayed in by accident were condemned to exile. The same concern for sacred wildlands even extended into international affairs; in 352 BCE, when people from Megara encroached on the *hiera orgas* west of Eleusis, Athens responded by mobilizing its army and threatening war.

Second, many of these sacred wildlands made very poor settings for the ceremonies and ritual feasts that defined the practice of ancient Greek religion. Many swamps belonged to the gods: Demeter, the wine god Dionysos, and Artemis, the goddess of wild animals, all had their sacred marshlands. Artemis and the wilderness god Pan laid claim to mountains, though the highest peaks belonged to Zeus. Worshippers who wanted to commune with these deities went to temples in the cities or the rural hinterlands, though, not to marshes or mountaintops. As we have already seen, some wilderness sanctuaries, like Zeus's precinct on Mount Lykaion, were off-limits to everyone.

Third, many of the wildland sanctuaries of ancient Greece make sense in a surprising context—the context of ecology. Demeter's groves offer the best example. Aside from the big urban temples in Athens itself and the sprawling temple complex at Eleusis, most sanctuaries of Demeter in Athenian territory lay on the border between hilly ground and the arable lowlands, where streams come rushing down from the rugged Greek mountains and groundwater breaks the surface to form natural springs. Elsewhere in Greece, look for the nearest large hill to any ancient city and odds are that in Pagan times it had a sanctuary of Demeter on top, overlooking the fields closest to the city.

What do these sites have in common? Erosion control and water management. On the thin soils and steep slopes of the Greek landscape, soil erosion is the farmer's worst enemy. Gullies and sheet erosion can strip fertile farmland down to bare rock in a few short years if they are left unchecked. Leave the most vulnerable areas wild, though, and native vegetation and unbroken soil soak up water during rainstorms, releasing it slowly afterward and minimizing the risk of erosion. Hilltops in the midst of farmland and slopes at the edge of the arable lowlands are the crucial checkpoints, the places where a few acres left to native trees and shrubs can hold soil and water with their roots and stop erosion before it starts. Those are the places the ancient Greeks gave to Demeter, the goddess who made the grain grow.

Patches of native vegetation near woodland offer plenty of other gifts to the farmer, as today's organic growers know well. The same water-retaining properties that slam the brakes on erosion also combat drought, channeling rainwater down into the soil and the water table instead of letting it run off into the rivers. Wild trees and shrubs also harbor predators of many kinds, from foxes to swallows to beneficial insects, who feed on farm pests and keep their numbers in check, and pollinators such as wild bees who play a crucial role in the life cycle of some crops.

When the ancient Greeks said a grove was sacred to Demeter, then, they may have meant something much more pragmatic than the phrase suggests to modern ears. The requirements the goddess of grain placed on her worshippers include the requirements of successful grain farming in the ecosystem of ancient Greece, and the network of sacred groves across the Greek landscape in Pagan times played a critical role not only in Greek religion but in Greek agriculture as well. That suggests that Demeter herself may have had a much more direct connection to grain farming than our current notions of religion imagine.

The ancient Greeks themselves said as much, but they did it in mythic language, and modern scholars have had a hard time taking that language seriously. One famous myth tells of Erysichthon, who cut an oak from one of Demeter's groves and paid a terrible price. The best surviving version comes from the Roman poet Ovid, who dressed up the tale in elegant Latin verse and put it in his collection of stories *The Metamorphoses*. It's a splendid story and Ovid made the most of it, crafting images that glint like polished stones: Erysichthon bellowing at his servants and seizing the axe; blood instead of sap dripping from the wounded tree; tree-spirits weeping before Demeter; the terrible calm of the goddess as her silent nod sent Erysichthon to his doom. The punishment she laid on him was hunger so terrible that he sold his only child into slavery to buy food, and he ended up devouring his own flesh.

It's easy to miss the implications of all this, and Ovid did his level best to help, equipping Erysichthon with a shape-shifting daughter and leading the narrative as quickly as possible into the realms of wonder tale. Still, the bones of the story echo an ancient warning the people of Greece knew better than to ignore.

Certain trees belong to the power that causes grain to grow: that is what the myth says. If you cut them down, you will starve.

▱

In the summer of 1868, a middle-aged German businessman swung down from the saddle of a rented horse and stood in the hot Greek sun, looking up the slopes of a rugged hill at the last fragmentary traces of a civilization that learned Erysichthon's lesson the hard way. In Corinth, not twenty miles north, guides shrugged when he asked the route there, but the traveler knew how to get to the right area from old records, and a local farm boy guided him the rest of the way. Gazing up at the ruined walls, the traveler knew he'd reached the right place: Mycenae, the stronghold of the warrior king Agamemnon who fought in the Trojan War.

The traveler's name was Heinrich Schliemann. Within a few years he would be famous as the discoverer of Troy, the man who proved Homer right. His excavations at Mycenae later on in 1876 turned into the stuff of legend when he found tombs packed with golden treasures that still awe visitors to Athens's National Museum. Yet the deeper implications of his discoveries surfaced later, as hundreds of further excavations allowed scholars to trace the outlines of the lost world Schliemann found.[61]

---

61. Wood, *In Search of the Trojan War*, is a good overview of the Mycenean era.

The Mycenean civilization, as it's now called, began around 1700 BCE and ended suddenly about five hundred years later. In the two centuries before it collapsed, it ranked as a major power in the eastern Mediterranean, carrying on diplomacy with Egypt and the sprawling Hittite Empire, which then ruled what is now Turkey and Syria. A federation of kingdoms ruled from fortified cities—Pylos, Tiryns, Orchomenos, Thebes, Argos, and Mycenae itself—the Myceneans could stand comparison with most of the civilized nations of their time. Their records, written on clay tablets in the famous Linear B script, reveal centralized states with small armies of scribes recording the details of agriculture and trade.

At the height of their power, the Myceneans dominated the Aegean Sea and fought with the kingdoms of what is now Turkey's west coast. One of these wars, sometime around 1260 BCE, ended in the conquest of a city named Taruisa in a kingdom called Wilusa. Centuries later, recalling old tales of a glorious past, a Greek poet named Homer wrote two long poems about that war, though he pronounced the kingdom's name Ilios and called the city Troy.

Less than a century after Taruisa's fall, all that was gone. Most of the Mycenean cities were gutted by fire right around 1200 BCE. A handful of Linear B texts from Pylos document the last days of the crisis, recording orders that sent soldiers and oarsmen running to their posts. A final half-finished clay tablet, written in a hurried scrawl, records sacrifices of gold vessels and slaves to Zeus and Hera. Soon thereafter, perhaps within hours, Pylos was a smoking ruin.

In the next two decades, a wider catastrophe swept the eastern shores of the Mediterranean. The Hittite Empire collapsed forever, the kingdoms of the Aegean coast vanished from history, and scores of city-states along the eastern Mediterranean became abandoned ruins. Nearly every archaeological site in the region shows the telltale marks of war and fire. Clay tablets from the archives of the city of Ugarit in northern Syria echo the records from Pylos, with soldiers and ships ordered to their positions as messages went out to allies, pleading for aid against a nameless enemy. Archaeologists found one last desperate letter from Ugarit's king to the king of Cyprus still in the tablet-oven. It had not yet been baked hard when Ugarit was destroyed.

Surviving records are so fragmentary that archaeologists are still arguing over exactly what happened, but vital evidence comes from Egypt, one of the few nations to survive the catastrophe. The great temple of Medinet Habu, erected by the pharaoh Ramesses III to commemorate his reign, records Egyptian victories in two immense battles in 1180 BCE against "the Peoples of the Sea." Who were they? The temple inscriptions list Tursha, Sherden, Shekelesh, Tjekeryu, Peleseti, Aqaiwasha, and Danuna, all mentioned in other Egyptian records as peoples of the northeastern Mediterranean; the last two names echo the Greek terms *Achaioi* and *Danaoi*, Homer's words for the Myceneans themselves. Carvings at Medinet Habu show the Peoples of the Sea in the armor and clothing of nearly all the peoples north of Egypt, including Myceneans. Women and children accompanied the fighters, clear evidence that this was no ordinary army but a migration of whole peoples seeking new homes.

Historians and archaeologists proposed many causes for the catastrophe of 1200 BCE, but as evidence piled up about the end of the Mycenean age, the role of ecological disaster became harder and harder to ignore. The smoking gun finally turned up in core samples of the sea floor from Greek coastal waters near the Mycenean heartland.[62] Layers dating from the Mycenean age proved to contain huge deposits of soil stripped from the nearby countryside. Evidently, erosion spun out of control and sent a sizeable fraction of Greece's sparse soil to the bottom of the sea.

In other words, like many other peoples before and since, the Myceneans ignored the hard reality of ecological limits and paid the inevitable price. Their civilization depended, like every agricultural society, on natural cycles that maintained soil fertility and made harvests possible. Once those cycles were disrupted, their civilization fell.

Probably no one noticed the slow breakdown of those cycles as the Myceneans cut too many trees, plowed too many hillsides, and pastured too many cattle. Only the telltale color change as clear rivers turned brown with eroded soil would have given warning at first, and the proud warlords and their busy scribes had other things on their minds. Still, faltering harvests likely had a role in sending Mycenean raiders across the Aegean in search of plunder to patch the cracks in a crumbling economy. The highest term of praise Homer gives his Mycenean heroes is "sacker of cities."

---

62. Fuchs, Lang, and Wagner, "The History of Holocene Soil Erosion in the Phlious Basin, NE Peloponnese, Greece, Based on Optical Dating."

Once the process had gone far enough, disaster was inevitable, though a shift in climate that cut Greece's annual rainfall probably triggered the final crisis. Once the harvests began to fail, the warlords turned on one another, fighting not for gold or glory but for sheer survival. As harvest after harvest failed, mass migration became the only option left, and Greece's crisis became an international disaster as the "sackers of cities" swept east into Asia and south along the Mediterranean coast, wrecking the ecological and social balance of drought-stressed urban societies across the region. Other peoples left homeless and hungry became refugees in turn, spreading devastation south and east, until finally a tidal wave of desperate human beings crashed into the ramparts of Egypt.

◇

The aftermath of the Mycenean catastrophe saw new kingdoms rise across half the Mediterranean. Defeated on the borders of Egypt, the surviving Peoples of the Sea scattered in all directions, looking for new homes. The Sherden ended up giving their name to Sardinia, the Shekelesh to Sicily. The Peleseti, originally from Crete, settled on the eastern shores of the Mediterranean and became the Philistines of the Old Testament. The Aqaiwasha and Danuna, Homer's Achaioi and Danaoi, vanished from history.

Meanwhile, Greece plunged into a dark age more than four centuries long.[63] Most of the Mycenean cities burnt around 1200 BCE were never rebuilt. A few, including Mycenae itself, struggled back to life, only to be destroyed again during the following century. Meanwhile, the number of Mycenean settlements plummeted. From the century before the catastrophe, archaeologists have found 320 inhabited sites; from the century after it, only 130—and from the century after that, only forty. Drastic depopulation set in. Whole regions of Greece were abandoned, and they stayed that way until Dorian immigrants from the north moved in much later. Elsewhere, survivors huddled behind half-ruined Mycenean walls, making a meager living from herds. The agriculture that fed the Mycenean warlords came to a halt as wheat and barley dropped out of cultivation, except in a few lowland areas. Writing became a lost art, and Linear B remained unreadable until Michael Ventris deciphered it in the 1950s. Looking

---

63. Snodgrass, *The Dark Age of Greece*, is a good survey.

back centuries later, the poets Homer and Hesiod knew only five craft professions—carpenters, blacksmiths, potters, weavers, and tanners—alongside farmers, herdsmen, and the omnipresent warriors. The complex Mycenean economy with its dozens of occupational specialties had vanished even from memory.

As they reflected on their past, the scattered Greek communities at the end of that dark age remembered that the earth had once been much greener and life less difficult. Hesiod, whose *Theogony* and *Works and Days* are among the oldest Greek poems, wrote of a Golden Age when the earth produced crops without toil. Hesiod himself lived during the eighth century BCE, the first century of real recovery after the Mycenean collapse, and his poems paint the struggle for survival in bitter colors. Yet that struggle was already easing in Hesiod's time, as two changes deeply rooted in ecology helped transform life for the desperately poor communities of Greece.

The first was olive cultivation, which was just beginning to spread across Greece in Hesiod's time. Olive trees thrived in the dry Greek ecosystem, and growing them on hillsides stopped soil erosion in its tracks. Olive oil was a valuable product that could be traded for food supplies from overseas, but olive cultivation also had rewards closer to home, since the tree roots held soil and water in place and helped spare the lowlands from flood and drought.

A little later, vineyards spread alongside the olive orchards, giving Greece a second lucrative trade crop and a second form of agriculture that did not cause soil erosion. As olive trees and grapevines spread across the Greek landscape, soils recovered and communities thrived.

There may well have been a third factor in the Greek recovery. This was the arrival of a new religious architecture from Egypt, bearing with it the secret of the temple technology. The transformation of Greek temples in what historians call the late Archaic period is well documented, and so is its source; the classic Greek temples that began to rise about this time, each one with its sacred greenbelt around it, are clearly modeled on Egyptian originals.[64] As I discuss in *The Secret of the Temple*, Egypt had had the temple technology for at least two thousand years by the time they exported it to Greece, as part of a broader transfer of Egyptian cultural ideas and influences that also set Greek philosophy in motion and inspired important shifts in Greek religious and

---

64. Hahn, *Anaximander and the Architects*, documents this.

magical thought. Since the temple technology was always understood in religious terms—"do this and the gods will bless your harvests"—it comes as no surprise that it would have been adopted by the Greeks, and its impact seems to have been considerable.

In his book *The Other Greeks*, American classicist Victor Davis Hanson has illuminated the central role of these changes in birthing classical Greek culture. He points out that most of the citizens of any Greek city were small-scale proprietors who owned and worked orchards, vineyards, and grain fields just outside the walls. Overseas income from the lucrative oil and wine trade helped these smallholders break the grip of the old feudal aristocrats, whose wealth came from pastureland and herds, and paid for the building programs that turned towns into walled cities crowned with marble temples. Those cities in turn fostered the blend of homegrown cultural initiatives and creative borrowings from overseas that made classical Greece the seedbed of Western civilization.

Hanson's otherwise-excellent book leaves out any discussion of the ecological side of the birth of classical Greece, and it has little to say about the religious side, either. He's hardly to blame for these blind spots. Most modern historians trace the causes of great social transformations to the realms of politics and economics, not to ecology or Pagan religion—much less to a fusion of the two. Here again, though, the ancient Greeks thought otherwise. To them, just as grain was the gift of Demeter, cities and urban culture were the gifts of Athena, the goddess of the olive tree. Temples to Athena, in the Greek way of thinking, were of crucial importance, the centers from which the blessings of urban life radiated across the landscape. They may have been correct in that assessment.

The legacy of the Mycenean collapse didn't turn the ancient Greeks into a nation of ecologists, to be sure. By the fourth century BCE, deforestation around Athens was common enough (and its effects clear enough) that Plato could put a thoughtful bit of ecological discussion into his dialogue *Critias*:

> *Some of the mountains can sustain only bees now, but it was not long ago that they were wooded, and even now the roofs of some of our largest buildings have rafters cut from these areas and those rafters are still sound. There were also many tall cultivated trees, and the land offered a vast amount of pasturage for animals. What is*

more, the land enjoyed the annual rain from Zeus, not lost, as now,
when it flows off of the bare earth into the sea. Rather, much of it
was retained, since the earth took it within itself, storing it up in the
earth's retentive clay, releasing water from the high country into the
hollows, and supplying all regions with generous amounts of springs
and flowing rivers. That what we are now saying about the land is
true is indicated by the holy sanctuaries, which are situated where
this water used to spring up.[65]

The effects of deforestation posed serious problems for the Greeks of Plato's time and afterward, but the "holy sanctuaries" Plato mentioned remained for centuries longer, maintaining the goodwill of Demeter and holding the lowland soil in place. When Pausanias wrote his *Guide to Greece* for tourists in the third century CE, Greece was part of the Roman Empire and Athens a provincial town dreaming of bygone days, but the sacred groves still remained, the olive trees still flourished, and the sacred ecology that underpinned classical Greece still functioned.

Two centuries later, Greece was once again hurtling toward collapse. A new religion had seized power in the Roman world and condemned sacred groves and their deities alike as remnants of an outworn, superstitious past. Christian axes felled the oaks of Dodona in 391, the last sacred groves became firewood under the Emperor Justinian in 571, and the old temple cult with its secret agricultural technology was banned at the same time. During these same years, the rural economy of Greece imploded.

The same researchers who found huge deposits of eroded topsoil on the bottom of the Aegean Sea from Mycenean times found another thick layer of soil from the late Roman period, dating from the years 400–600 CE. Though olive orchards and vineyards remained, the felling of the sacred groves and the closing of the temples undercut the Greek agricultural system and depopulation set in, leaving medieval Greece with a fraction of the population it supported in Pagan times. The same dismal story repeated itself across most of the Roman world as traditional religions attuned to ecological realities gave way to a new and intolerant faith that, at least in its first centuries, despised

---

65. Translated in Goldin, "The Ecology of *Critias* and Platonic Metaphysics."

nature and relied on the imminent return of its messiah to solve the world's problems.

◇

Ancient Greece was far from the only culture to evolve such a fusion of religious faith and ecological awareness. All across the old world in ancient times, religious traditions and environmental concerns mingled to an extent that can be hard to imagine today. Deities of wind and sea and fertile soil, gods who were buried with the seed and rose again with the new stalk, goddesses whose gifts to humanity were food plants, received the worship most modern people direct to the formless creator gods and moralizing prophets of monotheist religions. Each of the old nature religions embodied its own ecological wisdom, often in forms that show close kinship to the Greek model. In Pagan Ireland, for example, disrespect for sacred trees and groves carried the same harsh penalties as in ancient Greece. *Three unbreathing things paid for only with breathing things*, an old Irish maxim warns: *an apple tree, a hazel bush, a sacred grove.*

Yet these religions of nature weren't simply collections of ecological taboos. They reached straight to the same hopes and perplexities that motivate faith today. In Egypt, for instance, the archaeologists who opened the tomb of Tutankhamen found, here and there among the treasures, little figures of the god Osiris made of Nile mud. Each figure had barley seeds pressed into it, and the seeds had been watered until they sprouted. Osiris was the grain god of ancient Egypt, and the myth of his life, death, and rebirth tracks the life cycle of barley in the Egyptian ecosystem, but the little figurines—green with the sign of Osiris's yearly rebirth—show that ancient Egyptians turned to the cycles of nature for answers to humanity's deepest questions.

Such faiths are rare now. Two millennia of missionary zeal, politically enforced orthodoxy, and cultural imperialism have obliterated most of the old nature-centered faiths and forced alien ways of thinking onto many of the survivors. One of the few of the old religions that still survives more or less intact is Shinto, the old polytheist faith of Japan. Political pressures in the seventh century CE, when Buddhism first took root in Japan, forced the new religion to settle down alongside the old, rather than replacing it. Thereafter, Shinto cultivated links to its archaic heritage, making adjustments to fit the needs of the times while core traditions changed with glacial slowness. The results often look bizarre to foreigners—in one common Shinto ceremony nowadays, priests use prayers in ancient Japanese and centuries-old ritual to purify and bless parishioners' new cars—but they have given Shinto the resilience to keep its place in Japanese culture through centuries of change. Despite the spread of new religions, the ham-handed efforts of late nineteenth- and early twentieth-century governing elites to turn it into an imperialist ideology, and the social and technological revolutions that changed Japan from a third-world country in 1900 to one of the most urbanized, educated, and technologically advanced societies on the planet today, most Japanese still participate in Shinto ceremonies at least a few times a year, and a sizable number make Shinto part of their daily lives.

Even a casual comparison of Shinto and ancient Greek Paganism shows startling parallels. Both religions are diverse, tolerant polytheistic faiths that value ritual and custom above doctrine and belief. Both worship deities closely linked to the forces of nature; both use offerings of food and drink as the central act of their rites of worship, and both place great significance on sharing a part of the offerings among the worshippers. Both enshrine their deities in structures that make good use of the archaic temple technology while using local materials and architectural motifs. Both time their major festivals by the cycle of the agricultural year, turn to oracles to ask the gods for advice, and seek ceremonial purity from cold water—when Agamemnon and his warriors bathed in the sea to purify themselves before offering to Apollo in the first book of Homer's *Iliad*, they followed a custom still practiced near many Shinto shrines in Japan today.

The parallels run straight through the overlaps between religion and ecology we've already traced in ancient Greek tradition. Like Greek temples, Shinto shrines are traditionally surrounded by greenery, and many of the oldest and largest shrines stand in the middle of extensive sacred groves. Many Japanese hills and mountains are sacred to the *kami*, the divine powers of Shinto belief; logging, farming, hunting, and any other activity that might disturb the native plants and animals have been forbidden there since time immemorial.

The location of these shrines and sacred mountains displays a fine sense of ecological strategy. In a brilliant study of the ecological dimensions of Shinto, Minoru Sonoda has shown that in Yamato province, the heartland of early Japan, *yamaguchi no kami* (kami of forests and water) had shrines at the points where streams flowed out of the foothills into the irrigated lowland plains, while *mikumari no kami* (watershed kami) had shrines located at the four major river sources of the region.[66] Like the groves of Demeter in ancient Greece, the sacred precincts of the kami occupied exactly the places where native vegetation offered critical protection against soil erosion.

Deforestation and drought happened now and again in Japanese history, but Japan's rulers have had a better track record in dealing with these problems than the elites of most other nations. In 821 CE, for example, the imperial government took note of drought problems in the hills around the ancient capital at Nara and traced the problem straight to deforestation. An edict in that year ordered a halt to logging along rivers, streams, and irrigation ponds, and it commanded officials to plant trees to replace those that had been cut down. The language of the edict shows a clear grasp of what we would call the scientific dimensions of the problem:

> The infiltration of water depends on the combination of water and trees. Therefore you must make sure that trees grow abundantly along the banks. When clouds empty their rain on a [wooded] mountain, the river [emerging from it] will supply nine village units with water; when a mountain is bare and shaven of trees, its valley streams will dry up.[67]

Almost a thousand years later, after Tokugawa Ieyasu took power as shogun and brought Japan out of a long age of anarchy, the same story repeated itself. Lumber shortages in the mid-seventeenth century focused official attention to the fact that too many trees had been cut and too many forests cleared for farming. The shogun's government responded with edicts ordering trees to be planted and restricting unauthorized logging. These laws were so effective that even today, Japan has larger tracts of forest than most other industrial nations.

Meanwhile, Japanese rice fields have ranked as some of the world's most productive acreage for upward of two thousand years. Shinto tradition credits this productivity to the rice kami Inari, one of the most widely revered Shinto deities. Foxes are sacred to Inari, and few Japanese will harm or even inconvenience a fox

---

66. Sonoda, "Shinto and the Natural Environment."

67. Sonoda, "Shinto and the Natural Environment," 38–39.

willingly; many mountains overlooking the core agricultural regions of the old Japanese heartland belong to Inari, and they have stayed green with ancient forests since before the beginning of recorded history; thousands of Shinto shrines, each surrounded with its trees and gardens, have Inari as their patron deity.

All these things make the Shinto claim that Inari brings the rice harvest more than mere metaphor. The sacred mountains and shrines surrounded with greenery serve the same role in Japan they did in ancient Greece: preventing erosion and maintaining a stable water supply. Even the sacred foxes, who can often be seen trotting along the low earthen dikes between rice fields in rural Japan, have a crucial ecological role. They keep rodent populations in check, and so control the major threat to seed stocks and stored grain in the Japanese rural ecosystem.

Clearly, then, the worship of Inari in Japan—like the worship of Demeter in ancient Greece—can't simply be dismissed as outworn superstition. To this day it plays a significant role in maintaining the ecological balances on which the old agricultural economy of Japan depended for many centuries. Somehow, a great deal of subtle ecological knowledge entered the traditions surrounding these two deities, and not just these two alone. The same sort of ecological sophistication can be found in surviving traces of many other nature religions, along with the temple technology or a related system, mentioned earlier, that uses stepped pyramids or earth altars in place of enclosed temples.

Where did this knowledge come from? No one knows. In all probability, it was pieced together gradually over millennia as tribal peoples close to the land paid attention to what made the crops flourish and what did not. The temple technology, one of the core elements of the knowledge we are discussing, may well have originated in a single place as a result of a chance discovery, but it was adapted skillfully in different cultures to fit local environments and use local materials and architectural forms. All this shows that what was being passed on from one culture to another, and one age to another, was not merely a rote practice that happened to work, but a set of principles from which many applications could be unfolded. As we will see, it is only one of several such traditional sciences to have left visible traces in the Grail legends.

THE SECRET OF
THE BARROWS

"Before being discovered, the savage was first invented," wrote the Italian prehistorian Giuseppe Cocchiara.[68] He was quite correct. Rationalists who devoutly believed that history was a story of progress from primitive squalor to the glories of civilized life dreamed up an image of primal humanity—brutish, ignorant, living at war with nature—and then went looking for people who could be shoehorned into that image. Romantics who believed, just as devoutly, that history was a story of decline from an idyllic golden age to a corrupt present dreamed up an equal and opposite image of primal humanity—peaceful, innocent, living in harmony with nature—and then set out on the identical quest. These two images of the human past maintain their grip on the imagination of the modern world because they fulfill powerful emotional needs. As long as we cling to them, we will never understand the past.

Human beings in prehistoric times were just as intelligent, curious, and perceptive as we are today. They were perfectly capable of noticing what was going

---

68. Burl, *Prehistoric Avebury*, 7.

on around them, coming up with theories to explain what they saw, and figuring out ways to put those theories to work for them. They were also perfectly capable of making disastrous mistakes and then learning from the consequences. Until the invention of writing, they had to work within the limits of the human brain's capacity for information storage, but they accomplished impressive feats.

A properly trained member of a hunter-gatherer society—say, an elder of an Australian aboriginal band—likely knows as much as a professor of physics in a large Western city. The elder and the professor know different things, to be sure. The elder cannot explain the mathematics of gravity, but the professor cannot explain the intricate patterns of mythic geography that guide the band on its seasonal round and keep its members alive in a desert land. Both have specialized in types of knowledge relevant to their own needs and the needs of the people who come to them for instruction and guidance.

In the same way, and for exactly the same reasons, it's a mistake to think of technologies of hunter-gatherer peoples as primitive or crude. The boomerangs and woomeras (spear throwers) used by Australian aborigines to hunt are marvels of design, honed through thousands of years of experience to be extraordinarily efficient at doing what they do. Given the resources the aborigines had and the challenges they faced, these elegant weapons were the best that they could have come up with—and come up with them they did.

Boomerangs and woomeras are, in a certain sense, easy for us to understand. We know about hunting and most people in our culture enjoy eating meat, so we can grasp the motives that guided aboriginal craftspeople as they worked out the subtle issues of balance and heft that makes a woomera so effective at sending a stone-tipped spear soaring through the air to bring down a kangaroo in mid-jump. What's more, we understand the physics of spear flight, so it's not too hard for us to heft a woomera, fit the butt of a spear to its business end, and discover to our amazement just how sophisticated a technology a woomera actually is.

Imagine for a moment, though, that ancient peoples came up with technologies that are far less transparent to us. Imagine that certain technologies relied on principles we have not yet learned and evolved in directions we have never explored. Imagine, furthermore, that some of these technologies have to do with parts of human experience that our culture denies and rejects—aspects of the cosmos that have been ruled off-limits for centuries by rationalists and religious authorities alike. Given the widespread modern habit of despising what we don't understand, wouldn't these technologies be dismissed as "primitive superstitions," their material traces heaped up in museums as "ritual items," and any inconvenient data concerning their actual function consigned to the realm of mythology and legend?

This is not just a thought experiment. Ever since the nineteenth century, when Heinrich Schliemann showed that the locations described by Homer were real places rather than figments of a poet's imagination, scholars in dozens of fields have shown that tales dismissed as myth and legend are very often memories of actual events, and practices brushed aside as superstitious nonsense turned out to embody exquisitely precise knowledge of the natural world and the results of human interaction with it. Our ancestors knew more than most of us give them credit for, and some of their knowledge left detailed traces in the myths and rituals of an earlier day.

My earlier book *The Secret of the Temple* focused on a lost technology of exactly this kind. In that book, as already noted, I presented evidence for the existence of an archaic folk technology that used certain specially prepared buildings—made of certain materials, designed according to certain geometries, and used in certain ways—as resonance chambers to amplify naturally occurring energies that caused improved crop fertility in areas near the buildings. That was what was behind the claim, found with remarkable consistency over a wide range of Old World societies, that building temples and performing certain rites in them caused crops to flourish. That folk technology, according to the evidence I presented, survived in fragmentary form in Ireland through the Dark Ages, was filled out with further information brought from the Middle East in the wake of the Crusades, was embodied in the medieval churches built by the operative forerunners of today's Freemasons, and helped give rise to the legends of the Holy Grail that healed the Waste Land.

The temple technology was one of the great secrets of the ancient priesthoods. It was not the only such secret, however, nor was it the only one of the old priestly secrets that left its mark on the Grail legends. Another archaic folk technology—one of the most secret and, to modern minds, one of the strangest—also comes into our story. Like the temple technology, it had an architectural dimension, but its goals were not oriented to bountiful harvests. Its purpose was nothing less than the prolongation of human consciousness beyond physical death.

We can begin an exploration of this archaic priestly technology with a curious detail of Christian practice that few people today remember. According to the traditions of those Christian denominations that date from ancient times—the Orthodox and Catholic churches—the Mass can only properly be celebrated on top of part of a corpse. Every Catholic altar is topped with a stone slab containing two first-class relics, and traditionally at least one of those has to be part of the physical remains of a Catholic saint. Every Orthodox altar has spread upon it, just before the Communion service begins, a cloth called an *antimension*, and sewn into the antimension is a flat container with part of a saint's corpse in it.

The reverence for relics in today's Christianity, remarkable though it is, is a faint echo of what it was in earlier times. In the Middle Ages, the relics of saints were seen as talismans of immense power. A church or abbey with important relics could expect a steady stream of pilgrims who would come to invoke the saint and seek miraculous help. Certain medieval aristocrats were renowned for their collections of saintly body parts, some of which were obtained from churches by straightforward robbery.

While today's theologies by and large insist that God can act anywhere in the cosmos as easily as anywhere else, the Christians of the Middle Ages saw things differently. To be in the presence of the bones of a mighty saint was to enter a space where miracles were much more likely than elsewhere. Aristocrats who traveled with chaplains in their entourage routinely had portable altars, little flat boxes of stone and precious metals containing the relics of saints, which they took with them so Mass could be properly celebrated on the road and so the miraculous powers of a holy corpse could be close at hand at all times.[69]

This attitude toward relics is far from unique to Christianity. All across southern Asia, *stupas* containing some fragment of the body of the Buddha—a tooth here, a finger bone there—attract the devotion of millions of Buddhists. In Sufism, the mystical branch of Islam, the tombs of famous *shaykhs* (holy teachers) have a similar status and attract the same kind of attention.

---

69. One scholar, in fact, has argued that the Grail in Wolfram von Eschenbach's *Parzifal* was such a portable altar; see Murphy, *Gemstone of Paradise*.

Follow the thread back into ancient times and the veneration for relics begins to shade into something stranger. In ancient Greece, for example, the gods and goddesses of Mount Olympus and the spirits of mountains, forests, and rivers received worship, but so did a class of being who were known as heroes—in fact, the English word *hero* comes from the Greek word.[70] The heroes had been human beings at some point in the distant past, very often during the Mycenean era or in the dark age that followed Mycenae's fall. To the Greeks, however, they had long since become more than human.

Some heroes, though not all, had lived what we would now consider heroic lives. The thing that mattered was that their spirits remained awake and active, like the saints of Christian belief, so they could be invoked by the living. Thus, the grave of a hero became a sacred place where offerings were made to his spirit, and in exchange the local community could expect good harvests, healing from illnesses, omens for guidance, and success in war. The body of the hero was the essential focus of his power. When groups of people moved long distances and wanted to bring their heroes with them, the physical remains of the honored dead had to be dug up and taken along.[71] Where the corpses were, the heroes were.

Over much of the world, wherever archaic religious traditions have left traces, similar traditions can be found. In Ireland, the Greek heroes have their equivalent in the Tuatha de Danaan, the spirits of the people who lived in Ireland before the ancestors of today's Irish got there. It takes careful reading in scholarly literature to get past a thick layer of modern romantic fantasy and discover that the Tuatha de Danaan are in fact the ghosts of the ancient dead, and the hollow hills where they dwell are the burial mounds of the Neolithic inhabitants of Ireland, the people who lived there before today's Irish arrived. Cross the sea from Ireland to Brittany, the Celtic nation currently part of France, and matters are much clearer: the stories the Irish tell about the faeries and the Tuatha de Danaan are told in Brittany about Ankou, King of the Dead, and his ghostly followers.

---

70. *Merriam-Webster*, s.v. "hero (n.)," accessed March 11, 2022, https://www.merriam-webster
.com/dictionary/hero.

71. See Burkert, *Greek Religion*, 203–7.

Another echo of the same archaic tradition has left vivid evidence in the folklore and legends of many lands. Over much of the world, local tales describe hollow hills in which a king of olden times sleeps in a tomb full of treasure, surrounded by his warriors. They are not dead, and in due time they will awaken again, but no one knows when. King Arthur is the most famous of these figures, kings once and kings to be, but there are many others. Closely related to this motif is another that surrounds great wizards and loremasters of the past who have descended into the earth and remain there, not dead but passed into another mode of life. Merlin in Wales, the Buddhist wizard-saint Kobo Daishi in Japan, and Christian Rosenkreutz in Germany—the enigmatic medieval founder of the Rosicrucians—are all examples of this theme.

Where the traditions of mound burial can be traced, in turn, stories about the afterlife take on a distinctive and unsettling character. In the *Odyssey*, one of Homer's two great poems, the hero Odysseus has to travel to the land of the dead. When he does so, he finds himself in a place without sunlight, surrounded by the faint, feeble shapes of the dead, who flutter about him and squeak like bats. They remain unable to think or speak until they drink a blood offering that Odysseus makes to them, but once they taste the blood they are able to recognize him and answer his questions. While the epic frames the encounter with the dead with colorful details, it is clear from context that the house of Hades Odysseus enters is a burial mound. Wherever else mound burial was practiced, traditional lore describes the fate of the dead in the same way: pallid specters hovering in an underground place, dependent on offerings from the living for a semblance of life.

The further back in time we trace this body of traditions, the more complex, specific, and detailed it becomes. In ancient Egypt, as the bodies of the dead were mummified, priests performed rituals and carried out procedures that modern scholars still do not understand well, culminating in the process of Opening the Mouth, which made the spirit of the dead person capable of benefiting from offerings and communicating with the living. Just as the Tuatha de Danaan dwelt within huge mounds of earth and stone from which they could only venture forth by night, the Egyptian dead resided in pyramids or stone-cut tombs, sheltered from the sun's rays, and their ultimate hope—a blessing that only the gods could grant them—was enshrined in the Egyptian name of the Book of the Dead: *Pert em Hru*, the Book of Coming Forth by Day.

All this evidence can be summed up readily. Over much of the world, from very ancient times, people believed that it was possible to keep certain dead people conscious and able to interact with the living, provided that very precise procedures were followed. The body must be preserved intact, or nearly intact; it must undergo certain complex procedures closely linked to religion and magic; once these were done, it must be kept underground, sheltered from the sun's influence by massive structures of stone, brick, or earth. If this was done properly, the consciousness of the dead person became a living presence within the tomb and, at night, in its vicinity, could confer benefits on the living.

Whether or not this belief is literally true can be left for parapsychologists to investigate. What matters for our present purpose is that the belief was widely held over much of the Old World in the distant past. There were good reasons for at least some of the beliefs that gathered around this set of traditions, especially those having to do with agricultural fertility. Experiments with modern measuring equipment have shown that certain ancient customs around old mounds and pyramids—especially those that involve placing seed grain in specific places on or near them before planting—cause improvements in crop fertility, due to well-documented effects of geomagnetism on the seeds.[72] In an agricultural society that depended on each year's harvest for survival, that was good enough reason to keep up the traditional rites.

There may have been more to it than that—quite possibly much more—but again, that can be left to future researches. What matters for our present purpose is that the practices and folklore surrounding mound burial and the archaic cult of the dead offer unexpected insights into the legends that surround the Grail and its lost ritual. To make sense of these insights, we need to start by looking back more than six thousand years, before the pyramids, before Stonehenge, to the age when the first ancient earthworks rose in the lands that would later become central to the legends of the Grail.

---

72. Burke and Halberg, *Seed of Knowledge, Stone of Plenty*.

Those earthworks took many forms, each of them echoing patterns of religious belief and practice we can only guess at today. Among the oldest are cause-wayed enclosures, which first appeared around 4000 BCE. Imagine a hilltop rising green above a forested landscape. The top of the hill has been cleared of trees and the two deep ditches carved in the hilltop, one inside the other, form a double circle, marking out the hilltop as sacred space. Gaps in the ditches form causeways on which the tribespeople can cross onto holy ground. At certain seasons, the tribe gathers just outside its causewayed enclosure and celebrates ritual feasts, but during the rest of the years the enclosure is a place of the dead. The people of northwestern Europe in that time, like Tibetans and Zoroastrians today, did not bury their dead. Instead, they laid out the corpses in these hilltop shrines and left them until birds had picked the bones clean.

The bones of the dead also played an important, if enigmatic, role in an even more ancient class of monuments: the long barrows. By 4300 BCE, and possibly long before then, people across northwestern Europe had begun to build great earthen mounds up to a hundred yards long, twenty yards wide, and ten feet tall, with a chamber in one end lined with timber or stone, and a stone-paved court in front of the chamber for ceremonies and ritual feasts. There were an astonishing number of long barrows in megalithic times; some 40,000 of them still survive in Europe today, and there must have been many others that have eroded away or been destroyed by later building projects. In the regions where the tradition was practiced, every tribal village had one, and they kept it in use for many centuries.

As far as I have been able to determine, the long barrows were the first human structures to make use of the basic principles of the temple technology, and it is at least possible that the earliest builders of the barrows were the ones who discovered the effect that made the temple technology work. The barrows also had an important role in rites involving the dead, however. The bones of certain people—a tiny fraction of the total population of each tribal group, according to archaeologists—ended up in the chambers. Nor did the bones stay in the barrows once put there. Many of the bones in long barrows show signs of having been taken out of the barrow, used for unknown purposes, and brought back. The parallel with medieval Christian customs involving the bones of the saints, which were also taken out of their shrines from time to time and paraded through the streets of medieval cities, come to mind here.

Intensive study of ancient sites by archaeologists makes it possible to glimpse just a little of what went on at the causewayed enclosures and long barrows. The tribal peoples of that era seem to have practiced ancestor worship, holding sacrificial feasts at the causewayed enclosures and performing other rites in front of the long barrows to ask the spirits of the dead to bless and protect the crops, the herds, and the human community.[73] Certain ghosts were more central to these rites than others, but the difference does not seem to have been a matter of social status, as status markers are all but absent in the archeological remains of the age of long barrows.

Some other principle seems to have been involved in the selection. If certain occult traditions are to be taken seriously, specific family bloodlines were considered to be specially gifted at bridging the gap between the living and the dead, and their ghosts retained that gift after they died. Members of those families went into the long barrows to become what the ancient Greeks called heroes and modern Christians call saints: intercessors between humanity and the world of the unseen. They dwelt in an intermediate state between life and death within the hollow hills, where they could be approached by properly prepared worshippers and where their faint, fluttering voices could be heard. Those who went beneath the earth in this way did not remain there indefinitely; the traditions just mentioned suggest that each one served for a generation until replaced by another, and that their remains were then taken out of the barrow and exposed to the elements to free the ghost to go on to whatever fate awaited it.

The tribes who held ritual feasts outside causewayed enclosures and put the bones of the gifted dead in long barrows supported themselves in much the same way that the native tribes of the eastern woodlands of North America did long afterward. Farming provided part of their food, but only part. They also hunted, fished, and gathered wild plants, moving through a seasonal round that took them from one resource to the next. Theirs was a relatively egalitarian society, without drastic differences between rich and poor, and while the tribes doubtless warred with each other from time to time, there seems to have been no separate caste of warriors. It was a stable way of subsistence and it seems to have thrived for a very long time.

---

73. See, for example, Burl, *Prehistoric Avebury*.

Right around 3000 BCE, though, a radical religious and cultural change swept through northwestern Europe. The long barrows and causewayed enclosures were abandoned, and many of the barrows themselves were blocked up with huge stones, sealing them off from the living. New sacred spaces took their place: round barrows containing stone-lined chambers for the dead and stone circles oriented toward the turning heavens. Once again, only a small proportion of the dead ended up in these sacred spaces, but their bodies were no longer set on hilltops to be cleansed by birds, their bones were not taken out of the barrows for sacred rites, nor were they selected for their ability to interface between the living and the dead. The bodies interred in the round barrows belonged to chieftains, aristocrats, and warriors, and they were buried immediately after death with all the signs of material wealth: fine pottery, ceremonial weapons, and, once metalworking had reached Britain, precious objects of bronze and gold.

The new society also depended much more heavily on agriculture and herds than the people of the long barrows had, and much less on the hunting, fishing, and wild plants that had kept that earlier culture closely attuned to the natural world. Archaeologists back in the early twentieth century used to imagine the end of the long barrow era and the coming of the round barrow era as the arrival of a wave of conquerors, the Beaker folk, who rode roughshod over the native peoples. More recent research has cast doubt on this picture of events, suggesting that the transformation may have been considerably more gradual and less violent, but the arrival of genetically different populations from further east was certainly involved.

The Beaker folk have an important role in this story, though it is a far more nuanced one than an earlier generation of archaeologists thought. Around 2700 BCE, well after the first stone circles were built, the first of the Beaker folk arrived. Rather than conquerors, they seem to have been something like religious missionaries. They made exquisite pottery drinking vessels, probably for ritual use—these are the beakers for which archaeologists named them—and some scholars have suggested that they introduced beekeeping and the brewing of mead to the tribal peoples of the region. They settled down among the tribes, and thereafter their distinctive beakers show up routinely in burials in round barrows. Around the same time, the technology needed to work copper and gold nuggets into jewelry reached Britain, and megalithic society entered its golden age, the era of the great stone circles such as Avebury and Stonehenge.

Glorious as it was, that era lasted less than a millennium. The end came soon after 2000 BCE. The details have been pieced together a little at a time from archeological evidence. Around that time, farmers in Britain began to clear ground for planting in marginal areas such as Dartmoor and the Pennines, where soils were poor and crop yields low—a well-known marker of an agricultural society pushed to the brink. About the same time, stone circles stopped being built. By 1600 BCE the last round barrows had been raised, and not long afterward Stonehenge itself, the supreme achievement of the megalithic age, was abandoned, along with huge stretches of former farmland. The population of northwestern Europe suffered a frightful collapse, of a kind remarkably close to the one that overwhelmed the Mycenean civilization—or, for that matter, the one described in the *Elucidation* and the other Grail romances.

Exactly what happened is still being pieced together by archaeologists, but the clues point to a kind of crisis familiar from other historical examples, including those we have already discussed. The farmers of megalithic Europe had not yet learned how to replenish the soil with compost or manure, and they followed the very ancient custom of swidden farming: clearing a patch of farmland, burning the trees and brush on it so the ash will fertilize the soil, farming the land until fertility drops off, and then moving on to another patch and repeating the process, leaving the old patch to be overgrown by weeds and then trees and brush so that the soil has time to regenerate. This works well so long as there are few people. If the population expands, it becomes impossible to leave the abandoned patches of soil to recuperate long enough. The result is topsoil loss followed by failed harvests, starvation, and social collapse.

Something like that took place in the twilight of the megalithic age. In the wake of a long and bitter age of collapse and depopulation, the surviving population huddled in tiny villages scattered across a mostly empty landscape, making a precarious living by hunting, foraging, herding, and raising such crops as they could. Only after 1200 BCE did the darkness begin to lift again. The people who made that happen were the Celts, another wave of newcomers from Europe who brought the art of making iron tools with them. The

Celts had iron-tipped plows that could work the rich, heavy soils of the river valleys, untouched in earlier times, and they knew how to use animal manures to improve soil fertility. They settled down and intermarried with the survivors of the megalithic societies, and the Waste Land finally began to heal.

It is a familiar story, as we have already seen. For thousands of years after the invention of agriculture, crises of this kind happened routinely whenever population rose too fast for farming to keep up. Agriculture was, after all, a new technology—it was invented, building on older and less intensive ways of producing plant food, during the terrible global droughts that followed the end of the last ice age ten thousand years ago—and it took quite a while for all the bugs to be worked out so the system wouldn't crash. The computer metaphor is perhaps too lighthearted to fit the reality of the situation, since a system crash when the system routinely puts food on the table means starvation, mass death, and the collapse of a society.

It so happens, however, that the brutal subsistence crash that brought mega-lithic society to an end in northwestern Europe was the last crisis of that kind to take place in that part of the world. There were steep population declines in later centuries—the collapse of the Roman Empire in the fifth century and the Black Death in the fourteenth both sent population levels down steeply, for example—but never again did the exhaustion of the soil bring the conditions of the Waste Land back to the homelands of the Grail legend. This makes the Grail legend itself, and above all the version of it transmitted in the *Elucidation*, a record of immense importance, for it appears to contain a dim folk memory of the end of the megalithic age.

Reduce the narrative of the *Elucidation* to its most basic terms, and this is the story it tells. Once there was a time when customs having to do with hills made sure that everyone had enough to eat. Then kings and their vassals changed and abused the custom, and the result was environmental devastation and the destruction of the land of Logres. The archeological evidence says the same thing: the age of the long barrows gave way to the age of round barrows, a time of kings and warriors, and this was followed in turn by agricultural failure and population collapse. Take those facts, give them to storytellers, and pass them down through many generations, and the story recounted in the *Elucidation* is a likely result.

For that matter, the story of the Grail is far from the only echo of mega-lithic times to reach the Middle Ages and find a place in Arthurian legend. Several researchers have argued that dim memories of the building of Stonehenge itself may have survived in the same way, passed down in folklore that eventually reached the ears of medieval minstrels. In *Stonehenge Decoded*, Gerald Hawkins pointed out that the oldest surviving account of the building of Stonehenge, the version recorded in Geoffrey of Monmouth's *History of the Kings of Britain*, contains certain details that seem to reflect facts about the building of Stonehenge that no one in the Middle Ages had any way of knowing.[74] The most logical explanation is that Geoffrey had access to bits of folklore about Stonehenge that date back to megalithic times.

Furthermore, a recent study of folktales from societies speaking Indo-European languages found crucial evidence supporting the immense age of oral tradition. Using the same methods now used to trace the origins of prehistoric species, this study found that some of the stories the researchers examined could be traced back all the way to the Bronze Age—that is, to the era of the megalithic structures.[75] With this in mind, the possibility that the *Elucidation* might embody another set of fragmentary memories from that same distant period becomes harder to dismiss.

Three details of the *Elucidation*'s account are especially important for our investigation. First, the *Elucidation* stresses that the dwellers in the hills were women. We have no way of knowing what the social customs that surrounded the old long barrows might have been, and the whole issue of gender roles in prehistory has become a battlefield in which supporters and opponents of the theory of prehistoric matriarchy struggle with one another. Nonetheless, it is entirely possible that when the long barrows were in their prime, they were tended by priestesses or shamanesses rather than shamans or priests. That may be reflected in turn by the central role of women in the Grail romances as keepers of the Grail and teachers of its mysteries.

Second, the story told in the *Elucidation* is also an account of the first loss and recovery of the temple technology. The long barrows, as noted above, are

---

74. Hawkins, *Stonehenge Decoded*, 5–6.

75. da Silva and Tehrani, "Comparative Phylogenetic Analyses Uncover the Ancient Roots of Indo-European Folktales."

the oldest known human structures to have followed the basic design template of the technology, and it may well have been the ancient peoples of megalithic Europe who first noted that sacred structures built, aligned, and used in certain ways improved the fertility of the soil. That knowledge did not survive the coming of the age of round barrows. It's easy to imagine the kings and warriors of that age rolling their eyes at the thought that the old superstitious rites practiced at the long barrows could have anything to do with the annual harvest. Much later, a more advanced version of the same knowledge had to be brought back from elsewhere.

Third, the story told in the *Elucidation* may also include another echo of ancient ritual. The golden cups in which the maidens of the hills brought food correspond to the most common form of the Grail, of course, but they may also echo an ancient reality. The Beaker folk, as mentioned earlier in this chapter, got their name because of the decorated and exquisitely made drinking vessels they used for ritual purposes. Surviving examples of those cups were of pottery rather than gold, but oral tradition is famous for working changes of that kind, dressing up memories from an earlier period in the habits and costumes of a later age. In the cups of the maidens of the hills, we may have the last dim memory of religious rites of the Beaker folk, blended together in the imaginations of storytellers with the customs that once surrounded the long barrows of megalithic Europe.

THE SLEEPER
IN THE EARTH

What makes the evidence of megalithic Europe so fascinating in this context is that all the way on the other side of Eurasia, thousands of years later, a similar sequence of events took place—and gave rise to legends all but identical to the narrative of the *Elucidation*. The place in question is Japan, where standing stones and great earthen burial mounds dot the landscape just as extensively as they do in Britain, and where traditional stories that revolve around precious vessels from supernatural sources have been collected by generations of enthusiastic folklorists.

Folklorist Carmen Blacker summarizes these stories helpfully in her study of Japanese shamanism, *The Catalpa Bow*. These stories, which are found over much of Japan, recount how once in the past, certain supernatural beings would loan elegant lacquered bowls to human beings, provided that the cups were all returned intact. Inevitably, according to these *wankashi desetsu* ("bowl-lending legends"), someone failed to return one of the bowls or damaged one, and the custom ceased at once, never to resume.[76] Some of these stories claim that the

76. Blacker, *The Catalpa Bow*, 76–78.

bowl-lending spirits were found at lakes and pools, while other stories associate them with the great burial mounds; the parallel with the double meaning of the Old French word *puis*, "hills" or "wells," is unsettling.

To put these stories in their historical and legendary context will require a brief glimpse at Japanese prehistory. The earliest people known to have inhabited Japan, the Jomon culture, had a great deal in common with their opposite numbers in northwestern Europe, though they did not perform rites at long barrows—that technology arrived much later, as we will see. The Jomon lived in small communities scattered across the mountainous Japanese islands and supported themselves by a mix of small-scale agriculture, wild-plant gathering, hunting, and fishing. Such scraps of evidence that survive from Jomon times suggest that their religion was a shamanistic worship of nature spirits, in which priestesses played a central role.

The Jomon culture began to decline around 1000 BCE as settlers from the Asian mainland began to establish colonies in Japan, and by 300 BCE the Jomon period had given way to the Yayoi period, in which bronze and iron tools became common and agriculture became the mainstay of Japanese life. Six centuries later, as new ideas and cultural influences continued to arrive from the mainland, the Kofun period began; not long afterward, literacy began to spread and the first historical records appear. Some elements of the Jomon heritage remained part of Japanese custom, however. Shinto—the indigenous Japanese nature religion, which is still practiced by many Japanese today—became an important repository for these very ancient traditions. To this day *miko*, women who enter into trance to communicate with the spirit world, are an important part of some traditional Shinto ceremonies, and some elements of Shinto symbolism can be traced all the way back to objects found in Jomon archeological sites.

All this took place long after the rise and fall of the megalithic societies of northwestern Europe. Remarkably, though, there are close parallels between these two very different eras and societies. The *kofun* (burial mounds) of Japan, for which the Kofun period is named, are shaped like keyholes—as though to combine the long barrow and round barrow in a single shape—and for the first few centuries of the Kofun period, mounds had little, if any, treasure buried with their occupants. Later on, with the rise of a warrior aristocracy, pottery statues (called *haniwa*) of warriors and court ladies came to decorate the kofun, and lavish treasures of bronze and gold were buried there.

The difference of time had one significant impact, however. By the time agriculture reached Japan, most of the bugs had been worked out, so ancient Japan never seems to have gone through the kind of subsistence crash that ended the megalithic and Mycenean ages. This may be the source of the great difference between Japan's "bowl-lending legends" and the narrative of the *Elucidation*: the absence of the Waste Land theme. When the ritual practices dimly enshrined in both traditions came to an end in Japan, famine and the collapse of society did not follow. Better methods of agriculture were already in place, and so were the ecologically sound traditions discussed in chapter 5.

Only a few centuries after the end of the Kofun period, furthermore, Japanese monks studying the teachings of esoteric Buddhism in China seem to have come into contact with one form of the temple technology, which had arrived in China with heretical Christian missionaries of the Nestorian sect not long before. The Chinese themselves never adopted the temple technology— they had a different technology already in place, one that used stepped "earth altars" that are smaller equivalents of the ziggurats of old Sumeria and Babylonia—but Japanese Buddhists and Nestorian missionaries in China are known to have met and exchanged ideas. At Koyasan in southern Japan, the great complex of Buddhist monasteries and temples belonging to the esoteric Shingon sect, a Nestorian Christian monument can still be found today among the Buddhist structures and statues.

The esoteric Buddhist schools in Japan also had close ties with Shinto. It was after they brought Nestorian influences back to Japan that Shinto shrines began to be designed, built, and operated in accordance with the temple technology. The result, as discussed earlier in this book and in *The Secret of the Temple*, was the great productivity and stability of Japanese traditional agriculture, which has weathered the ups and downs of Japan's tumultuous history largely intact.

Another of the ancient technologies discussed in this book also seems to have arrived in Japan at some early date, and it left significant traces behind. It is because of these traces that we know as much as we do about the secret technology of the burial mounds that was intended to make consciousness transcend death.

Koyasan, the great complex of Shingon Buddhist temples and monasteries mentioned previously, has another feature that attracts its quota of pilgrims each year: the founder of the Shingon school, Kobo Daishi, is still there. According to secular histories, he was born in 774 and died in 835, but devout Shingon Buddhists believe he is not dead. At the end of a busy and successful life, he retired into a little cave at Koyasan and entered into meditation. He is still there, in a state of suspended animation called *nyujo* in Japanese. The mouth of the cave now has a stone structure like a small cottage built over it, and a gate and high walls surround Kobo Daishi's place of meditation so that no one will interrupt him. Shingon tradition has it that he will remain in profound meditation for millions of years to come until the arrival of Miroku, the Buddha of the far future.

According to Japanese legend, Kobo Daishi is far from inactive in his timeless trance. Stories all around Japan, some dating from shortly after the end of his outward life, some dating from much later, describe how a plump and smiling little monk appears out of nowhere to bind demons, break curses, and solve otherwise insoluble problems through powerful prayers and shrewd common sense. Once all is well, the monk vanishes just as suddenly as he appears. Then, of course, someone who encountered the monk sees a statue or scroll painting of Kobo Daishi and realizes who it was that saved the day. The legends that have gathered around Kobo Daishi and his magical powers make it appropriate to refer to him as the Merlin of Japan.

Kobo Daishi has countless equivalents in traditions around the world, of course. King Arthur is merely one of the most famous figures of old who is thought to be waiting in a state between death and life for the hour when he will again walk the earth. Another, much closer to Kobo Daishi in many ways, is Christian Rosenkreutz, the legendary founder of the Rosicrucian Fraternity. Like Kobo Daishi, he traveled to a distant land in order to learn traditions of spiritual wisdom, brought them back to his homeland, and founded an organization to pass on what he had learned. According to the *Fama Fraternitatis*, the original manifesto of the Rosicrucians, he then arranged to be buried in a secret vault beneath the College of the Holy Spirit, the Koyasan of the Rosicrucians. The discovery of the vault, and of Rosenkreutz's perfectly preserved body, inspired a later generation of Rosicrucians to announce their existence to the world.[77]

Merlin is another figure of the same type. There are two traditional accounts of Merlin's death, both of which will concern us later in this exploration, but the one that most people know today has him buried alive beneath the earth, where he still remains. The *Didot Perceval*, a very early version of the Grail legend written between 1190 and 1215, gives an unusually complete account of Merlin's fate:

> And then Merlin came to Perceval and to Bleyse his master, and he took leave of them and told them that Our Lord did not wish that he should show himself to people, yet that he would not be able to die before the end of the world; "but then I shall enjoy the eternal joy, and I wish to make a lodging outside your palace and to dwell there and I will prophesy whatever Our Lord commands me. And those who see my lodging will name it the esplumoir of Merlin." Then Merlin made his esplumoir and entered within and never since then has he been seen in the world.[78]

The Old French word *esplumoir* has puzzled scholars for centuries. No one is sure exactly what it means, but it occurs in several places in Arthurian legend, always with reference to Merlin's final resting place. The word *merlin* is the name of a small falcon, and some researchers have suggested that it might be a pun suggesting that Merlin, like a falcon, needed a place to shed his feathers (*plumes* in French as well as English). Is this the original meaning, or simply a bit of wordplay like the folk term "sparrowgrass" for asparagus? Nobody knows. Like so much that surrounds the Grail legend, it whispers of archaic mysteries that we may never be able to solve completely.

Yet it is clear from the passage that to some extent, we are on familiar ground. Like the visionary dead in the age of the long barrows, or for that matter like Kobo Daishi and Christian Rosenkreutz, Merlin announces that he is passing into a state of being between life and death, where he will remain until the end of the world. He will not be seen by anyone, but his voice will

---

77. See Yates, *The Rosicrucian Enlightenment*.

78. Skeels, *The Romance of Perceval in Prose*, 93–94.

be heard, uttering prophecies—and he will dwell "outside your palace," that is, outside the castle of the Grail, for Perceval by that point in the story has become the Grail King.

How much of this legend echoes dim folk memories from megalithic times is impossible to say for certain, but the presence of the same themes in many lands across the whole length of Eurasia suggests that we are dealing with an ancient and widespread tradition. To judge by the evidence of archeology, that tradition began in Egypt sometime before 6000 BCE with the construction of the first mastabas—square or rectangular burial structures of mud brick, the earliest ancestors of the pyramids. The tradition spread west to Europe sometime before 4300 BCE, when the first long barrows were raised. Its peregrinations in other directions are harder to trace, but by 300 CE, as we have seen, the tradition of mound burial had been adopted in Japan.

The legends surrounding Kobo Daishi suggests that the deeper and stranger dimensions of that tradition arrived at or near the same time. Those legends have an uncanny echo in an isolated and legend-rich region of Japan, at a place called Senninzawa—a name that literally means "Wizards' Valley."

Dewa Sanzan, the Three Mountains of Dewa, are among the holiest places in Japan. Located in Yamagata Prefecture, in the northwest of the main island Honshu, the mountains—Mount Haguro, Mount Gassan, and Mount Yudono—have been a major site of pilgrimage for Shinto and Buddhist seekers alike since 594 CE, when the imperial prince Hachiko came there to take up a life of prayer and austerity. Kobo Daishi went there in search of spiritual power, and so did En no Gyoja, another famous Buddhist magician of ancient Japan. To this day *yamabushi*, mystics who practice ascetic disciplines in the mountains, gather at the Dewa Sanzan every autumn to perform rituals of initiation that have a great deal in common with the ancient Greek Mysteries.[79]

Within sight of the three holy mountains, the little valley of Senninzawa winds through forested hills. Two Buddhist temples in Wizards' Valley, and a third temple in the nearby town of Sakata, contain gruesome relics that may represent the last survival of the practices of the long barrows and the pyra-

---

79. See the account of the Autumn Peak in Blacker, *The Catalpa Bow*, 208–34.

mids. The relics in question are five Buddhist priests of the secretive order of monks that is based on Mount Yudono. They are still seated in the lotus posture, still dressed in the ornate robes and headdresses of Buddhist abbots. They died in the seventeenth, eighteenth, and early nineteenth centuries, as a result of a set of practices meant to bring about self-mummification.

The method was as follows. Late in life, after many years of mystical practices and austerities, they took up a carefully designed diet that consisted mostly of tree products—nuts, seeds, berries, pine needles, and edible bark. Over a period of one thousand, two thousand, or three thousand days, they cut back on the amount of food they ate a little at a time, ending in total fasting for many days. All the while, as their bodies shriveled around them, the practitioners spent every waking hour reciting special mantras and engaging in other intensive mystic practices.

If everything went well, the practitioner died peacefully of starvation on the last day of the process, still upright and seated in lotus posture. His body was then placed inside a wooden coffin and buried in a stone chamber underground for three years. At the end of this period, if his body showed no signs of decay, the practitioner was held to have succeeded in his quest: he had entered into nyujo, the same state of suspended animation between life and death that Kobo Daishi also achieved. There he will remain, according to traditional belief, until the future Buddha Miroku arrives countless ages from now. In the meantime, the body was placed in a temple in the place of reverence usually reserved for statues of the Buddha, where it radiated spiritual power as a *sokushinbutsu*, a "buddha in this very body."

How much of this macabre tradition dates back to distant antiquity is anyone's guess. The sanctuary on Mount Yudono holds many secrets to this day. Set apart from the secular world, it is off-limits to photography and video recording, and only qualified ascetics are permitted on some parts of the mountain. Yet it is clear from the legends surrounding Kobo Daishi that something akin to the traditions of Senninzawa was already known and understood a thousand years before the self-mummified monks performed their terrible austerities.

Equally, a wealth of data, extending from the legends surrounding Merlin's esplumoir to the abundant archeological evidence for ancient Egyptian burial practices, shows that many other peoples across the Old World shared a common belief that certain practices could permit certain people to survive as conscious entities after biological death. The most reasonable explanation for these shared ideas and practices is that there was a common tradition of great age that spread to many different lands, taking on varying shapes according to local religious ideas but retaining the same basic structure throughout.

Yet a fissure runs through the middle of this tradition, and it can be traced in examples we have already studied closely. The self-mummified monks of Senninzawa were not members of the *daimyo* (nobility) or samurai classes. They did not belong to the ruling elite of their society. Like Merlin or Christian Rosenkreutz, they earned their posthumous status through personal discipline and hard work, not by being rich and powerful. As far as archaeologists can tell, the same thing was true of the anonymous figures who left their bones in the long barrows of northwestern Europe. The round barrows of the time of Stonehenge, the pyramids of Egypt, and the kofun of ancient Japan were on the other side of the fissure. Those who went into these monuments were not monks or wizards but the kings and aristocrats of their time. The powers they controlled were political, not spiritual.

In retrospect, it is easy to see what happened. A set of practices originally designed to enable a small number of spiritually advanced individuals to step out of the flow of time and become the inner guardians of their communities, intercessors between the human world and the world of spirits and deities, was hijacked by an ascendant class of wealthy magnates who hoped to use it to escape death and whatever judgment might lie beyond. The same story can be seen reflected in the old Christian churches of Europe, which started out as repositories for the bones of saints and ended up as the favored burial venue for the wealthy and famous in every walk of life, whether or not the least shred of holiness showed in their lives or clung to their memories.

This same story, as we have already seen, is at the heart of the story of the *Elucidation*: what was once a gift given out by the priestess-guardians of the hollow hills was seized and turned into a possession of kings and their vassals. Yet, this is not the only trace of these archaic mysteries in the Grail legends. At the heart of the legend itself is an echo of the same ancient traditions we have been discussing.

▱

Richard Wagner gets very little favorable attention these days, and it's only fair to say that he did everything he possibly could to make that happen. Vain, bombastic, selfish, manipulative, and vindictive, he was a thoroughly unpleasant human being. It doesn't help matters any that he also embraced a variety of attitudes toward race and gender that were common in his time and have become deservedly unacceptable in ours. His life and writings are a pointed reminder that creative geniuses do not have to be nice people.

A genius he unquestionably was. His operas had an immense impact on nineteenth- and twentieth-century music, art, and literature, and that impact continues today. Next time you watch a movie or a television drama, for example, notice the little repetitive musical themes that show up on the soundtrack to set the mood when something is about to happen. Those are called leitmotifs, and Richard Wagner invented them.

Among his many interests were the myths, legends, and folklore of the German-speaking peoples of central Europe and their Scandinavian neighbors. Those sources provided the raw materials for the most famous of his creations, the four-opera cycle *The Ring of the Nibelung*, and for his last and most intellectually complex opera, *Parsifal*, his version of the Grail legend. Yet he was also interested in those materials for their own sake. In 1848, while he was in the middle of the studies that would result in *The Ring of the Nibelung*, he penned an essay that points to crucial dimensions of the Grail legend rarely discussed elsewhere. The essay is titled "The Wibelungs: World History as Told in Saga."[80] It is not easy reading—none of Wagner's essays are—but it provides essential clues in our search.

Throughout the old cultures of Europe, Wagner points out, great cycles of legend center on a magical treasure that can only be won by the greatest of heroes. In Norse and German legends, this treasure is the golden hoard of the Nibelung dwarfs, guarded by the terrible dragon Fafnir, and in the Arthurian romances, as we have already seen, it appears as the Grail. Though he apparently did not know this, the same pattern of legend can be found across Eurasia from end to end. In Iranian legend, which preserves themes of immense antiquity, it is the Hvarena, the "Glory," while in the Finnish Kalevala—another repository of astonishingly ancient traditions—it is the many-colored Sampo.

---

80. Wagner, "The Wibelungen," is a good English translation.

In every case, it is the goal of a mighty quest, and in most cases it is claimed and fought over by two kingdoms, a kingdom of light or summer and a kingdom of darkness or winter.

Whether this treasure of sovereignty is a ring, a cup, a mass of gold, or something harder to describe, it is a potent force on the inner side of existence. Those who win it become kings—and more than kings. A spiritual glory surrounds the hero of the summer kingdom who claims the treasure for his own. Yet those who win the treasure are doomed, for in some strange sense it belongs to the winter kingdom and drags each hero down into the darkness. Of Siegfried, the greatest of German heroes, Wagner writes:

> When Siegfried slew the Nibelungen-dragon, he further won as victor's spoil the Nibelungen-hoard it guarded. But the possession of this hoard…is also reason of his death; for the dragon's heir now plots to win it back. This heir dispatches him by stealth, as the night the day, and drags him down to the gloomy realm of Death: Siegfried thus becomes himself a Nibelung. Though doomed to death by acquisition of the hoard, each generation strives to seize it.[81]

All this, it bears remembering, was written before Sir James Frazer wrote the first sentence of *The Golden Bough*. Yet the parallels between Wagner's narrative and Frazer's are close and important. Like the priests of the grove at Nemi that Frazer studied and analyzed, the heroes who contended over the Nibelungs's hoard each took possession by killing the previous owner of the treasure. Like the priests of Nemi, they were fated to die at the hand of the next hero who sought the same role: at once hero and sacrifice, surrounded by a nimbus of spiritual glory that was also a mark of doom.

Map this same pattern onto certain parts of the Arthurian legends and the parallels are hard to miss. I have already mentioned the curious Grail-like story of Ywain, who conquers the knightly guardian of a well and becomes the guardian of the well and the lover of its mistress. Here the story is stripped down to its most basic elements, and nowhere is it hinted that Ywain will be defeated and killed in turn by some other knight. The story of the Grail has suffered the same sort of stripping-down process, but a crucial detail remains:

---

81. Wagner, "The Wibelungen," 276; emphasis in original.

the condition of the Fisher King, the guardian of the Grail who is healed and replaced by the successful knight.

In the versions of the story that give the role of Grail knight to Gawain—the earliest of all, according to Jessie Weston—the Fisher King is quite simply dead. In one, the lord of the castle where the Grail is found is strong and uninjured, but he is never called the Fisher King, and he shares space in the castle with a dead knight on a bier, the victim of the Dolorous Stroke that elsewhere afflicts the Fisher King. Weston comments sensibly enough that in this version, the dead knight fills the Fisher King's role.[82] In the other surviving Grail story that gives the central role to Gawain, Heinrich von dem Türlin's *The Crown*, the Fisher King appears to be alive but is actually dead, held in a ghostly simulacrum of life until Gawain frees him by asking the necessary question.

In the versions of the story that give the lead role to Perceval, the Fisher King is not dead but wounded. He has been struck in the thighs or the genitals with a wound that will never heal and continues to bleed. This in itself offers a remarkable parallel with the tale told in the Mysteries of Cybele, in which both Acdestis and Attis are wounded in the same way. (The possibility that all these images may be linked symbolically to menstruation has not, I think, been given enough attention by scholars.) The Fisher King in these legends is not dead, but the death he suffers in the Gawain versions has been reflected outward onto the world of nature in the form of the Waste Land.

In the late versions of the story that give the lead role to Galahad, finally, the Fisher King is usually in the same condition as in the Perceval stories, but he has multiplied himself! In some of them there are two Fisher Kings, both of them wounded and unable either to be healed or to die, and in others there are three such figures. What makes the Galahad stories fascinating in the context we are discussing is that as soon as he finds the Grail, Galahad dies. Of course this is presented in orthodox Christian terms—having achieved the Grail quest, there is nothing left for Galahad to do but ascend to heaven in an odor of sanctity so overwhelming that it becomes a stench—but it is intriguing that here again, the Grail and death are so closely interwoven.

---

82. Weston, *From Ritual to Romance*, 115.

There is at least one straightforward explanation for all these strange inter-weavings of symbol and legend. If the legend of the Waste Land found in the *Elucidation* and elsewhere represents a dim folk memory of the history of the megalithic age, from the abandonment of the long barrows and their forgotten rites to the terrible subsistence crisis that brought the age of Stonehenge to its end, then it is worth suggesting that the role of the Grail knight in that legend may represent an equally dim recollection of that age.

If the traditions mentioned earlier are to be taken seriously, those who went into the long barrows to intercede between the people and the spirit world were replaced at intervals of a generation or so. We have no way of knowing what methods were used to select the next person who would take on that role, but the possibility that each such person had to accomplish a quest or test of some kind is at least worth considering. Once chosen, they would have had the same status Wagner describes in his essay, at once holy and doomed—the same status that the self-mummified monks of Wizards' Valley had as they pursued their quest for Buddhahood. Whether the chosen ones starved them-selves in the same way as the monks did, we will probably never know. One way or another, however, they died, and their spirits were believed to remain in the long barrows, caught between death and life, until their successors came to replace them and they went on to whatever further destiny awaited them.

The Grail legends are far from the only folk memories of this same body of custom. The reverence for the relics of saints in Christianity and other faiths, the veneration of heroes in ancient Greece, the beliefs surrounding the spirits of the hollow hills in Celtic countries, and many other bodies of traditional lore in many lands all point back to the same archaic source: a lost technol-ogy for the prolongation of human consciousness beyond death. We can trace it through these echoes from its first known appearance in predynastic Egypt through its spread over much of Eurasia, its distortion and abuse at the hands of ruling elites, and its gradual abandonment, until the last lingering traces remained in a few isolated areas.

This same trajectory was also followed by the temple technology, and doubt-less by many other archaic technologies as well. It is entirely possible that the same thing will happen in due time to the technologies of our own age, and that scholars in some distant time will be left to speculate, on the basis of fragmen-tary remains in isolated regions, about the strange practices their distant ancestors carried out that made use of roads, gasoline, and certain legendary objects of metal and glass called "cars." That was certainly the situation that faced Jessie Weston in the early years of the twentieth century as she set out to reconstruct the ritual that lay behind the Grail legends.

A crucial question thus comes to mind. If these traditions and teachings were once so important, how were they forgotten? What history lies behind the abandonment of the secret traditions we are discussing—and how is that history reflected in the legends of the Grail? To find answers to these questions, we will have to venture into another branch of the lost knowledge of the archaic world.

THE WHEEL OF
THE AGES

For as long as we have been human, people have looked up at the starry heavens in search of the meanings of events on Earth. Back when chipped stone tools were considered high tech, our ancestors knew that changes in the position of the Sun were linked to the cycle of the seasons, and the phases of the Moon seemed to correspond to the tides and the menstrual cycle. Bones marked with tallies, found at prehistoric sites, show how people in the Stone Age kept track of solar and lunar cycles. Later still, improvements in record-keeping technologies made it possible to compile data in much greater volume. The clay tablet libraries of Sumer and Babylon were largely given over to astronomical records, which contributed mightily to the rise of astrology in later times.

Between scratches on bones and intricate characters on clay tablets, however, a different information technology saw extensive use as a way of storing astronomical data. This was the technology of storytelling. The sheer scale of the oral starlore of the ancient world remained largely hidden until two historians of science, Giorgio de Santillana and Hertha von Dechend, published the results of decades of research in their deservedly famous book *Hamlet's Mill*. They showed that many of the figures of myth and legend are lightly disguised emblems of the planets visible from Earth, and the adventures of these figures pass on details of astronomical knowledge in the same way that the story of "The Strange Musician," discussed in the prologue of this book, communicates the right way to stretch old-fashioned gut strings on a fiddle.

One example cited by de Santillana and von Dechend is a colorful detail from the Kalevala, the great epic poem of Finland. This describes a hero-child of supernatural strength whose wicked uncle, in the traditional manner, repeatedly tries to kill him. One of these failed attempts involves flinging him into the ocean. The wicked uncle's henchmen are startled to find the hero-child unharmed, sitting on a wave and measuring the whole ocean with a ladle. It comes to a little over two ladles full.[83] What is it that measures the Great Deep in a little more than two measures? The planet Mars, with its orbital time of 2.2 years.

In the great mythological cycles of antiquity, each planet has its own cycle of myths and legends, and the attentive student who approaches old stories with this key in mind can quickly learn to catch the symbolic and numerical clues that tell you which planet's movements and encounters with other planets are being discussed. The same analysis, interestingly, can be applied just as precisely to the Arthurian legends. Perceval is a classic figuration of Mars, for example, with the immense strength and utter cluelessness that always goes with the mythic images of that planet. Gawain with his many amours is the planet Venus, always circling close around Arthur the Sun, though not as close as Sir Kay-Mercury. Lancelot is Jupiter; Guenevere is the inconstant Moon; and Merlin is Saturn, the lord of time and fate, who sets the Arthurian cycle in motion and then withdraws into contemplation in a classic saturnine fashion. The other knights and ladies? Some of them are duplicates—Sir Tristram, for example, is another Venus knight, and the Fisher King is another image of Saturn—while others fill different roles in the intricate tapestry of the Arthurian legend.

Yet the planets are far from the only subjects of astronomical myth, nor are they the most important. That latter status belongs to the precession of the equinoxes, the slow wobble of the earth's axis that makes the Sun's position against the background of stars at the equinoxes and solstices shift slowly around the

---

83. de Santillana and von Dechend, *Hamlet's Mill*, 28.

heavens. Five thousand years ago, for example, if you stood facing east on a clear night just after sunset on the day of the spring equinox, you would see the stars of Aries glittering low in the west once the sky darkened enough to reveal them. Two thousand years later, Aries would have vanished behind the sun, and the first stars visible after sunset would have belonged to Pisces. Meanwhile, at dawn on the same day, the stars of Taurus—hidden behind the sun for 2,160 years— would be visible low in the east just before sunrise as the sky turned pale.

Another two thousand years later, people in the Dark Ages who waited for the coming of spring watched the stars of Aquarius rising just before the sun and the stars of Aries setting just after sunset, for the sun on the day of the spring equinox was located in the constellation Pisces and so the stars of Pisces were hidden by sunlight on that day. Now? Aquarius is sliding out of sight behind the Sun as the age of Aquarius dawns, and the first stars of Pisces are becoming visible again just before dawn.

The current consensus among historians of science is that precession was first discovered in ancient Greek times. De Santillana and von Dechend showed, however, that many of the most puzzling features of mythology become instantly clear once they are taken as references to precession, nor would it have been especially difficult for ancient peoples to detect it. It takes seventy-two years for the sun's position at the equinoxes and solstices to shift by one degree against the background of stars and 25,950 years for the Sun to slip through the entire circle of the zodiac and return to its starting place. So long as people had some way to record which stars appeared just before sunrise on the days of the solstices and equinoxes, however, they would figure out within a few generations that the slippage was happening, as bright stars that were once visible low on the horizon just before sunrise on the dates in question vanished from sight.

That process of discovery is much easier if you have a way of determining the equinoxes and solstices that isn't dependent on the Sun's position among the stars. One of the things that makes Stonehenge a masterpiece of prehistoric engineering is that it does precisely that. The standing stones mark out the positions of the rising and setting Sun on the equinoxes and solstices so precisely that the structure's designers could have tracked precession with great accuracy. It may be that this is one of the reasons why Stonehenge was built in the first place.

They had ample reason to do so. Precession may seem like an abstruse detail of astronomy of no practical use to anybody, but in an age before printed calendars it threw a wild card into the vital process of timing the spring planting and carrying out other seasonal tasks that community survival depended on. If you kept track of the arrival of spring by watching which stars rose just before the Sun, the way most ancient peoples did, a shift in those stars would make you plant too early, when frost might damage the crops. On a deeper level, in societies that saw human life as an echo of the cycles of the heavens, seeing those cycles go out of joint must have been traumatic, and it would have inspired earnest and sustained attempts to figure out what was happening to understand what message it had for human life.

◻

These days, pop-culture talk about the astrological ages—and the age of Aquarius in particular—assumes by default that the coming age of the world must, by definition, be better than the one winding down around us at present. The same sentiment could be heard here and there back when it was the age of Aries that was winding down and the age of Pisces was expected to be a wonderful new era free of the burdens of the age just past. The Roman poet Virgil, not long before the beginning of the Christian era, put that belief into one of his poems: "Now the Virgin returns, the reign of Saturn returns, now a new generation descends from heaven on high. Only do thou, pure Lucina, smile on the birth of the child, under whom the iron brood shall first cease, and a golden race spring up throughout the world!"[84]

Behind these lines hovers the phantom of a much more troubling prophecy, the cycle of ages traced out by the ancient Greek poet Hesiod more than seven centuries before. To Hesiod, the course of history leads steadily downhill. First was the golden age, when the earth produced crops without human labor and people were naturally wise and just. Next came the silver age, when people were foolish and passionate and would not worship the gods. After that was the bronze age, an age of strange powers and mighty warriors who slaughtered each other in terrible conflicts. Fourth came the age of heroes—the heroes discussed earlier in this book, whose tombs became places of worship. Fifth was

---

84. de Santillana and von Dechend, *Hamlet's Mill*, 244.

the iron age, Hesiod's own time, an age of bitter poverty, labor, and misery, which would eventually end in human extinction. If Hesiod expected anything better to come afterward, he did not mention it.[85]

Virgil, like some people of his time and many in ours, refused to accept this grim prospect. He insisted that "the iron brood" would end sometime soon, perhaps in his own lifetime, and a new golden age would dawn again, stocked with a better grade of human beings. In Roman legend, the original golden age had been ruled by the god Saturn, and Virgil therefore called for the reign of Saturn to be renewed. The reference to the Virgin points to the underlying logic behind the whole structure of predictions, however, because the zodiacal sign Virgo, the Virgin, was entering into a special role when Virgil wrote.

Precession, as already noted, moves the Sun's stations at the equinoxes and solstices backward through the constellations of the zodiac. In Virgil's time the station of the spring equinox was slipping from Aries into Pisces, and the autumn equinox was accordingly moving from Libra into Virgo. Imagery centered on the fish or fisherman and the virgin as the symbol of the coming age was already common by the time Virgil wrote.[86] Shortly afterward, of course, the same imagery would be picked up and deployed systematically by the newborn Christian church, with its messiah born of a virgin, who recruited his apostles from among fishermen and fed multitudes with fish, and whose followers used the symbol of the fish and an acrostic based on ΙΧΘΥΣ (ichthys), the Greek word for fish, which spells out the initials of the Greek words for "Jesus Christ, God's son, Savior."

The extent to which Christianity adopted the emblems of astrology to shore up its claim to be the religion of the coming Piscean age clearly shows just how pervasive the symbols of the stars had become in the ancient world. The same conclusion could have been drawn from the writings of Hesiod, however, for the same astrological pattern underlies his sequence of ages. The underlying structure is shown in the diagram below.

---

85. Hesiod, "Works and Days," 61–65.

86. Eisler, *Orpheus the Fisher.*

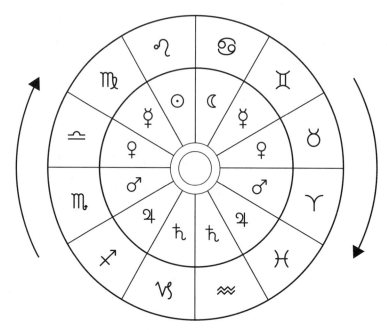

Wheel of Time diagram

In astrological tradition, each sign of the zodiac is ruled by one of the planets, and in ancient times—before the discovery of Uranus, Neptune, and Pluto—those rulerships were set out as shown in the diagram. Each planet was also traditionally associated with a metal: the Sun with gold, the Moon with silver, Mercury with alloys of two or more metals, Venus with copper, Mars with iron, Jupiter with tin, and Saturn with lead. Any literate person in ancient times would have associated Hesiod's golden age with the Sun and the age of Leo, the silver age with the Moon and the age of Cancer, and the bronze age—since bronze is an alloy—with Mercury and the age of Gemini.

The age of heroes, to which Hesiod does not assign a metal, would nonetheless have been just as obvious to readers in ancient times, because in Greek mythology the heroic age began when Zeus took the form of a bull, the symbol of Taurus, in order to mate with Europa and carry her away from Asia to Greece. The heroic age ended, in turn, once a later generation of heroes sailed aboard the Argo to seek the Golden Fleece: a ram's fleece, indicating the coming of the age of Aries the Ram. Iron, finally, was the metal of Mars, the ruler of Aries and of the iron age in which Hesiod believed he lived.

Hesiod did not expect the human race to survive to see the end of the iron age. Virgil, like some other intellectuals of his time, hoped to witness a better age dawn once the age of Aries gave way to that of Jupiter, the planet of organized religion and of justice. Neither of them were right. On the one hand, more than two thousand years after the end of the age of iron, our species is still here. On the other, while the Piscean age followed its astrological symbolism in important ways—organized religion was far more powerful during that era than it had been in earlier precessional ages, and a concern with justice and equity led to such radically new developments as the eventual abolition of slavery and the emergence of the concept of human rights—it certainly was nobody's idea of Utopia.

◇

In ancient times, Virgil's view of things belonged to a minority. Most people in ancient times believed that for the foreseeable future, at least, the cycle of precession would make things get worse. That attitude can be hard for modern people to understand since our culture provides us with the opposite expectation: a faith in progress that assumes that over time, things necessarily get better.

That was not how the ancient world saw things, however. Many people these days are familiar with the Hindu concept of the yugas, the four great ages of the world. In order, these are the Krita Yuga, the Treta Yuga, the Dvapara Yuga, and the Kali Yuga. The first of these corresponds very closely to the golden age as Hesiod describes it, and the last corresponds just as closely to Hesiod's iron age. According to the *Puranas*, the great collection of Hindu myth and tradition, the Kali Yuga began in 3125 BCE and will continue for a very long time—360,000 years, according to one account. Only when it has run its course will a new Krita Yuga begin.

Much the same way of thinking shapes the time theory of Buddhism. According to Buddhist teachings, Buddhas appear at long intervals, and their saving influence only lasts for a limited time before the forces of ignorance sweep it away. By the time Buddhism established itself in the countries of East Asia, many Buddhists believed that the dreaded Latter Days of the Law— *Mappō* in Japanese—had already arrived. As a result, according to this tradition, it was no longer possible to attain salvation through the ordinary practice of the

Buddha's teachings. That was why Kobo Daishi entered into the state of nyujo to wait for the arrival of the future Buddha Miroku, and why the self-mummified monks of Senninzawa set out to accomplish the same thing. By entering into suspended animation, they hoped to wait out the Mappō and attain salvation once the next Buddha arrived.

The Kali Yuga and the Mappō show no obvious signs of being linked to the cycle of precession. De Santillana and von Dechend showed, however, that many other accounts of decline in ancient sources were in fact derived from precession, and that these two East Asian traditions contained scraps of imagery and lore that were clearly connected to the same thing. They proposed that all these teachings were fragments of the old lore of the stars, more or less distorted by the influence of later religious beliefs. Behind these visions of decline, and Hesiod's as well, is an older account of the fate of the world—and it can be read precisely from the wheel of zodiacal signs.

In that diagram, the signs Cancer and Leo, traditionally ruled by the Moon and Sun respectively, are on top, while the signs Aquarius and Capricorn, traditionally ruled by Saturn, are on the bottom. The Sun and Moon in astrology are called the luminaries, and they are the sources of light in a spiritual as well as a physical sense. To pass from the luminaries down the arc of the wheel to the rulerships of Saturn is to move to the outer limits of the solar system as it was understood in ancient times. It was to go from light to darkness, and from the genial rule of the Sun and Moon, into the realm of cold, silent Saturn, the lord of time, death, and fate. That eventually the wheel would turn upward again was scant consolation to those who could expect to live during any part of the 4,320 years the earth would spend under Saturn's unyielding rule.

This was a live issue in the ancient world, for educated people in Greek and Roman times still understood the old astrological lore. De Santillana and von Dechend commented that they found every detail of the archaic lore of precessional myth set out in the writings of Plato.[87] Plato's writings were essential reading all through the alternative spiritual traditions of the ancient world and had a powerful impact on many new faiths, including Christianity.

The Christian doctrine of the Second Coming can be seen, in fact, as a response to the idea that precession was taking humanity further and further

---

87. de Santillana and von Dechend, *Hamlet's Mill*, 311.

away from the sources of light and life. To the devout Christian, once Christ returns from heaven and vanquishes the forces of evil once and for all, time will dissolve into eternity and nothing will ever change again. This is perhaps the most radical alternative to historic change ever proposed. The only problem with it is that almost two thousand years have passed since Jesus of Nazareth died on the cross, most of a precessional age has passed, and the Second Coming hasn't happened yet.

The claim that time itself would be no more once the Second Coming took place can be seen as a desperation move on the part of people terrified by the direction that the cycle of precession was taking them. It was matched by another, equally desperate attempt to insist that the precessional cycle would stop and the Sun's position at the spring equinox would begin slipping forward again. The technical term for this back-and-forth movement was *trepidation*, and you can find learned discussions of trepidation all through the astrological literature of late antiquity and the Middle Ages. In most parts of the world people assumed, or hoped, that trepidation would stave off the final descent into the realm of Saturn all by itself. In some—notably in the New World—the belief spread that only human sacrifice would convince the implacable gods to stop the precessional machinery, with gruesome results.[88]

Yet the most significant of all the attempts to escape the implications of precession is found in the writings of some of the Gnostic sects of ancient times. In these documents, the attentive reader will find references to the ruling spirits of the seven planets, to the ages of the world, and to other elements of the old astronomical vision. Very often, however, those references recast the old lore in a harsh new light. The spirits of the seven planets were understood as gods by most ancient peoples—we still call most of them by the names of deities—but many of the Gnostics stood this tradition on its head.

To them the rulers of the planets were the archons, the ruling powers of the world of matter, who had imprisoned human souls in that world and kept them from returning to their home in the world of light from which they had come. They pursued spiritual practices for the same reason that the monks of Senninzawa embraced the terrible discipline of self-mummification: as a way to escape a world in which the sources of life and light were slipping ever further

---

88. Sullivan, *The Secret of the Incas*.

away. Was this why kings and aristocrats in late megalithic times seized the old technology of mound burial in an attempt to overcome physical death? The surviving data does not say, but the possibility is a real one.

That view can be found all through the Gnostic writings found at Nag Hammadi, and it also underlies the teachings of the Cathars whose doomed heyday paralleled the rise of the Grail legend. To judge by the Naassene document and the few other sources that have survived, however, it was not shared by the Naassenes. Nor is it found in Hermetic writings such as the *Krater*, which, as we have seen, also fed into the Grail tradition. In these traditions, the path of spiritual attainment remains open even in the present age.

This difference is not accidental. Central to the Naassene teachings, as Mark H. Gaffney points out in his study of their tradition, is the concept of divine immanence—the idea that the divine is not "out there" in some distant heavenly realm, but present all through the world of matter.[89] This concept underlies the Naassene acceptance of the rites of generation of the ancient Mysteries as spiritually valid, the First Gate that awaits aspirants to gnosis. From this standpoint, the cycle of precession does not take us away from the spiritual realm, it simply requires us to relate to that realm in a different way, in its expressions in matter rather than in its pure form as spirit. In the precessional ages of Saturn, the First Gate of gnosis, the gate of material generation, would be even more important than it was in ages closer to the luminaries.

Another factor may also have helped shape the difference in attitudes just indicated. Though he is the lord of time, fate, and death, Saturn was also described in mythology as the lord of the golden age. This is why Virgil, predicting the coming of a better world with the end of the age of Aries and the coming of the age of Pisces, included the line "now the reign of Saturn returns." An undercurrent in the old starry lore suggests that the reign of Saturn may not be the era of unrelieved grimness that so many people seem to have thought it would be.

As de Santillana and von Dechend showed, a great many myths and legends from around the world touch on the precession of the equinoxes in one way

---

89. Gaffney, *Gnostic Secrets of the Naassenes*.

or another. There are at least two reasons why this should come as no surprise. First, since the constellations rising just before dawn were used as a calendar all over the world in ancient times, knowing that the stars could be expected to slip out of sync with the seasons over time was a basic piece of practical knowledge, the kind of thing that needed to be passed down to future generations. That made precession an obvious piece of data to include in stories.

Second, the same slow movement of the constellations provided a convenient way to mark events in the distant past and anchor predictions in the far future. The Greek legends of Europa and the Golden Fleece mentioned earlier are, among other things, good examples of this process at work. Back before literacy came to Greece, when these stories embodied the knowledge of the past that anyone had, those who knew the secret of precession could place events in the heroic age in their proper location during the age of Taurus. Other markers such as planetary conjunctions (transmitted in the stories in the form of encounters between gods and heroes) were used to date things more precisely.

This way of keeping track of time in oral tradition seems to have been in common use all over the ancient world. It is not surprising, therefore, that the stories of King Arthur and his knights include scraps of the old starry wisdom. The Celtic storytellers whose tales became the raw material for Arthurian legend were steeped in oral traditions dating back to the distant past, and they wove material from much older stories into the tales of Arthur. We have already seen this at work in the survival of scraps of megalithic lore in Arthurian romance.

This brings us back again to the *Elucidation*, for that cryptic tale also includes material from archaic starlore. Among these are the seven guardians of the world, who are also the seven cloaks and the seven natural stories that proceed from the Grail. In the light of the material we have just examined, these references take on an obvious meaning. The astrological beliefs of the ancient world saw the planets as seven great spiritual powers guarding the world. Their orbits traced out seven coverings or veils between earth and heaven, and each planet was the subject of a cycle of stories that recounted its movements and conjunctions in the guise of heroic events.

There is, however, another crucial detail in the *Elucidation* that reached back to the old starlore and went forward in turn to help inspire the labors of Jessie

Weston. It centers on the enigmatic figure of the Rich Fisherman, whose court was once the source of abundant wealth in the age before King Amangons violated the ancient custom of the hills and brought ruin on Logres. Once that happened, the *Elucidation* tells us, the court of the Rich Fisherman could no longer be found. Seen from the standpoint of the old mythologies of the stars, this is a statement of simple astronomical fact expressed in terms of symbolism. In the starry heavens, the court of the Rich Fisherman is the constellation Pisces, the Fishes—and during the Piscean age it "could no longer be found" because at the spring equinox, as we have seen, the stars of that constellation were hidden behind the Sun.

One implication of this symbolism is that the *Elucidation* may have been intended as prophecy rather than history. During the Middle Ages, the Sun at the spring equinox was solidly placed in the midst of Pisces. If the hiding of the court of the Rich Fisherman was meant as a precessional reference, the discovery of the court by Arthur's knights could not happen until the Sun had passed onward to the previous sign. Only then could watchers gazing west after sunset on the spring equinox hope to see the stars of Pisces show themselves low and pale near the horizon, heralding the end of the Piscean age. Then, quite literally, the reign of Saturn (the ruler of Aquarius) would return, and the greening of the land could be expected.

Whether the prophecy turns out to be correct in any other sense—whether the secret customs of the hills in megalithic times will be recovered in any sense, and whether the Waste Land that industrial humanity has made of the earth will turn green again—will have to be seen as the Aquarian age unfolds around us. In Jessie Weston's time, however, such predictions had a special importance. Many people in the occult community of late nineteenth and early twentieth century Britain believed that the Aquarian age was dawning around them. It was in that time, as we will see, that the ceremony of the Grail was revived and certain aspects of the traditions that surrounded it were explored by Weston and others.

Their explorations had a dimension that has rarely been grasped by more recent students of the Grail legend. In the course of her researches, Jessie Weston came to believe that the secret of the Grail was concealed and passed down through the years in a specific geographical region in Britain. It is to this that we now turn.

PART THREE
THE
KEEPERS OF
THE SECRET

THE LAND OF
THE MABON

Even today, the border counties where England and Scotland meet are a place
apart. They are among the least thickly inhabited regions in the British Isles,
a land of bleak, windswept hills and treacherous bogs where ruins left behind
by a long and complex past far outnumber the tiny villages and scattered farm-
houses of the present inhabitants. From the fortress town of Berwick on the
North Sea to the village of Gretna on Solway Firth—long famous as a destina-
tion for eloping English couples—the border slants northeast to southwest, following lines traced out by rivers and hills, reinforced here and there by ancient
earthen dikes. Even in Britain, many people lose track of where it is. Hadrian's Wall, the boundary between Roman Britain and the wild Pictish tribes two
thousand years ago, is still what most English people imagine when they think
of the line between their country and Scotland, but the old Roman wall is well
to the south of the current border.

From the Middle Ages up to the edge of modern times, the border counties were also a dangerous place to be. The border reivers made it that way.
The reivers were clans on either side of the border who raided the other side
for cattle and movable goods, and they were not averse to adding murder and

arson to their activities when the opportunity presented itself. Unconcerned with the laws of the kingdoms to either side of them, the reivers had their own body of traditional law passed down by word of mouth, which established certain "trysting places" along the border where the clans could meet without danger of violence, and set aside certain crossings where merchants and travelers could pass from kingdom to kingdom in safety.

The border laws had another, stranger detail. They set aside a certain small region near the southwest end of the border, thirteen miles long and five across at its widest, which belonged to neither England nor Scotland.[90] By mutual agreement of the reiver clans, no building—not even the smallest shed—could be built there, the earth could not be plowed or dug, and animals could be pastured there during the daylight hours but had to be gone by sunset.

This "Debatable Land," as it was called, is only a few miles northeast of the English fortress city of Carlisle, in the midst of an area full of traces of ancient Pagan worship. Its southwest end, a short walk from Gretna, is marked by the Clochmabenstane—a great boulder, once surrounded by a stone circle, that was the site of Pagan rites in ancient times. The name Clochmabenstane means "the stone of Mabon's head," and the stone and the circle around it are a sacred place dating perhaps from the late Stone Age.[91]

The word *Mabon* is the title of a Celtic god worshipped by the ancient Druids. It literally means "the Son." The ancient Celts liked to keep the actual names of their gods and goddesses secret, and so the terms they used for deities in public were titles rather than names: Cernunnos means "The Horned One," Lugos means "The Shining One," Esus means "Lord," Epona means "She of the Horse," and so on. Mabon is another of these titles. It appears in ancient inscriptions and also features in one of the stories of the *Mabinogion*, the great treasury of Welsh legend, where a character is named Mabon ap Modron, "Son, son of Mother."

Shrines to Mabon, or as the Romans called him, Maponus, existed here and there in those Celtic countries that were conquered by the Roman Empire. One of these was in the area we have just been discussing, where Scotland and England come together. That shrine was called *Locus Maponus*, "the place of

---

90. Robb, *The Debatable Land*, discusses this remarkable territory.

91. Robb, *The Debatable Land*, 98.

Mabon," in a late Roman geographical document. Nowadays the name has been rounded off to Lochmaben, which is the name of a town in the region. Roman records also indicate that a certain place in southern Scotland was considered "the land of Mabon," a region specially sacred to the Son.[92]

The traditions surrounding the Debatable Land go back a very long way, as shown by archeological evidence and historical records alike. Excavations have found that from the end of the Bronze Age to the beginning of the sixteenth century, there are no traces of human activity in this strange region. Just southeast of the Debatable Land, across the river Liddel at Netherby, a Celtic stone sculpture of a man's head with ram's horns was found buried; archaeologists have concluded that it was the image of a Pagan god.

Beginning early in the Middle Ages, moreover, a ring of churches and chapels surrounded the forbidden zone. No one knows why. They were located as close to the border as possible without violating the ancient law forbidding building on the ground.[93] Some of these religious structures are parish churches, but normally a parish church lies toward the middle of the parish, not all the way over to one edge, as these are. They look for all the world like spiritual fortresses meant to keep someone—or something—penned up within the Debatable Land.

There are, of course, parallels to this sort of sacred space in other parts of Pagan Europe. The most famous was the *hiera orgas* north of Eleusis in Greece, the sacred zone of wilderness set apart for the goddesses Demeter and Persephone, where no plowing or settlement was permitted. There were other such places scattered across the ancient world. There are still such places today in Japan, where so many other archaic customs relating to Pagan worship have been preserved. The Debatable Land is almost certainly another of them— as far as I have been able to determine, the only one of these sacred nature reserves in Europe that survived the coming of Christianity.

It is quite possible that we know the name of the deity to whom this forbidden ground was consecrated in Celtic times. As already noted, Roman records refer to a place somewhere in what is now southern Scotland, which was known as the Land of the Mabon. The Debatable Land includes the Clochmabenstane

---

92. Tolstoy, *The Quest for Merlin*, 206.

93. Robb, *The Debatable Land*, 100.

at its southwestern tip, as we have seen, and not far away is Lochmaben, the old *Locus Maponus*. It would make sense of all the evidence, therefore, to suggest that the Debatable Land was once known as the Land of the Mabon, a region set apart for the worship of the Celtic god known as the Son.

The Debatable Land and the area immediately around it have yet another body of connections to Pagan Celtic tradition. During the early centuries of the Dark Ages, this part of Britain was a battleground swept repeatedly by waves of political and religious conflict. In the poetry of old Wales it is part of the broader region called *y Gogledd*, "the North," the zone of conflict where Celtic warriors of the generations after Arthur fought and died in a vain but heroic effort to hold back the invading Saxons. One of the core reasons the defense of the North failed, in turn, is that the defenders were divided against one another, and one of the main divisions was between Christian and Pagan.

The crucial event in that long struggle was the battle of Arderydd in 573 CE. In that struggle Gwenddolau, the last Pagan Celtic king in the region, faced a Christian Celtic army led by several rival kings. To judge by the references to the struggle in old Welsh poetry, the battle was unusually fierce even by the standards of that harsh time. One of Gwenddolau's warriors, Dreon the Brave, held the approaches to Arderydd until he and all the warriors with him were killed. In the battle that followed, Gwenddolau died and his warriors were slain with him. With them the last bastion of Celtic Pagan religion went down in defeat.[94]

Gwenddolau has a strange reputation in later Welsh poetry. He was said to have a magical chessboard that played by itself, a detail that, curiously enough, appears more than once in the medieval Grail legends. He is also described as having two magical birds who wore a yoke of gold and who ate human flesh. Pairs of magical birds linked by gold or silver chains appear in old Irish literature, so we are probably dealing with a mythic image from the old Celtic religion, misunderstood or distorted by later Christian writers. The echoes of Pagan symbolism are strong here.

---

94. Tolstoy, *The Quest for Merlin*, 43–56.

Another aspect of Gwenddolau's reputation takes us even closer to the archaic Pagan traditions of the Celts. According to some of the oldest surviving Welsh poems, it was Gwenddolau, not the earlier war leader who came to be remembered as King Arthur, who was the patron of Merlin, the great poet, prophet, and enchanter of British legend. A handful of very ancient poems attributed to Merlin or, as his name is spelled in Welsh, Myrddin, have to do with Gwenddolau and the battle of Arderydd, and with Merlin's madness and flight to the woods after Gwenddolau's death. For that matter, one of the oldest references to Merlin in British sources is an old Welsh chronicle that gives the following entry for the year 575 CE: *Bellum Erderit inter filios Elifer et Guendoleu filium Keidiau, in quo bello Guendoleu cecidit. Merlinis insanus effectus est.*[95] (The battle of Arderydd between the sons of Elifer and Gwenddolau son of Ceidio, in which battle Gwenddolau was killed. Merlin became insane.)

The religious dimension may help to explain the unusual savagery with which the battle of Arderydd was fought. In most of the battles of that era, the death of one side's king was enough to end the fighting. In this case, however, that did not happen. A Welsh triad speaks in awed tones of "the retinue of Gwenddolau son of Ceidiau at Arderydd, who continued the battle for a fortnight and a month after their lord was slain."[96] A local tradition has it that the retinue was finally forced to surrender after a siege of many days, and the victors slaughtered them and buried them on the spot. This again was not the way that wars were normally conducted at that time. Religious hatred is one of the few plausible explanations.

Many of the battles of Dark Age Britain have proved difficult to place on the ground, but the site of the battle of Arderydd was located by the famous antiquarian W. F. Skene when Queen Victoria was still on the British throne. In documents from the Middle Ages, he found references to a place on the English-Scottish border called Arthuret and another not far away called Carwindlow or Carwenolow. Arthuret was simply an alternative spelling of Arderydd, and Skene was a good enough linguist to recognize in Carwenolow the rounded-off remains of the name Caer Wenddolau, the Castle of Gwenddolau.

---

95. Tolstoy, *The Quest for Merlin*, 45.

96. Tolstoy, *The Quest for Merlin*, 54.

Further research allowed him to track down both places. Arderydd today is called Arthuret Knoll, a low hill with the remains of an ancient stronghold on top, and Caer Wenddolau is now known as Liddell Moat, a steep-sided hill that rises where a stream called Carwinelow—another echo of the ancient name—flows into the Liddel River. Skene's discovery has been supported by further research, giving one of the crucial battles of Britain's Dark Age history a firm geographical location.

What makes this important in terms of this book's project is that Arthuret Knoll and Liddel Moat are right up against the southeastern border of the Debatable Land, and between the two is Netherby, where excavations turned up the statue of a Celtic god. From the battlefield of Arthuret it takes only a few minutes to walk to the River Esk and look across it to the ancient Land of the Mabon, and from Liddel Moat the edge of the Debatable Land is closer still, practically a stone's throw. The last stand of Celtic Paganism in the border country, in other words, took place on the edge of a tract of land that was apparently sacred to a Celtic god. Was the war caused by an attempt by the Christian kings to desecrate the Land of the Mabon in order to break the back of Pagan resistance to the new faith? We will almost certainly never know, but it seems likely.

One way or another, the region around the Debatable Land was a crucial Pagan stronghold in the sixth century, and it seems to have kept that status to some degree even after the Christian army defeated Gwenddolau and slaughtered his warriors, and Merlin fled to the safety of the forest. As late as the eighteenth century, antiquarians noted that the area on both sides of Solway Firth, just west of the Debatable Land, preserved certain very ancient customs from Celtic Pagan tradition.[97] The tenacity with which the border reivers kept up the old custom that prohibited building and farming on the Land of the Mabon for almost a thousand years after the Battle of Arderydd supports this idea.

So, in another way, do the medieval Christian churches and chapels that surround that tract. Elsewhere in Britain, Pagan holy places were simply taken over, and churches were built in place of the old shrines and sacred groves. The famous Twelve Hides of Glastonbury in southwestern England had roughly the same status as the Land of the Mabon on the Scottish border—until the dis-

---

97. Tolstoy, *The Quest for Merlin*, 50, note 23.

solution of the monasteries under Henry VIII, it was formally outside the juris-
diction of the king of England—but it was under the authority of the abbot of
Glastonbury Abbey and thus of the Christian church.[98] The Land of the Mabon
also had a Christian monastery in its midst, Canonbie Priory, but this was on a
little wedge of property that was surrounded on three sides by the Debatable
Land but not actually part of it. All this would make sense if Pagan religion
remained a living presence in the area well into the Middle Ages, and if local
Pagans were prepared to push back with force against any Christian attempt to
trespass on their sacred ground.

$$\square$$

Certain events that took place in the region just before the coming of the Dark
Ages give a remarkable degree of support to this possibility. To make sense
of those events, we will need to glance at the guarded frontier that once cut
across the region a little to the south of the Land of the Mabon.

When the Romans invaded and conquered Britain, most of the area that
is now England was a civilized society with thriving towns and a complex
farming economy, while the region that is now Scotland had fewer people,
fewer resources, simpler societies, and a much more deeply rooted habit of
tribal raiding and warfare. The Roman province of Britannia thus stopped at
a line some distance south of today's English-Scottish border, and under the
Emperor Hadrian a wall of stone and brick, reinforced by observation posts
and forts, was built to keep the northern tribes on their side of the border.
Even with the wall, the border was vulnerable enough that around 15 per-
cent of the entire Roman Imperial army was stationed permanently in Britain,
mostly in the northern part of the province.

The garrisons along Hadrian's Wall itself were not Roman legionaries, however. They were auxiliaries—troops recruited from all over the Empire to serve
as backup for the Roman legions. Some 10,000 of these auxiliaries guarded the
border, while two legions were stationed at the fortress cities of Deva (today's
Chester) and Eboracum (York) to deal with serious trouble. Among the auxiliaries stationed along the wall were units recruited from Belgium, North Africa,
Romania, Spain, and Syria. By the last century or so of the Roman presence in

---

98. Michell, *New Light on the Ancient Mystery of Glastonbury*, i–ii.

Britain, the auxiliary forces were thoroughly Romanized, proud members of the imperial army with regimental traditions dating back centuries.

Their status changed around 370 when Magnus Maximus, the commander of Roman forces in Britain, reorganized the northern frontier defenses after another round of raids by the northern tribes. Between increasing pressure from beyond the border and the worsening economic and political troubles of the Empire, the situation had become unsustainable, so Maximus made two dramatic changes. The first was that he turned the army guarding Hadrian's Wall into a permanent local force, giving the officers and auxiliaries farmland in exchange for their military service.[99]

That was a step with immense consequences for the future. Maximus, like other Roman generals who did the same thing elsewhere in the western Empire, was planting the seed from which the Middle Ages would grow. For more than a thousand years afterward, the right to hold land in exchange for military service was the keynote of feudal society. Yet it also had a more local importance in the areas where it was first established, and nowhere more so than on the northern borders of Britannia. As a result of Maximus's policy, after all, ten thousand auxiliary soldiers and their officers settled permanently in the country near Hadrian's Wall, and their descendants stayed there even after the Empire fell. Whatever traditions and practices they brought with them from their homes elsewhere in the Empire had a good chance of remaining in place for a long time thereafter.

Another project Maximus pursued to stabilize the northern border had similar effects. On each of the four Celtic tribes immediately north of the wall, he imposed the rule of a tribal prefect, a Roman officer who functioned as the ruler of the tribe.[100] Despite the obvious difficulties of such a project, all four of these officers were able to maintain control over their tribes even after Maximus and his army left Britain, and they seem to have spread certain elements of Roman culture among their Celtic subjects. As the power of Rome waned further, they and their descendants became kings, and they duly appear in Welsh and Scottish royal genealogies for many centuries thereafter.

The effect of both these policies was to give Roman culture a staying power in the border region that it would not have had otherwise, and did not always

---

99. Turner, *The Real King Arthur*, 30–31.

100. Morris, *The Age of Arthur*, 17–19.

have in other parts of Britain or the Empire as a whole. When the last of the Roman legions pulled out of Britain in 403, the auxiliaries who had settled along the northern border stayed behind, and so did the tribal prefects and their half-Romanized subjects north of the Wall. What makes this relevant to our theme is that members of the Roman garrison along Hadrian's Wall were known to be initiates of the Mysteries of Mithras.[101] Of the five known Mithraea in Britain, in fact, three of them were located at Roman forts along Hadrian's Wall, at Housesteads, Rudchester, and Carrawburgh. Statues and other artifacts of the Mysteries of Mithras have also been found at the great legionary fortresses at Chester and York, and an inscription twenty-two miles north of Hadrian's Wall at High Rochester shows that the Mysteries even spread to the tribes north of the border.

The worship of Mithras was not an exclusive faith. Initiates of Mithras also took part in the worship of other gods and goddesses as part of the ebullient polytheism of Roman culture. At Housesteads, statues of the Roman gods Mars and Victory and the Celtic god Cocidius were found inside the Mithraeum itself, and at the Mithraeum in London, statues of the Roman deities Minerva and Mercury and the Egyptian god Serapis were hidden beneath the floor, possibly to keep them out of the hands of Christian persecutors in the bitter twilight years of classical Paganism.[102] While no archeological finds show a connection in Britain between the Mysteries of Mithras and those of Cybele and Attis, finds elsewhere show that the latter Mysteries also had a presence in Roman Britain, and the connection between the two is well documented elsewhere in the Roman world.

This is important to our theme, because the Mysteries of Mithras themselves did not set down deep roots in British soil. The Mithraea of Roman Britain were all abandoned well before the end of the Roman military presence in Britain, and scholars have suggested that the worship of Mithras may have been a personal interest of certain Roman officers, which flourished while those officers were in command of this or that Roman military base, and shut down promptly once they died or were transferred elsewhere.[103] Elsewhere in

---

101. Drummond, "Mystery Cults in Roman Britain," 28–47.

102. Drummond, "Mystery Cults in Roman Britain," 37, 44–46.

103. Drummond, "Mystery Cults in Roman Britain," 56.

the Roman world, the Mithraic Mysteries endured longer, but they seem to have vanished generally not long after the Christian church seized power in the Roman world.

Where the Mithraic Mysteries flourished, however, the Mysteries of Cybele and Attis usually accompanied them, and the latter—along with the Eleusinian Mysteries—are known to have survived long after the Christian takeover, practiced quietly in a much-simplified form in private homes. No one knows how widespread these last forms of the Mysteries became or how long they were practiced. If Jessie Weston is correct, something like this simplified form of the old rites lingered in the region near Hadrian's Wall. Given the permanent settlement of Roman auxiliaries and their families there, and the spread of Roman culture into the four tribes north of the Wall that accepted tribal prefects, this is by no means impossible—and it would explain another curious body of folk tradition that Weston began to research late in her career.

◇

Mention the words "sword dance" and most people who know anything about British culture at all will usually think of the Scottish sword dance, one of the traditional performance arts of the Highland clans. It is performed by placing two swords crosswise on the ground. A single dancer then leaps and spins above the swords, setting their feet down inches from the sharp blades. It's a beautiful and demanding dance and deserves the attention it has received.

Another kind of sword dance, however, can be found a little farther south. These dances involve six or seven ornately costumed men, each carrying a sword. They dance in a ring, leaping and flourishing their blades, and at the conclusion of the dance suddenly bring their swords together into an interlocked pattern, usually a five- or six-pointed star. These sword dances are mostly found today in the northern English county of Yorkshire, a little south of Hadrian's Wall; some of the dances have been performed by teams from specific villages since at least the Middle Ages. They are performed at the beginning of the agricultural season, often on Plough Monday (the first Monday after the Christian feast of the Epiphany, January 6), the date on which English farmers traditionally began to work their fields.

What makes these dances especially relevant to our theme is that they are often performed as a little play or ritual drama in which one member of the dancing group, usually the leader, is symbolically beheaded by the others and then revived. As Jessie Weston points out, these dances have many close similarities to another set of English folk rituals, the mummers' plays, and to the colorful morris dances, both of which are found much more widely distributed across England and which also have a place in the agricultural cycle.[104] In some areas the sword dances are performed as part of mummers' plays, while in others they are a routine included in the repertoire of morris dancers. Weston's suggestion was that all three are remnants of a single ancient ritual practice that has become fragmented over the course of the centuries.

The mummers' plays are important in this context because nearly all of them are reenactments of the same ritual drama. In most versions of that drama, St. George, the famous dragon slayer and patron saint of Britain, does battle with an enemy knight, who is defeated and killed. The mother of the victim then bewails her fallen son, a doctor comes on the scene and resurrects the victim, and a figure dressed up as the devil then collects donations from the audience. While St. George is the ostensible hero of the play, the knight he defeats is the center of the dramatic action. More to the point, he also fills a role we have seen before.

The knight of the mummers' plays, like the leader of the sword dances, dies and then rises again, as Persephone did in the Eleusinian Mysteries and Attis did in the Mysteries of Cybele. In the death and resurrection acted out in the sword dances and mummers' plays of northern England, is it possible that we have the last garbled and fragmentary remnant of the Mysteries of Attis, enacted at the beginning of the agricultural year to bring fertility to the fields and reenact the once-sacred drama? That was Jessie Weston's theory.

It might be argued that the sword dances are a matter of folk tradition, part of the enduring heritage of British folk culture, rather than a relic of something as outré as the celebrations of the ancient Mysteries. As historian Ronald Hutton has shown, however, a great deal of folk culture originally started out much higher up the social ladder and worked its way down to isolated rural communities over the centuries. The morris dance itself, practically the epitome of English folk culture today, was danced at the royal court of England many years before it found its way to provincial towns and then to the coun-

---

104. Weston, *From Ritual to Romance*, 81–100.

tryside.[105] If the ceremony of the Grail was practiced in the twelfth century among aristocrats—and the prevalence of the Grail romances in courtly circles in that century suggests that this may well have been the case—its gradual descent and transformation into a Yorkshire country custom followed the same trajectory through time.

Weston saw the ancient Greek Mysteries as part of a much broader realm of fertility rituals, in which sword dances and ritual plays of various kinds play an ancient and well-documented role. The evidence she studied in folklore and in Arthurian legend convinced her that a ritual of this kind had survived into the Middle Ages: a ritual that started out as a simple fertility ceremony evolved from there into one of the most widely celebrated of the Greek Mysteries and was then adopted by at least one sect of Christian Gnostics as an expression of the Lesser Mysteries, the Mysteries of nature, the first gate which had to be experienced and understood before the initiates of the gnosis could proceed to the two higher gates.

Weston believed that the specific ritual that was preserved in this way belonged to the Mysteries of Attis and the Great Mother. Her colleague and rival W. A. Nitze argued that the ritual belonged instead to the Eleusinian Mysteries, and both Weston and Nitze were able to offer evidence to defend their point of view. It seems to have occurred to neither of them that they might both be correct. Rituals are fragile things, and they routinely change from generation to generation. It is hardly inconceivable that among the small communities of secret Naassenes who preserved these two mystery traditions, practicing them in private homes like the last Pagans of Greece, the two ceremonies would have eventually blurred together, picking up bits of symbolism and imagery from the surrounding culture, and gradually mutated over time into the ceremony of the Grail as it was known to the Middle Ages. From the point of view of the Naassenes, certainly the combined ritual would still have served to initiate members into the first gate of the Fleshly Generation, and prepared them to pass through the second gate of Christian ritual to the third gate of gnosis.

Those gates were slammed shut more than once over the troubled history of the Western world. The persecution of the Mysteries and Paganism gener-

---

105. Hutton, *The Rise and Fall of Merry England*, 55–61.

ally in the last centuries of the Roman world was echoed later on by the persecution of the Cathars and the Knights Templar, as well as many less-famous outbursts of violence against those who refused to limit their spiritual horizons to the narrow range of possibilities permitted by the established church. It was only in modern times, when Christianity finally lost its grip on political power, that those gates could be opened again in public.

It will come as no surprise to readers who have followed the narrative this far that the first movements toward opening those gates began in a part of the world next to the one we have discussed in this chapter, the area of southern Scotland immediately north of the border. It was further south in London, however, that those first movements came together to create one of the most controversial institutions of the modern world. In that creation, the ceremony of the Grail we have been seeking again comes into sight.

THE MASON'S WORD

London in the autumn of 1717 was a bustling place. Already the largest and most crowded city in Europe, it was among other things full of clubs, societies, and associations of every kind, where gentlemen could spend a pleasant evening with like-minded friends. As far as anyone today knows, nobody paid the least attention on the evening of June 24 of that year, when small groups of men made their way up the stairs of the Apple Tree Tavern in London's Covent Garden neighborhood to the rental rooms above, where private parties and clubs met nearly every night. Probably not one person in that tavern on that memorable evening, including those who climbed that stair, had even the slightest suspicion that the chain of events set in motion by that meeting would bring kingdoms crashing down and transform the intellectual and religious climate of the entire Western world.

Nonetheless, that was what happened. The men who gathered in one of the private rooms at the Apple Tree tavern that evening belonged, according to later tradition, to four stonemasons' lodges that had existed in London, as the saying was, "since time immemorial." At that meeting, they created the Grand Lodge of England, the first-ever national organization of the movement that has since come to be known as Freemasonry.

The origins and history of Freemasonry have been a playground for eccentric scholars and paranoid conspiracy theorists since not long after that memorable June day. Serious historians, however, have also tackled the rise of the Masonic movement, and the broad outlines of its history are, at this point, well known. All through the Middle Ages, when every skilled craft was organized in guilds, stonemasons had their own guilds, which were responsible for secular and religious building projects all over Europe and which developed their own rich heritage of ritual, symbolism, and tradition. Like all guilds, the stonemason's guilds had three degrees of membership, through which each member passed in turn. Apprentices carried out unskilled labor while learning the basics of carving and building with stones. Journeymen, fellows, or fellow crafts—the term varied from guild to guild—had learned enough to carry out skilled tasks under the supervision of a master, and they developed their skills until they could create a masterpiece (that's where this word comes from) and be accepted as masters. Masters taught apprentices, employed fellow crafts, and carried out the most challenging work. It was an effective system and it flourished for centuries.

The sweeping economic changes that followed the end of the Middle Ages brought the guild system crashing down over most of Europe, but guilds managed to survive in certain places. In Scotland, which was an independent kingdom in those days, the stonemasons' guild was one of the survivors. One of its assets was that it had a curious reputation as a repository of strange secrets. As a result, educated gentlemen interested in secret lore arranged to join the guild as what we would call honorary members; the term for this in sixteenth- and seventeenth-century Scotland was "accepted masons," as distinct from the "operative masons" who actually built things from stone and mortar. Over the years that followed, the number of working operative stonemasons in the lodges declined while the number of "accepted masons" rose, until eventually the Free and Accepted Masons in southern Scotland had only incidental and symbolic connections to the building trades. Meanwhile, the same thing began to happen in several other parts of Britain, especially the English cities of London and York. It was at this stage that the four lodges in London met to form the Grand Lodge of England.

Most Masonic lodges these days have little or nothing in the way of secret teachings to offer their initiates. They perform elaborate rituals of initiation,

most of which center on the history of the building, destruction, and rebuilding of the Temple of Solomon in Jerusalem, and they present to new initiates
a series of emblems and symbols, which are typically explained in terms of
entirely conventional moral teachings. For example, the trowel, the working
tool assigned to the third degree of initiation—the degree of Master Mason—
is supposed to symbolize brotherly love, which unites the members of a lodge
the way that mortar spread by the trowel unites the stones of a building.[106]
Similarly, the sprig of acacia, which plays a memorable role in one stage of the
ritual for initiating Master Masons, is supposed to represent faith.[107]

And the secrets of Freemasonry? Officially, they consist of the rituals of
initiation; the passwords, grips (secret handshakes), and signs (secret gestures)
of the degrees; the private business of each lodge; and the private business of
each member of the lodge. These are the things that each Mason pledges to
keep secret from everyone in the world who is not a properly initiated Mason.
The rituals, passwords, grips, and signs have been revealed in print hundreds of
times, and you can find them online without the least difficulty, but no Mason
who takes his word of honor seriously will divulge them to anyone who is not
a Mason in good standing.

Since not long after the founding of the Grand Lodge of England, however, rumors have been in circulation claiming that the Freemasons have other,
deeper secrets. Speculations about what those secrets are or might be have
filled enough books to stock a good-sized library. There is a rich irony here
because, according to the rituals and teachings of Freemasonry themselves,
those deeper secrets exist, but today's Masons no longer know what they are.

This is the theme of the most important Masonic initiation ritual, the
degree of Master Mason. All Masonic initiation rituals are essentially ornate
ways of telling a story, and this one is no exception. According to the story of
the Master Mason's ritual, a man named Hiram Abiff was the chief architect
at the building of the Temple of Solomon. He alone knew all the details of
the project, and the secrets of a Master Mason—above all, the Mason's Word,
the innermost secret of the Craft—could only be passed on to qualified Fellow
Crafts by him. Three Fellow Crafts, unwilling to wait for the completion of the

---

106. Roberts, *The Craft and its Symbols*, 65.
107. Roberts, *The Craft and its Symbols*, 80.

Temple to receive the secrets of a Master Mason, ambushed Hiram and tried to extract the secrets from him by threatening his life. He refused to reveal the secrets, and each of the three hit him with a different weapon, killing him. The three Fellow Crafts then hid his body and tried to make their escape.

When Hiram could not be found, King Solomon sent search parties after him, and one of the parties discovered Hiram's grave. Since the true Mason's Word was lost, King Solomon established a new, substitute Word to be used by Masons until the Lost Word could be found. This substitute Word is the one that is given to every Master Mason at his initiation. The true Word, and the other secrets of a Master Mason, remain lost to this day.

This strange and haunting narrative has certain, very puzzling features. To begin with, while the vast majority of Masonic rituals are based squarely and precisely on narratives from the Bible, the story of Hiram Abiff is not. The name of the central character of the story is based on that of a minor figure in the Old Testament, a man named Hiram or Huram, who is mentioned in 1 Kings 7:13–14, 2 Chronicles 2:13, and 2 Chronicles 4:11.[108] According to these passages, he was the son of a widow who lived in Tyre, and he was summoned by King Solomon to take charge of all the metalworking needed for the Temple. That is what the Bible knows of him. Nowhere in the Bible does the story of the three villainous Fellow Crafts and the murder of Hiram Abiff appear, nor does the Bible give Hiram the central role in the building of the Temple that Masonic ritual assigns him.

The Mason's Word, the substitute Word passed on in the Master Mason degree, is another mystery. There are many passwords in Freemasonry, enough of them that the Masonic scholar Albert Pike filled a book with them. The vast majority of them are ordinary words in Hebrew, Greek, or Latin, but the Mason's Word is not a word in any of these languages.

To refer to it as a single word is a bit of a misnomer, because there are at least a dozen different versions of the Word in use among various branches of Masonry.[109] Among the forms of the Word that have been published in writings

---

108. I have used the Revised Standard Version for all Bible quotes.

109. As a Freemason, I have pledged my honor never to reveal the Mason's Word to anyone who is not a Mason, and I have kept that pledge to the letter. None of the versions of the Word given here is the one that I received when I was raised a Master Mason.

on Masonry down through the years are "Mahabyn," "Machaben," "Mach-benah," "Matchpin," "Ma-ha-beneh," and "Marrow-bone." (This diversity is hardly surprising; since the Word was passed on purely by word of mouth for centuries, it's astonishing that it didn't become even more thoroughly garbled.) All known versions of the Word, however, are recognizable variants of an original word that we have already encountered in a different context. That word is *Mabon*.

This brings up possibilities that have not yet been explored in Masonic writings. Over the years since the first Grand Lodge of England was founded, hundreds of theories have been proposed to account for where Freemasonry came from and why it has the peculiar features that it does. The ancient Mysteries have been included tolerably often in this quest, as have the Knights Templar, the medieval guilds, and a great many more unlikely sources. Yet one thing that has been neglected almost completely in this context is the geographical region in which Freemasonry as we know it first took shape.

What makes this relevant to our quest is that southern Scotland, just north of the Land of Mabon and many other traces of ancient Celtic Paganism, was also the homeland of modern Masonry, the place where the old stonemasons' lodges began the transformations that turned them into Freemasonry as it exists today.[110] Scotland was an independent nation until the Acts of Union joined it with England in 1707, and a great many Celtic traditions and practices survived there long after they had vanished everywhere else. As late as the early twentieth century, W. Y. Evans-Wentz found many people in rural Scotland who worshipped the fairies using rites that were clearly descended from ancient Celtic Pagan spirituality.[111]

The area of Scotland close to the border was especially well supplied with these traces, as we have seen. The Debatable Land; Lochmaben, the sacred place of the Mabon; Hart Fell, where medieval legends say Merlin lived, and where the ancient Celtic god remembered in the Merlin legends likely had a sanctuary in Pagan times; Rosslyn Chapel, with its important connections to

---

110. See Stevenson, *The Origins of Freemasonry*, where this is exhaustively documented.

111. Evans-Wentz, *The Fairy Faith in Celtic Countries*.

the origins of Freemasonry; and the locations of the oldest-documented Scottish lodges to welcome accepted members from outside the building trades—all of these are found within a relatively small geographical region. You can reach them all in a few hours by car today, and even in the days when travel meant going by foot or horseback, a few days of travel was enough to go from one end of the region to another.

We know that sometime around 500 CE, southern Scotland was known even in distant Rome as a place where the god known as Mabon received a great deal of worship. We know that a little after 1717, a word that sounded very much like "Mabon" was being passed on to newly initiated Master Masons as the Mason's Word, the innermost secret of the stonemason's craft. The gap of twelve centuries between these two dates is considerable, but plenty of other archaic traditions have survived for much longer than this.

In the town of Gubbio in central Italy, for example, a traditional procession in honor of the local saint, St. Ubaldo, has been held on May 15 since time out of mind. Among the tourist attractions in that same town is a set of bronze tablets more than two thousand years old which record, in a language older than Latin, the rituals performed in what was then the city-state of Iguvium by a Pagan priesthood many centuries before the coming of Christianity. Some of the ceremonies recorded on these Iguvine Tablets, as they are called, were still to be found in recognizable form in the procession honoring St. Ubaldo in the late nineteenth century.[112]

For that matter, the Roman ceremony of the Ambarvalia, a procession through the fields to invoke blessings on the crops, survives to this day in Britain and several other European countries as the "beating of the bounds," in which the minister and congregation of the parish church walk in procession around the parish boundaries, praying to the Christian god for the same benefits their ancestors sought from Ceres.[113] So it is by no means unlikely that traces of old Celtic rites might have found their way into Masonry across a similar gap in time.

For many centuries, however, openly worshiping a Pagan deity in Scotland was a crime punished by the death penalty. Just as the old gods of Iguvium

---

112. Bower, *The Elevation & Procession of the Ceri at Gubbio.*

113. Laing, *Survivals of Roman Religion*, 48–52.

were replaced by St. Ubaldo, other traditional cultures placed under the Christian yoke have practiced what William Sullivan, in his study of astronomical myths in ancient and modern Peru, has called "guerrilla syncretism": the concealment of Pagan deities and legendary figures behind a thin veneer of Christianity.[114] It's often possible to see through the disguise, in cases like this, by finding places where Christian symbolism has obviously been stretched out of shape to fit a Pagan original.

The Masonic figure of Hiram Abiff shows ample traces of this process at work. As we have already seen, the account of Hiram the metalworker in the Bible lacks nearly all the features assigned to Hiram Abiff in the Master Mason ritual. To see through the "guerrilla syncretism" to the original figure behind the mask of Hiram, all that is necessary is to make a list of the things that were added to the biblical narrative. According to the Masonic version, Hiram Abiff

- was the master builder of the Temple of Solomon, Israel's chief holy place;
- advised King Solomon, the most famous monarch of Israel;
- was killed by being struck three times by three different weapons;
- revealed the secrets of Masonry, in a certain sense, from his grave.

To this, we can add the fact that he was a widow's son.

There is, as it happens, a figure who matches all these criteria precisely, once they are translated into the language of British legend. Like the widow's son, he had a mother but no living (or earthly) father. He was reputed to be the master builder of Stonehenge, ancient Britain's chief holy place. He advised King Arthur, the most famous monarch of Britain. According to a strange legend that can be traced back to the same region of southern Scotland we have already discussed, he was killed in three different ways at the same time: by stoning, falling, and drowning. Other legends claim that he remained alive in a crystal cave beneath the earth, from which his voice could be heard. According to some researchers, he was the Mabon, and thus bore the title that comes down to us in the form of the Mason's Word.[115]

---

114. Sullivan, *The Secret of the Incas.*

115. Tolstoy, *The Quest for Merlin,* is among the works that discuss this.

The figure we are discussing has another name, though, or more properly a title in the old Celtic fashion. In ancient times that title was Moridunos, "He of the Sea-Fortress," a god of magic and prophecy who ruled over the island of Britain before the first human beings set foot on it. Nowadays, time has rounded off that name to Merlin.[116]

The idea that Merlin, the great enchanter of British legend, might have originally been a Pagan god may be surprising at first glance, but there are many other cases of gods and goddesses being redefined as legendary human beings once the arrival of Christianity restricted the term *god* to one and only one deity. The transformation of Pagan gods to Christian saints is extremely well documented. In Greece, for example, Demeter was transformed into St. Demetrius, the patron saint of agriculture. St. Dionysius was revered as the patron of vineyards, filling the role of the god Dionysus, and St. Artemius received the veneration once directed toward Artemis. In the same way, St. Elias, the Elijah of the Old Testament, neatly replaced Helios the sun god. St. Elias was—and in some Greek districts still is—credited with control over sunlight and weather, and prayers for fair weather rise up to him exactly as they rose up to his Pagan equivalent two millennia ago.[117]

Nor is this sort of retrospective humanization limited to saints. Christian scribes during the Middle Ages, when the legend of Merlin was born, routinely converted Pagan gods and goddesses into human characters who could then be assigned places in history and legend. The Norse god Odin, for example, appears in Snorri Sturluson's chronicle *Heimskringla* as an ancient king in Asia whose descendants became the royal house of Norway. In much the same way, the medieval Irish *Glossary of Cormac* turned the Irish sea-god Manannan mac Lir into a famous sailor of the distant past whose exploits led later generations to call him the god of the sea.[118] The god Moridunus could easily have been transformed into a human enchanter the same way.

And the Merlin who went mad after the battle of Arderydd, and who was credited with poems grieving for the death of Gwenddolau, the last defender of Celtic Paganism in Britain? Nikolai Tolstoy, whose book on the Merlin leg-

---

116. I have discussed this in detail in Greer, *The Mysteries of Merlin*, 19–40.

117. Hyde, *Greek Religion and its Survivals*, 41–85.

118. Stewart, *The Book of Merlin*, 152.

end is essential reading in this connection, has suggested that he was a historical figure, one of the last of the old Druids, who served Gwenddolau as a priest and diviner, and who fled from the battlefield to the forests around Hart Fell after the disaster at Arderydd. It was common for the ancient Celts to take the names of gods for their own; Roman records, for example, mention Celtic chieftains named Brennius and Belinus, Latin versions of the divine names Bran and Beli. Thus, the Druid Myrddin could easily have had the same name as the god he worshipped, and the two of them would have been jumbled together in folk imagination during the Dark Ages with other figures of legend and myth to create the vivid figure of Merlin the mage, the counselor of Arthur and the builder of Stonehenge.

Thus the Master Mason's degree of contemporary Freemasonry appears to be descended from an archaic ritual once celebrated in honor of a Celtic god—the god whose myths come down to us in garbled form, by another route, as the legends of Merlin. The obvious question is how such a ritual could have gotten into the hands of the stonemasons whose lodges evolved into Masonry. Plenty of Masonic historians would like to know the answer to that same question. The fact of the matter is that no one knows where the Master Mason's ritual came from or how it got into the hands of the Masons. Nor, for that matter, does anyone know the origins of the narrative at the heart of the ritual—the story of the murder of Hiram Abiff.

According to surviving Masonic records, the four lodges that joined forces in 1717 to create the Grand Lodge of England worked only two degrees, the ancestors of today's Entered Apprentice and Fellow Craft initiations. They continued working along these lines until 1725, when all at once the records indicate that the degree of Master Mason was being conferred. There is no reference to where the degree came from or why, or what led to it being adopted by the four London lodges; it simply shows up without explanation.

All this is extremely strange. All the old craft guilds had three degrees of initiation, not two, and everything we know about the old stonemasons' lodges indicates that this was as true of them as it was of any other guild. To open a lodge—whether it's a lodge of operative stonemasons or a lodge of Free and Accepted Masons—requires the presence of Master Masons, so it's hard to take seriously the claim that there were four lodges meeting in London "since time immemorial" that somehow had no way to initiate Master Masons. What is more, the legend of Hiram Abiff does not appear anywhere in the "Old Charges"—the official documents of the stonemasons' guilds of the Middle Ages—which have been studied systematically by Masonic historians eager to trace the origins of their Craft.

Clearly the chain of events that led to the founding of the first Grand Lodge in 1717 had dimensions that didn't make it into the official Masonic records. In my previous book *The Secret of the Temple* I have argued that the Grand Lodge, and thus Freemasonry as we now know it, were founded as elements of an attempt to recover the lost secrets of the temple technology. Those secrets were closely linked to the Temple of Solomon, the central theme of Masonic symbolism, in two ways. First, the original Temple itself was designed in accordance with the tradition, and according to passages in the Old Testament, the Talmud, and Jewish legend, it had the effects on agricultural fertility that the temple technology was intended to produce. Second, it was in the ruins of the Temple of Solomon that the Knights Templar discovered certain keys to the temple technology and brought those back to Europe, where they were passed on to certain monastic traditions and to the stonemasons who were responsible for building churches that made use of the technology.

The evidence suggests, however, that the temple technology was not the only thing the Templars brought back with them from the Middle East. When the Templars were rounded up to be tried before the Inquisition, some of the charges brought against them referred to the temple technology, as filtered through the minds of medieval theologians—they were accused, for example, of worshipping an idol that they believed caused flowers and trees to grow—but others reflected the actual practice of dissident Gnostic sects such as the Cathars. On the basis of this and other clues, many researchers into the Templar tradition have argued that during their time in the Holy Land, the Templars became converts to a Gnostic sect. It was not the Cathars, certainly, because what is known of the Cathar faith contradicts the scraps of knowledge about the heresy of the Templars that survive in the records of the Inquisition. Yet there were many other forms of Gnosticism, as we have seen, and some of them were more easily hidden beneath a cloak of Christian orthodoxy.

The survival of the Knights Templar in Scotland after their order was proscribed in 1311 has been discussed in many recent books. One detail not always remembered by incautious writers is that the Templars already had a substantial presence in Scotland long before their order fell afoul of the King of France and the Pope. The village of Temple, four miles from Rosslyn Chapel and thus squarely within the region of southern Scotland that gave birth to modern Freemasonry, got its name because it was the headquarters of the Templars in the Kingdom of Scotland. In the Middle Ages it was the center from which Templar officials managed their substantial Scottish landholdings, and where money, supplies, and new recruits for the Templar Order were brought together from Scottish Templar preceptories and manors to be shipped to the Holy Land by sea by the Templar fleet.

The suggestion made by several historians that Templar teachings and symbolism found their way into Scottish stonemasons' lodges in the Middle Ages, and were then passed on from the operative stonemasons to the accepted masons who created modern Freemasonry, gains plausibility from these simple facts of geography.[119] No lengthy quests into foreign countries would have been required. The Templars had their own architects and builders since they were constantly building and repairing their own castles, churches, and other buildings, and Scotland had enough of a Templar presence that the order would have needed a staff of stonemasons there to construct new buildings and maintain the ones already in place. If the Templar architects and builders in Scotland went to work as ordinary stonemasons after 1311 and joined the local stonemasons' guilds in the normal way of things, that all by itself would account for the presence of a Templar heritage in Freemasonry.

In my previous book *The Secret of the Temple*, I have shown that certain Masonic rituals contain information that only the Knights Templar or their heirs could have had: descriptions of tunnels under the Temple Mount in Jerusalem. Those descriptions appear in rituals that already existed in 1771, even though the tunnels themselves were not rediscovered until 1968. (We know the Templars knew about them because there are artifacts in the tunnels dating from the time of the Crusader Kingdom of Jerusalem, when the Temple Mount was the headquarters of the Knights Templar.)

---

119. See especially Robinson, *Born in Blood*.

Certain scraps of lore relating to the temple technology also appear in Masonic ritual and symbolism, but there is no actual description of the technology anywhere in the lore of Freemasonry. There are also important elements of the temple tradition that can be traced in detail in other sources but that appear nowhere in Masonry. The ritual of the Master Mason's degree, furthermore, has nothing to say about the temple technology, nor does it have any apparent connection to the Knights Templar or to the Gnostic heresy they seem to have embraced. Instead, it appears to have a different origin, though that origin can also be traced back to the same region of southern Scotland where Freemasonry was born.

There is at least one straightforward explanation for these curious details. When those four London lodges organized the first Grand Lodge of England in 1717, as we have seen, they did not have the ability to initiate Master Masons. By 1725 they had obtained a ritual for the purpose, but it lacked certain features that, according to other lines of evidence, should have been present. Is it possible that they got the wrong ritual?

THE ROSY CROSS
OF HEREDOM

The suggestion that the Master Mason's ritual of modern Freemasonry was not the original ritual, but a substitute, may seem surprising at first glance. Put the events of 1717 in their historical context, however, and the possibility takes on intriguing dimensions. When the first Grand Lodge of England was founded, England had just closed the door on a long era of revolutionary violence and convulsive change. Two centuries before, in the midst of the Protestant Reformation, King Henry VIII turned his back on the Catholic church and embraced Protestantism for himself and his nation. For a century and a half thereafter, the kingdom whipsawed back and forth from one religious extreme to another—a more radical form of Protestantism under Edward VI, a Catholic reaction under Mary, a return to Protestantism under Elizabeth I, and then growing pressure from the extremist Puritan wing of the Protestants, leading to the English Civil War of 1641–1645 and a Puritan dictatorship under Oliver Cromwell.

The return of the monarchy in 1660 under the nominally Protestant king Charles II brought a temporary truce to the religious struggle, but that conflict broke out again in 1688. In that year, Charles's Catholic brother James II was overthrown by a revolution and his Protestant sister Mary, along with her Dutch husband William III, took his place. The heirs of James II, backed by the Catholic church and the King of France, established a government in exile and recruited a network of followers throughout the British Isles. These followers—called Jacobites, after *Jacobus*, the Latin version of James—hoped at first that they would be able to return to power peacefully, for William and Mary had no heirs and neither did Mary's sister Anne, the last of the Protestant Stuarts.

The Jacobites fatally misjudged the climate of English opinion, however. When Queen Anne died in 1714, too many people in England feared that the return of a Catholic Stuart to the throne would result in Catholicism being imposed by force, and that religious liberty in Britain would be abolished the same way it had been a few decades earlier in France. To prevent this, the English parliament voted to give the crown to a Protestant prince from a small German kingdom who became England's George I, founder of the House of Hanover.

The Jacobites, taken by surprise, tried to stage a rebellion against the new king the next year. Unfortunately for their hopes, the rising of 1715 found few supporters outside of Scotland and Ireland, and the rebels were easily scattered by loyal military units. In the wake of that defeat, thousands of Jacobites fled England for France and other Catholic countries. Not until 1745 did the Jacobites manage another rebellion, under the leadership of James II's grandson Charles—the Bonnie Prince Charlie of Scottish legend—and that uprising suffered an even more crushing defeat at Culloden in 1746. The House of Hanover remained secure on the British throne thereafter until the death of Queen Victoria in 1903.

By 1717, in the wake of the Jacobite defeat two years previously, many people in England finally felt confident that the terrible religious wars of the recent past were finally over. The new king added to that belief by proclaiming religious liberty for most of his Christian and Jewish subjects. It was a good time for religious dissidents to come out into the open, and a great many of them did: the century or so after 1717 in England saw the birth of scores of new sects and denominations, and the formal establishment of many others that had been launched in secret in the years beforehand. (It was during that period, for example, that the first modern Druid organizations were founded.)

Yet it was also a time when many old traditions were in danger of being lost, and many others had already disappeared.

Earlier scholars such as Elizabeth I's court astrologer John Dee and the alchemist and historian Elias Ashmole had rescued what they could, preserving and transmitting various branches of medieval lore, but the long years of sectarian warfare and religious persecution had taken a heavy toll. The Jacobite rising of 1715 and its aftermath added to that toll because some of the most influential students of occultism and secret traditions in Britain at that time were Jacobites, and their flight to Europe took many traditions out of the reach of British students. More generally, the bitter animosities between Jacobite and Hanoverian parties thereafter became a barrier across which very little could be transmitted.

The founding of the Grand Lodge in 1717 is thus best understood as a salvage operation, carried out by people who had inherited the surviving fragments of an ancient tradition and were trying to reassemble those fragments in a form that could endure: an event of a kind that has happened many times in the history of the world's secret teachings. Whatever ritual the old London lodges had used to confer the rank of Master Mason until sometime before 1717 had clearly been lost. The most likely possibility, given the historical context, is that the handful of Master Masons in London who knew it were Jacobites, and they fled to France after 1715. Whatever the facts of the matter, it was necessary for the members of the newly founded Grand Lodge of England to recover the ritual—or at least to find something to put in its place.

The evidence suggests that the latter is what happened. A suitable ritual was found. Doubtless, as has happened in countless other cases, it was modified as needed to make it fit the requirements of the emerging Masonic fraternity. The London Masons may even have received it from Scottish stonemasons or from documents preserved by Scottish operative lodges, though this is pure speculation at this point. All we can say for certain is that the Word passed on to initiates and the story reenacted in that ritual both point back toward the region of southern Scotland where the Mabon was worshipped and where the legends of Merlin have their home.

The ritual itself, however, bears witness to a pervasive sense of loss. That may have been one of the things put into the ritual when it was adapted for use by the London lodges that gave rise to modern Freemasonry. Among Masons thereafter, it became axiomatic that the True Word of a Master Mason was lost, and a substitute Word—drawn from a tradition rooted in Celtic antiquity, but without the links to the temple technology—was put in its place, until the True Word could be discovered.

The three degrees of Entered Apprentice, Fellow Craft, and Master Mason remained the stock in trade of regular Masonry thereafter, but other rituals existed, and they began to surface in France and Germany in the wake of the Jacobite defeat of 1715. Most of them can be linked directly to Jacobite exiles in those countries or to people who were in contact with the Jacobite underground. The standard name for them at the time—"Scottish Masonry"—is also a giveaway, since Scotland remained a hotbed of Jacobite support all through the eighteenth century. The *hauts grades* ("high degrees"), as these further initiations were also called, remained highly secretive until after the second Jacobite rising in 1745.

Historian Marsha Keith Schuchard has presented ample evidence in her many writings on the subject that covert Masonic lodges working these higher degrees were used for networking purposes by Jacobite rebels to assemble money, weapons, and allies for the planned rising.[120] Only after the rebellion failed and the Jacobite cause was lost for good did these lodges open their doors to Freemasons in general, and by then the manufacture of new hauts grades had practically become an industry among European Masons. By the early nineteenth century there were so many Masonic initiations available in Europe that one organization, the Rite of Memphis and Misraim, offered its initiates no fewer than ninety-nine degrees of initiation. That sort of exuberance didn't last indefinitely, but the Scottish Rite of thirty-three degrees, the York Rite of ten degrees, and several other smaller rites such as the Knight Masons remain active today in the United States and elsewhere, each conferring a selection of the hauts grades created during those years of ritual enthusiasm.

The early hauts grades, the ones that may have been brought over from Britain with Jacobite exiles after 1715, cast an intriguing light on our subject. The first of these to surface was the Scots Master degree, which first appears

---

120. See especially Schuchard, *Emanuel Swedenborg*, and Schuchard, *Restoring the Temple of Vision*.

in Masonic records in 1733. By 1744, to judge by surviving records, it had its name changed to Knight of the Sword, and it survives today as the Order of the Red Cross in the York Rite, the Fifteenth and Sixteenth degrees of the Scottish Rite, and the three Knight Mason degrees.[121] Its origins are entangled with Rosslyn Chapel—the one text carved into the structure of that enigmatic ruin just happens to be the biblical text at the center of the degrees just named—and a case can thus be made that the Scots Master ritual may be one of the few remnants of the traditions that once surrounded Rosslyn Chapel and the attempted revival of the temple technology there in the fifteenth century.[122]

The second high degree to surface in Masonic history is the Royal Arch degree, which first appears in Masonic records in 1743. It is one of the degrees that most clearly shows echoes of the secret of the Knights Templar, for it describes the discovery of a secret cache of documents in a buried chamber beneath the ruins of the Temple Mount in Jerusalem. It is also the most widely conferred of all the higher degrees and is found in some lodge organizations that have no connection to Freemasonry at all. Within Masonry, it is widely considered to be the completion of the Master Mason's degree, for it purports to reveal the True Word that was lost at the death of Hiram Abiff.

In fact, it gives its initiates two words, one of them one of the standard Jewish names of God, the other a strange word that appears in slightly different forms all through the older degrees of Masonry in many different contexts.[123] These forms include *Jubelo*, *Jubela*, and *Jubelum*, the names of the three assassins of Hiram Abiff in some but not all versions of the Master Mason's degree, and *Giblim*, a secret word in another Masonic degree. All of them are variations on the Arabic word *jebel*, "mountain," with one or more suffixes whose meanings can no longer be teased out. This suggests that the original version may have been among the things brought back by the Knights Templar from the Holy Land. My guess, though it is only a guess, is that this was in fact the original Mason's Word, and it most likely refers to a mountain or hill in the Holy Land where the secrets of the temple technology were once preserved.

---

121. Greer, *The Secret of the Temple*, 17–18.

122. Greer, *The Secret of the Temple*, 219–25.

123. As a Royal Arch Mason, I am prohibited by my obligations from giving the word as I received it. The alternative versions listed here are close enough to make the necessary point.

The Royal Arch degree is accompanied, in most of the Rites where it appears, with another ritual that gives more information about the secret passages under the Temple Mount. Here again, the traces of the Templar secret are strong, for these rituals—the degree of Select Master in the York Rite and that of Perfect Elu in the Scottish Rite—describe horizontal tunnels extending from the palace of King Solomon to the hidden chamber under the Temple. Except for Freemasons who had been initiated into those degrees, no one knew about those tunnels until they were rediscovered by Israeli archaeologists in 1968.

These early rituals, then, are among the most compelling pieces of evidence for a Templar connection in modern Freemasonry and, through that connection, a link with the lost temple technology that was once put into practice at the Temple of Solomon. The hauts grades invented after 1745, even those that claim a Templar connection—and there are quite a few of these—have nothing similar to show the researcher, and it's tolerably clear that they were made up by eighteenth-century Freemasons who enjoyed putting on colorful initiation ceremonies and decided to try their hand at writing some. There is another hauts grade, however, which dates from before 1745 and deserves careful attention here. One of the most colorful of all Masonic degrees, it does not contain any signs of Templar ancestry—quite the contrary—but it points directly toward the object of our quest. This ritual, the degree of Knight Rose Croix of Heredom, is not the ceremony of the Grail, but the evidence suggests that it was created in imitation of the lost ceremony we are seeking.

To understand what the degree in question has to reveal, it's necessary to start with a circle of Lutheran intellectuals at the University of Tübingen in Germany at the beginning of the seventeenth century.[124] That was an exhilarating time for Protestants. The Reformation had made inroads in many European countries, and for the first time since the heyday of the Cathars, religious dissidents could exist in some parts of Europe without facing the threat of being burned at the stake for heresy. The inevitable backlash was on its way—the Thirty Years' War in Germany, the Wars of Religion in France, and the bitter struggles between Jacobite and Hanoverian factions in Britain—but it had not

---

124. My discussion here is based largely on Yates, *The Rosicrucian Enlightenment*.

yet arrived. Optimistic Protestants hoped that it might never arrive or, failing that, that their movement would survive the struggle. (History shows that they were wrong about the first but right about the second.)

During those years a significant number of Lutherans took an active interest in magic, alchemy, astrology, and other arts forbidden by Rome. The members of the Tübingen circle belonged to that number. Sometime in the first decade of the seventeenth century, they worked up a set of ornate parables about a German mystic named Christian Rosenkreutz (that is, Christian Rosy-Cross), the mysterious Rosicrucian Fraternity he founded, and the wonderful secrets the members of the Fraternity knew. They published the first of them, the *Fama Fraternitatis* (*News of the Fraternity*), as a cheap pamphlet in 1614 and the other two, the *Confessio Fraternitatis* (*Confession of the Fraternity*) and *Chymische Hochzeit Christiani Rosencreutz* (*Alchemical Wedding of Christian Rosy-Cross*) in the two years that followed. Plenty of similar works appeared in those same years, and the members of the Tübingen circle probably thought that their creation would be just one more addition to the lively pamphlet literature of the time.

That wasn't what happened. It would be fair to say that these three publications—the Rosicrucian manifestos, as they were later called—turned into the Harry Potter series of the seventeenth century. The only difference was that people across Europe were convinced that the Rosicrucian equivalent of Hogwarts was real, and a great many of them set out to find it, either to join the Fraternity or to burn its members at the stake. Small presses, the seventeenth-century equivalent of the internet, accordingly flooded Europe with hundreds of pamphlets praising or condemning the mysterious Rosicrucians.

Then 1618 arrived and the Thirty Years' War began, plunging central Europe into a maelstrom of chaos and bloodshed. Nearly a third of the population of Germany died during those ghastly years. By the time peace finally arrived with the Treaty of Westphalia in 1648, the occult wing of Protestantism in Germany had long since gone to ground. It was more than a century later, after the collapse of the Jacobite cause, that Rosicrucian groups began to surface. The Royal Order of Scotland, which confers a Rosicrucian degree, was active in Paris in 1749, and the *Orden des Gold- und Rosenkreuz* (Order of the Golden and Rosy Cross) was founded in Germany sometime in the 1750s.

The degree of Knight Rose Croix of Heredom also emerged at this same period. The Rite of Perfection, the ancestor of today's Scottish Rite, was founded in Paris in 1754 by the Chevalier de Bonneville, and in its early days it met at the College of Jesuits in Clermont, France. It worked a system of twenty-two degrees of initiation, and the Knight Rose Croix of Heredom degree was one of these.

According to the 1783 Francken manuscript, one of the few surviving sources for the details of the eighteenth-century hauts grades, the Rose Croix of Heredom degree is the original form of Scottish Masonry, and it was at that time worked by some branches of Masonry as the fourth degree, by others as the seventh degree, and by still others as the eighteenth. According to the manuscript, it was also called by a variety of different names—Knight of the White Eagle, Knight of the Pelican, Perfect Mason, or Knight of the Rose Cross.[125] All this suggests that the degree had been in circulation for some time before the Rite of Perfection started celebrating it.

It is, to be quite frank, a very odd degree. The version of the initiation included in the Francken manuscript begins with the candidate led into a room in darkness, draped in black, where the tools and symbols of Freemasonry lie scattered and broken on the floor and the officers of the lodge are in mourning. From there the candidate sets out on a quest for the new Word that will replace the old Word of Freemasonry. During this quest he is brought into a room that represents Hell, complete with devils and roasting sinners. Finally he reaches a third room in brilliant light, draped in white, which represents the burial place of Christ. Here he receives two words drawn from ordinary Christian tradition and is enjoined to practice the Christian virtues of faith, hope, and charity.

What is lacking from the ritual is even more striking than what is present. By the time the Rite of Perfection came into being, the Rosicrucian movement had its own set of symbols and imagery, of which the central emblem of the Rose and Cross was only one. The burial vault of Christian Rosenkreutz, which has a central role in most Rosicrucian traditions, is nowhere to be seen in the Rose Croix of Heredom degree. Nor are other standard Rosicrucian emblems such as the beehive and the symbols of alchemy. Mount Abieg-

---

125. Francken, *The 1783 Francken Manuscript*, 496.

nus, the symbolic Rosicrucian mountain of initiation, is also absent, replaced by an equally mysterious mountain variously called Heredom, Heroden, or Harodim, located "between the west and north of Scotland," whatever exactly that means.[126]

The version found in the Francken manuscript already shows signs of substantial reworking to fit the symbolism of Masonry, and the versions conferred nowadays have undergone even more revision to conform with Masonic expectations. The original form visible through all these variations, however, might best be described as straightforwardly anti-Masonic. The first chamber shows the symbols of Masonry fallen and broken, and they are not raised up again. In their place, after a visit to a typically Christian version of Hell, the candidate is presented with the symbols and ideals of conventional Christianity and told to follow those in place of the rituals and emblems of traditional Freemasonry. In its oldest surviving form, furthermore, the degree has no obligation—that is, no oath of secrecy and brotherhood.[127] Every other Masonic degree, by contrast, has an obligation of this kind.

It is not surprising that ever since this degree first appeared in the eighteenth century, rumors surrounding it have claimed that it was originally created by the Catholic Church in an attempt to lure Masons away from the Craft. This is by no means impossible. The absence of an obligation is telling, since Masonic oaths of secrecy are among the things that the Catholic Church has always found most objectionable about the Craft. The theme of the ritual more generally also offers some support to this old theory.

That claim also gains credibility from the place where the Rite of Perfection first met. Well before 1754, Roman Catholics were strictly forbidden from having anything to do with Freemasonry; a papal edict in 1738 excommunicated all Freemasons without exception, and it reserved to the Pope alone the power to forgive them. The Jesuit order was traditionally given a great deal of leeway in its work, but hosting an organization that had been explicitly banned by the Pope was more than even they could get away with—unless they had some secret agenda in mind that had been approved by the church hierarchy.

---

126. Croteau, Foulds, and Newell, *The 1783 Francken Manuscript*, 499.

127. Croteau, Foulds, and Newell, *The 1783 Francken Manuscript*, 515.

Four years after it was founded, however, the Rite of Perfection had been absorbed by another Masonic body, the Council of Emperors of the East and West, which quickly became embroiled in rivalries with another organization titled the Council of Emperors of the East. In 1764 the Jesuit order itself, accused of various forms of political and financial chicanery, was expelled from France. If the Rite of Perfection was created by the Jesuits for their own purposes, it slipped out of their hands very quickly. Thereafter the degree of Rose Croix of Heredom was taken up by a variety of Masonic bodies, and today—after many further revisions—has an honored place in the rituals of the Scottish Rite.

Compare the degree of Rose Croix of Heredom to the ceremony of the Grail described in the *Elucidation*, however, and a fascinating possibility emerges at once. As described earlier, the Grail ceremony—like the ancient Mysteries on which it is modeled—begins in darkness and mourning beside the bier of a slain knight. After the vigil in the Chapel Perilous, the candidate proceeds to a second stage of the ritual where he takes part in the feast of the Grail and asks the question that heals the Fisher King and the Waste Land alike. Once this has taken place, the third stage of the ritual—"the great wonder to which no other can be compared"—takes place, and the questing knight is crowned and becomes the next Keeper of the Grail.

In eighteenth-century Masonic rituals, the usual way to handle a ritual divided into separate parts like this was to assign each part to a separate room or chamber. Thus we have the first chamber, draped in black and full of signs of grief and mourning; the second chamber, set up for a feast; and the third chamber, on the model of the last stage of the ancient Mysteries, draped in bright colors and full of signs of celebration and triumph.

This pattern should be familiar to those readers who have been paying attention. Replace the second chamber with a representation of Hell, and you have a close equivalent of the three chambers of the Rose Croix degree.

The similarity is unlikely to be accidental, for this arrangement of stages and chambers is found nowhere else in the earliest hauts grades. The *Elucidation*, for that matter, was completely unknown when the grade of Rose Croix of Heredom was written, and scholarly interest in medieval Arthurian literature did not become a significant factor until the next century. (Nor, for that matter, do any other of the old Masonic degrees relate to a legendary mountain reminiscent of the Munsalväsche of the Grail legends.) We are left with puzzling parallels between two ceremonies: one in a medieval document later studied intensively by Jessie Weston, the other in a Masonic ritual that all the available evidence suggests she never read.

There is a straightforward explanation for this puzzle, and it also explains some of the strange events surrounding the sudden appearance of the Master Mason degree in early Masonry. Suppose for a moment that a ritual descended from the one described in the *Elucidation*, a ritual that had been performed by the Knights Templar and had survived in the isolated region where Scotland and England meet, had also come into the possession of a few very old lodges of stonemasons in London. Suppose that the handful of members who knew the ritual were Jacobites and fled to France after the failure of the 1715 revolt, leaving the other members of the lodges scrambling to find a ritual they could use to raise members to the degree of Master Mason. The London lodges eventually settled for a different ritual, an early version of the present Master Mason degree, with its links back through time to archaic Celtic rites. Thereafter Masonry went its own way, conferring a substitute Word, while the remembrance that there was a true Word that might one day be recovered gradually faded, and various other substitute Words were added to the mix by the authors of assorted hauts grades.

And the original ritual? It went to France with the Jacobites—and stayed there. If the Master Masons from London who knew it performed it in Jacobite Masonic circles in Paris or elsewhere, no record remains of it. Sometime around 1740, however, as preparations for Bonnie Prince Charlie's doomed mission reached fever pitch, someone who knew about the old ritual drew up a ritual based on it, but rewritten to conform to Christian orthodoxy. The Jacobite movement had used Masonry systematically to prepare for the uprising, but the Catholic Church's ban on Masonry must have been on many minds just then. The new degree was meant as the final step of Jacobite Scottish Masonry, the step that would lead its adherents out of Masonry altogether and back into the arms of Mother Church.

Then catastrophe struck. The great uprising failed, the Jacobite army was annihilated at the battle of Culloden, and Prince Charles barely escaped alive to return to France. With the total failure of "the '45," the dream of a Jacobite restoration vanished forever. Jacobites across Europe, with their dreams of a return to power shattered, had to get by as best they could, and one way some of them did so was to start offering initiation into the haut grades to wealthy Freemasons who were willing to pay large initiation fees.

The degree ritual that became Rose Croix of Heredom got caught up in that process. Whether or not the Rite of Perfection was originally directed by Jesuits for reasons of their own, its degrees soon became part of the stock in trade of high-grade Masonry in Europe. Today every initiate of the Scottish Rite in the United States experiences a version of that degree, neatly modified to make it fit the broader symbolism of Freemasonry, and goes on to take in other degrees of various origins, each of which has its own symbolism and its own lessons to teach.

And the original ritual that had been used to initiate new Master Masons before 1715, with its inheritances from the Naassenes, the ancient Mysteries, and the teachings of the megalithic age? It survived in some form, probably in a manuscript in some European library or private collection, where it would be found more than a century later. Not until the late nineteenth century, however, would scholars turn up the *Elucidation* and the fragmentary records of the Gnostics and the ancient Mysteries, the keys to the ceremony of the Grail— and not until the early twentieth century would Jessie Weston find those keys and put them to use.

PART FOUR

THE
COMPANY OF
THE GRAIL

JESSIE WESTON'S
SECRET

The years between 1913 and 1920, as we have seen, saw Jessie Weston's vision of the Grail ritual shift in important ways. In her 1913 book *The Quest of the Holy Grail*, she still saw the ritual as the last legacy of a dying faith, which had lingered in isolated mountain valleys in Wales long enough to inspire the earliest writers of Grail romances. In *From Ritual to Romance*, published in 1920, her focus had shifted to the border country where England joins Scotland, and the Grail ritual was suddenly revealed as a living presence in her own time. That dramatic change echoed another, deeper change, which is reflected in both these books. Weston's earlier publications had by and large come from scholarly presses. *The Quest of the Holy Grail*, by contrast, was published as part of a series of volumes on occult topics curated by G. R. S. Mead, and Mead is cited repeatedly in *From Ritual to Romance* as an authority on Gnosticism.

Though he is largely forgotten today outside of the contemporary Gnostic revival, Mead was an important cultural figure in Weston's time, a leading scholar on Western esoteric traditions and a major presence in the British occult scene. He was born in 1863, graduated from Cambridge in 1884 with an honor degree in Classics, and went to Oxford to study Asian philosophy under the famous professor Max Muller. Early in his studies, however, he decided that practicing mysticism was more important than studying it in an abstract sense, and he joined the Theosophical Society.

Many people nowadays have a hard time grasping just how revolutionary the Theosophical Society was when it first appeared. Founded in New York City in 1875, the T. S. (as it was usually called) taught occult philosophy right out in public—the first organization to do so in the Western world since the twilight of classical Paganism fifteen centuries earlier. As branches sprang up across North America, Europe, Australasia, and India, people interested in occultism and mysticism in all these regions joined it as a means of networking, even if they had no interest in the specific doctrines taught by the T. S. For a decade to either side of the dawn of the twentieth century, the T. S. thus became a venue for many of the most creative spiritual ventures of the age.

It was a propitious time for such ventures. As I have mentioned already, many people in the very late nineteenth and early twentieth centuries believed that the age of Pisces had ended and the age of Aquarius was dawning in their own time. One common claim, repeated a little later on by the influential occultist Rudolf Steiner, was that the change of ages had happened in the autumn of 1879. Certainly many people then and in the decades that followed were eager to embrace a tolerant approach to spirituality that was based on experience rather than dogma—and G. R. S. Mead was one of them.

Mead's interest in the T. S. was not limited to its networking potentials. Within a few years of joining he had demonstrated a solid commitment to the teachings of the Society and so was permitted to join the Esoteric Section, the inner circle of members who were allowed to study and practice the more advanced teachings the T. S. had to offer. In 1889 he became one of the secretaries of the Esoteric Section, responsible for distributing the inner teachings, and in the same year he became the personal secretary of T. S. founder Helena Blavatsky, a position he held until her death in 1891. Under her successor, Annie Besant, he became the chief editor of the Society's monthly magazine, *The Theosophical Review*.

It was after Blavatsky's death that Mead began producing the books for which he is best known, a series of English translations of classic Western mystical texts, focusing especially on the Gnostics. His volume *Fragments of a Faith Forgotten*, published in 1901, was for many years the only good introduction to

Gnostic ideas in the English language, and he followed it up with an eleven-volume series of translations of Gnostic texts titled *Echoes from the Gnosis*. Until the Nag Hammadi manuscripts were discovered in Egypt in 1945, Mead's translations included literally every scrap of surviving Gnostic literature that was known to exist.

When Jessie Weston described Mead as an authority on the Gnostics, in other words, she was not exaggerating. In particular, he was thoroughly familiar with the Naassene document quoted by Hippolytus, which he translated and annotated in great detail. He was also aware of the possible connection between the Grail and the Krater of Hermes Trismegistus, and he discussed this at length in his book *Thrice Greatest Hermes*, which is still the most complete book in English on Hermetic literature from ancient times. He was familiar, in other words, with much of the story we have described in these pages— more familiar with it, in fact, than any other scholar in Britain in his time.

1909 brought a shift in Mead's career that is of great importance in our story. Annie Besant's erratic leadership of the T. S. and her attempts to turn it into a dogmatic religious organization had become increasingly unpopular among longtime members, Mead among them. Crisis hit in 1906 when Besant's ally Charles Leadbeater was caught fondling the children of several T. S. members and was expelled from the Society. In early 1909, Besant ordered him readmitted. Mead was one of seven hundred outraged British Theosophists who resigned in protest. He immediately set out to start a new organization, the Quest Society, to fill the same niche the T. S. had previously had as a gathering place for occultists and mystics of all kinds.

The Quest Society was an immediate success. Under Mead's direction it launched a quarterly magazine, *The Quest*, which quickly became one of the leading occult periodicals of its time and held that status until the Great Depression forced it to shut down in 1931. It presented a regular lecture program at Kensington Town Hall in London, which drew crowds. It started a book publishing program, also titled *The Quest*, which released many of Mead's own later works and also published many other titles on subjects of interest to occultists and mystics. One of those, of course, was Jessie Weston's *The Quest of the Holy Grail*.

It was probably inevitable that Mead and Weston would meet and collaborate. Both were independent scholars producing quality work outside the official channels of the universities. Both were interested in the byways of Western spiritual history and in traditions that had been silenced by the heavy hand of orthodox religion. They had another point of contact, however, because Mead married a fellow Theosophist, Laura Cooper, and Laura had a sister who was one of the most intriguing figures in early British Theosophy.

Her name was Isabel Cooper-Oakley, and she was a scholar and author who contributed many articles to *The Theosophical Review* during Mead's editorship. Cooper-Oakley's interests focused on Western occult traditions, as did Mead's, but she was particularly interested in the survivals of the ancient wisdom in the Middle Ages. Inevitably this led her to two of the themes we have already discussed—the origins of Freemasonry and the legends of the Holy Grail. Five essays she wrote on these subjects appeared in *The Theosophical Review* in its early issues. In 1900, they were released in book form as *Traces of a Hidden Tradition in Masonry and Medieval Mysticism*.

This book has received remarkably little attention from later students of the inner dimensions of the Grail legend. This is unfortunate, because it lays out in some detail much of the story covered in the first part of the present book. From the ancient Mysteries to the Gnostics, from there to an assortment of heretical medieval groups including the Cathars and the Knights Templar, and from there to the traditions out of which Freemasonry emerged, Cooper-Oakley traced a familiar trajectory, in which the legend of the Grail played a significant role. She was aware of Jessie Weston's work, furthermore, and her essays on the Holy Grail cite Weston as an important authority on the subject. While I have not been able to find documentary proof that Weston and Cooper-Oakley met or corresponded, it seems very likely that they did so, and that Cooper-Oakley was the link that brought Weston and Mead into contact.

By 1913, as we have seen, Weston was certainly close enough to Mead to publish a book on the Grail legends in his Quest series. In 1914, Cooper-Oakley died suddenly while traveling in Europe. It was after her death that Weston's essays and books about the Grail legend began to move in new directions. She continued to labor over scholarly studies of individual legends and historical questions, but her views concerning the origins and history of the Grail tradition changed in a way that echoed the themes that Cooper-Oakley had explored. Did Cooper-Oakley leave Weston some collection of unpublished information about the Grail legend, either directly or through Mead? Some such event would explain the remarkable transformations in Weston's work in the years that followed Cooper-Oakley's death.

◇

The first significant expression of Weston's new concerns was a short piece of hers that appeared in 1916 in Mead's magazine *The Quest*. Its title was "The Ruined Temple." It was a work of fiction—the only short story, as far as I know, that Weston ever published—about the ceremony of the Grail. In *From Ritual to Romance*, Weston described it as "a hypothetical reconstruction of the Grail Initiation."[128] As we will see, it was considerably more than that.

In the story, an unnamed traveler in Weston's own time comes to a headland reaching out into the sea from a moorland full of gorse and heather. He finds scattered blocks of stone and masonry on the headland, with a stone altar overgrown with bracken in the middle of it. He sits down with his back to one of the stones, thinking about the ruined temple and tracing it back to a forgotten Phoenician colony on the British coast, which brought the Mysteries of Adonis with them. He dozes off and dreams that he is passing through the initiation of the Grail.

First he keeps vigil in the first chamber, the Chapel Perilous, which is hung in black and features the traditional dead body on a bier between two lit candles. There he comes face to face with the terrible reality of death and affirms the equal and opposite reality of everlasting Life. Next he comes into the second chamber, a hall of feasting, where he is seated next to a kingly host, witnesses the miraculous presence of the Grail, and asks the expected question. Next he is tempted by a group of beautiful maidens, and he resists their blandishments. Having done so, he is clothed in white and enters a final chamber, where the Grail and the bleeding spear are displayed and he receives a final revelation of the nature of Life. Finally he awakens, and though he does not remember the details of the initiation, he knows that a powerful blessing of some sort has been given to him.

It is a remarkable story, though it cannot be taken quite at face value. Neither the temptation by the maidens nor the final scene with the Grail and the spear can be found in the medieval Grail legends. They come instead from

---

128. Weston, *From Ritual to Romance*, 183.

Richard Wagner's opera *Parsifal*, which made a deep impression on many people in Weston's generation. In the older legends, the *Elucidation* among them, the bleeding spear was present in the first chamber and was also brought past the guests at the feast in the second chamber. In the third and final chamber, to judge from all the available evidence—the medieval Grail legends, the records of the ancient Mysteries, and the parallel structure of the Rose Croix of Heredom degree—amid rejoicing over the healing of the Fisher King and the Waste Land, the successful candidate would have been crowned and taught the symbolon and the other secrets of the initiation, and he would have received the word that should properly have become the true Word of a Master Mason.

Another detail of the story that is crucial for our researches is that it never mentions the Naassenes, the Gnostics, the Knights Templar, or any of the other stages in the evolution of the tradition that Isabel Cooper-Oakley traced out in her writings. If Weston knew about these, she kept them secret, though four years after the publication of "The Ruined Temple" she discussed them at great length in *From Ritual to Romance*. In the story, she still associates the Grail legend with the dying god Adonis rather than with Attis, and she credits the ancient Phoenicians with the introduction of the ritual to Britain. With one exception, we are still in the world sketched out by Weston's earlier writings, and especially her book in Mead's Quest series, *The Quest of the Holy Grail*.

The one exception is the setting. Her traveler does not discover the ruined temple in some isolated valley in the mountains of Wales. Instead, it is on a headland somewhere on the western coasts of Britain—the unnamed traveler watches the setting sun sinking toward the ocean, framed by two standing stones—and the land behind it is described as "a wild moorland studded with clumps of gorse and heather" in which the traveler had not seen a single tree during that day's hike. It is, to be precise, a typical landscape in the northern parts of Britain, especially common in the area where England and Scotland come into contact.

The headland is described in some detail. It is covered with a tangle of gorse and heather and ends in cliffs that plunge down into the sea. A row of standing stones leads out to the ruined temple, which was apparently circular in form. It has an altar at the center and two pairs of standing stones, one to the east and one to the west, through which the sun shines at rising and setting. Keep this description in mind; we will be encountering it again.

In the four years between the appearance of "The Ruined Temple" and the publication of *From Ritual to Romance*, Weston changed her view of the origins of the Grail ceremony in almost every detail. Point for point, she adopted the ideas presented by Isabel Cooper-Oakley in *Traces of a Hidden Tradition in Masonry and Medieval Mysticism*. It was during these years that she identified the Mysteries of Cybele and Attis, rather than those of Adonis, as the source of the Grail ceremony. It was during these years that she brought the Gnostics and the Knights Templar into the picture. She also noted, for the first time in her writings, that the four suits of the minor arcana of the tarot deck correspond precisely with four symbolic items found in many of the Grail romances: the lance to the suit of wands, the Grail as cup to the cups, the sword to the swords, and the Grail as dish to the disks, coins, or pentacles.

Her source for at least some of this information reveals more than the information itself. In *From Ritual to Romance* she cites several sentences from a personal letter she received from William Butler Yeats, "whose practical acquaintance with Medieval and Modern Magic is well known."[129] That is quite an understatement. Yeats is remembered nowadays as one of the great poets of the twentieth century, but he was also a senior member of the Hermetic Order of the Golden Dawn, the most prestigious occult order in late nineteenth and early twentieth century Britain, and a very public exponent of occultism in the literary world of his time. When *From Ritual to Romance* appeared, he had already published several essays on magic, and a few years afterward he published an intricate work of occult philosophy titled *A Vision*.[130] During the years when Weston was pursuing the secret of the Grail ceremony, Yeats also worked on and off on a set of initiation rituals of his own for an Irish magical order called the Castle of Heroes, in which a symbolic spear, cauldron, sword, and stone—elements also found in the older stratum of Grail legends—played crucial ceremonial roles.[131]

---

129. Weston, *From Ritual to Romance*, 79.

130. Yeats, *A Vision and Related Writings*, has several of his other occult essays along with *A Vision*.

131. Yeats's rituals are collected in Kalogera, "Yeats's Celtic Mysteries."

Weston's contact with Yeats, like her interactions with Mead, thus make it clear that well before the publication of *From Ritual to Romance*, she had moved away from a purely academic approach to the Grail legend. She was seeking the Grail in earnest by then, and was evidently willing to follow the trail wherever it led—even if it took her into the burgeoning occult scene of early twentieth century Britain, as it clearly did.

Her involvement in occultism led her in strange directions. Perhaps the strangest has to do with a passage in the Grail romance called, after its main character, the *Perlesvaus*. The version of the *Perlesvaus* that survives comes from the latter half of the era when medieval Grail romances were being written and is full of conventional Christian morality, but it contains a very odd legend toward the beginning. According to this part of the story, a young squire named Chaus was told by King Arthur to be ready to ride with him at dawn to the mysterious Chapel of St. Austin.[132] Anxious for the adventure, Chaus lies down fully dressed in the hall and goes to sleep. Then, as it seems to him, he wakes up in the morning to find Arthur already gone. He hurries to the stable, saddles his horse, and rides after the king, following the track of his steed.

In due time Chaus comes to the fearful Chapel, which is surrounded by a graveyard. He goes inside to find the usual dead knight on the usual bier, with golden candlesticks at head and foot. King Arthur is nowhere to be found. Chaus takes one of the candlesticks and rides back along the track in search of the king. Before he gets far he meets the guardian of the chapel, who demands the candlestick from him; when Chaus refuses, the guardian stabs him with a knife. With a loud cry the squire awakes; he is still in Arthur's court and has dreamed the whole sequence of events, but he has been mortally wounded by the knife, which is still in the wound, and he still has the golden candlestick.

It's a fine spooky story, of a kind that can be found quite often in medieval legend. Weston's interpretation of the story, however, is that of an occultist: "For this is the story of an initiation…carried out on the astral plane, and reacting with fatal results on the physical."[133] She argues, furthermore, that the story is based on a real occurrence. Her justification for that surprising claim is that it appears as such in at least two other sources from the Middle Ages—the

---

132. That is, St. Augustine; this name was usually shortened to "Austin" in medieval English.

133. Weston, *From Ritual to Romance*, 182.

chronicle of John of Glastonbury, which claims that it happened in the vicinity of Glastonbury, and the biographical epic *Histoire de Fulk Fitz-Warin*, based on the life of one of the great barons of medieval England, which places it in a location called the Blaunche Launde in Shropshire, just east of the border of Wales.

The *Histoire de Fulk Fitz-Warin* also recounts a very curious story about the Blaunche Launde. According to that story, that country had been haunted by an evil spirit named Geomagog and his fellow demons. They built a wall and ditch around the place so that every human was kept out of it, while the Launde itself was full of evil spirits. Many bold knights came there to try to defeat the evil spirits, but none succeeded until the twelfth century, when Payn Peverel, a cousin of England's King Henry I, vanquished Geomagog. Long before then, the demon confessed, a Christian missionary named Augustine had come to the Blaunche Launde, baptized many people, and built a chapel of St. Austin there.[134] The story of a land inhabited by demons and closed off to human beings sounds remarkably like an echo of the Debatable Land in its ancient role of Pagan sanctuary, as seen through Christian eyes, and it is a curious coincidence—if it is no more than that—that Canonbie Priory, the monastery on a spit of land surrounded by the Debatable Land on three sides, was founded by the Order of St. Augustine.

The Blaunche Launde in Shropshire, now known as Whittington, has its own robust body of traditions about the Grail and a viable candidate for the Grail itself. In 1934, a small chalice of Roman style made of green alabaster was discovered hidden in a statue of St. John near Whittington; it had apparently been there since the 1850s, when the statue was made. Its history before then has proven difficult to trace exactly, but one author, Graham Phillips, makes a plausible case that it had been kept by a local family until the 1850s, when the last member of the family arranged to conceal it in the statue.[135]

Glastonbury, for its part, has more Arthurian traditions per square yard than any other place in Britain. The form of the *Perlesvaus* that exists today, according to most scholars in Weston's time and today, was written at Glastonbury and includes extensive references to the landscape surrounding the town.

---

134. Weston, "Notes on the Grail Romances," 423–24.

135. Phillips, *The Chalice of Magdalene*.

John of Glastonbury's claim that the strange story of Chaus and Arthur had originally taken place at Glastonbury thus seems relatively plausible—more plausible, at least at first glance, than Weston's decision to relocate the legend into an isolated corner of northern Britain close to the Scottish border.

Yet relocate it she did. Her arguments for the northern location are, however, curiously incomplete. She notes that there was a Blaunche Launde, now Blanchland, in the far northern English county of Northumberland, due east of Carlisle and thus within an easy ride of the Debatable Land and the other sites we have discussed on or near the English-Scottish border. She notes that both these White Lands (the meaning of the French phrase *blanche lande*) have traditions claiming that they had that name already in the days of King Arthur. She notes that there does not seem to be any sign of a chapel of St. Austin in the part of Shropshire identified with the Blaunche Launde, while there are chapels and other religious sites dedicated to St. Austin in the Northumbrian Blanchland.

Finally, she notes that in the *Perlesvaus*, Arthur is said to be staying at Carlisle when the adventure of Chaus took place, and from Carlisle to the Northumbrian Blanchland is a much shorter journey than from the same city to Shropshire. Since Chaus's journey was a dream journey or, in occult terms, a journey made on the astral plane, I am not sure that the physical distance matters that much. Yet she seems utterly certain that the Northumbrian Blanchland is the original Chapel Perilous, the place where the first stage of the Grail ritual took place. It looks very much as though she had some other reason for choosing that location—a reason that she was not willing to mention in print.

There are few things more difficult to extract from publicly available data than a secret that has been systematically concealed by a small group of people. This is especially true if the people who guarded the secret considered it to be of immense importance and kept it private among themselves. The inner secrets of the ancient Mysteries remain unknown to this day for exactly this reason. So, too, does whatever lay behind Jessie Weston's evasive hints about a Grail ceremony being practiced in her own time.

What we know is this. Weston was aware of a group of people who, around 1920, celebrated a ceremony of the Grail that she believed was the original ceremony, handed down from the Middle Ages. At the time she made these comments, she had been in contact for some years with the occultist and scholar G. R. S. Mead, the head of the Quest Society, and through him—if by no other means—she would have had contact with the work of his sister-in-law Isabel Cooper-Oakley, whose researches into the suppressed Gnostic traditions of the Middle Ages covered much of the same ground as Weston's final book on the Grail.

In that book, *From Ritual to Romance*, she describes the fate of Chaus in terms that were standard among occultists in her time, but not at all common—or even acceptable—among ordinary scholars in the cultural mainstream. Finally, and crucially, she says absolutely nothing about the reference to gnosis as a cup in the Naassene document, even though she was clearly familiar with the document's contents and that reference would have clinched her case, and she engages in what looks very much like evasive maneuvers around her information for the location of the Chapel Perilous.

There is one explanation that would make sense of all these clues. That is the suggestion that in the last years of her life, Jessie Weston became a member of the group that had possession of the ceremony of the Grail in her time—a group we may as well call, in the language of the Middle Ages, the Company of the Grail. She received the initiation of the Grail from them, and thereafter was bound to secrecy about certain elements of the tradition by the oaths of initiation she had taken.

G. R. S. Mead and Isabel Cooper-Oakley were certainly members of the Company of the Grail, and Mead was probably its head, the heir of the Fisher King. Weston considered the Company's claim to have the original Grail ritual to be valid. Since she was a careful scholar well versed in the Grail literature, her judgment here cannot simply be dismissed out of hand. Clearly whatever documents the Company of the Grail were able to show Weston, she found them convincing enough to stake her reputation on them.

The ritual or the documents or traditions connected with it clearly had some link to the Blanchland in Northumberland, which convinced Weston that this was the site of the original Chapel Perilous, rather than Whittington in Shropshire or Glastonbury far to the south in Somerset. For reasons we will discuss shortly, it also seems to be connected to an actual place somewhere in the north of Britain that corresponds closely to the description Weston gave in her story "The Ruined Temple."

Did the teachings passed on by the organization I have described include material relating to the archaic traditions discussed in part II of this book—or, for that matter, to the temple technology, the ancient secret that had once used natural energies to make the fields flourish? So far, at least, I have been able to find no evidence that any of this material was known to Mead, Weston, and their fellow participants in the ceremony of the Grail. Most of the research into agricultural electricity, terrestrial magnetism, and paramagnetism that made it possible for me to reconstruct the temple technology in my previous book had not yet been published in their time. Nor had the fragmentary remains of megalithic earth magic and starlore explored earlier been pieced together yet. They had only part of the riddle, though it was enough to inspire them to preserve and enact the ceremony of the Grail in their time.

It is possible to say a little more about the secretive organization I have called the Company of the Grail, though as with so much of the material in this investigation, the suggestions I have to offer must remain speculative for the time being. It was standard practice in late nineteenth and early twentieth century British occult organizations to use a two-level structure, with a lower tier that was relatively public and a higher tier that was strictly private, open only to individuals who had passed through the lower tier and proven themselves to be worthy students. The Theosophical Society is of course a classic example here: members of the T. S. studied the public teachings of the organization and practiced a variety of basic spiritual exercises, and those who proved that they were willing to take on the labor of study and practice were then quietly welcomed into the Esoteric Section, where they were given the inner teachings of Theosophy.

In exactly the same way, the Hermetic Order of the Golden Dawn, the leading occult order in Britain at the turn of the century, had an Outer Order where initiates passed through ornate ceremonies and studied the basics of occult philosophy. Those members who displayed a commitment to the work in the Outer Order were admitted to the Inner Order and given a systematic course of training in ceremonial magic—on the condition that they bind themselves never to reveal any of it to Outer Order members or to the general public.

To all outward appearances, at least, the Quest Society was an exception to this rule. The publicly available information on the Society includes only the outer side of its work—the magazine, the book publishing program, the regular lectures at London's Kensington Town Hall, and the rest of it. There is no visible trace of an Esoteric Section or Inner Order, the higher tier of study and practice available to select members in the other occult organizations of the time. The logical conclusion is that the Quest Society, being smaller and less prone to political splits than the T. S., the Golden Dawn, or most of the other occult groups of its place and time, succeeded in keeping its inner section secret—*and that this inner section was the group I have called the Company of the Grail.*

The name of Mead's organization is, among other things, a pointer to this. Several other groups split off from the Theosophical Society during the early decades of the twentieth century. Most of them took names very closely linked to the original—the United Lodge of Theosophists, the Anthroposophical Society, and so on. Then there was the Quest Society, which discarded the word *theosophy* entirely and replaced it with something that was evocative in a different sense. In 1909, due to the enthusiasm for Arthurian legends and stories in popular culture all through the English-speaking world, the word *quest* almost automatically brought up the concept of the Grail, and it seems improbable that Mead would have named his organization without taking this into account.

This would imply that by 1909, Mead already had access to the ceremony of the Grail and so had something to offer prospective members of the Quest Society's inner circle. Another line of evidence suggests that this was in fact the case, for a famous and highly influential figure closely associated with the early Theosophists in Britain also seems to have had access to the ceremony. He was one of the titans of late Victorian British artistic culture, a passionate student of the Middle Ages and the author of Arthurian poems famous in their day. His name was William Morris, and the greatest of his fictional works, *The Well at the World's End*, includes details taken straight from the traditions that we have been following down through the centuries.

THE WELL AT
THE WORLD'S END

Most people have at least one creative talent, and some have more than one. A few have several. Then there was William Morris, who had so much talent in so many fields that it would be easier to list the few creative things that he *couldn't* do well. A force of nature who transformed nearly the entire range of Victorian arts and design, breaking new ground in fields that ranged from poetry through landscape architecture to political activism, his life was a dizzying whirlwind of raw creativity. It's typical of the man that he finished the revisions of his last novel while on his deathbed.

Of all the interests of his omnivorous mind, the one that sprang up earliest and continued longest was a fascination with the Middle Ages. Born in 1834, he caught the Victorian passion for all things medieval in its first great upsurge, and the Arthurian legends in particular became one of his lifelong obsessions. His first literary success was a volume of poetry titled *The Defence of Guenevere*, and the most famous production of the Kelmscott Press, his publishing firm, was a gorgeous edition of Malory's *Le Morte d'Arthur*. That was far from his only literary interest—he was among other things a passionate fan of the old Norse sagas, and he worked with an Icelandic scholar to produce the first English translations of several of these poems of the Viking age—but few people in Victorian Britain could match his encyclopedic knowledge of the legends of King Arthur.

Toward the end of his life, after failing health forced him to set aside his more strenuous activities, he got bored with retirement and invented modern fantasy fiction just to give himself something to do. (See what I mean?) He was inspired partly by the Arthurian legends and partly by the Norse sagas, which is why so much fantasy fiction ever since has remained stuck halfway between the two. His first fantasy novel, *The Wood Beyond the World* (1894), was a fine example of the type, a straightforward tale of adventure and love in a more or less medieval setting, though its forthright handling of sexuality and its strong female characters will startle readers who have absorbed too many modern notions about the Victorian period. With one exception, his other fantasy novels were cut from the same cloth.

That exception was *The Well at the World's End*, which was published a few months before his death in 1896. It ranks alongside Tolkien's *The Lord of the Rings* as one of the greatest of all English fantasies. It is, among other things, a summing up of Morris's own life, and his own passionate commitments to art, literature, and politics come in for examination and critique in its pages. It is also—though few modern literary critics seem to have noticed this—a Grail legend.

For reasons that will become clear a little later in this chapter, a basic summary of the plot of *The Well at the World's End* will be useful at this point. The tale begins with Ralph of Upmeads, a supremely clueless young man who is the youngest son of a very minor king, who leaves home to seek his fortune. His godmother has given him a curious rosary of blue and green beads that is linked to the mysterious Well at the World's End, about which Ralph knows absolutely nothing. It is not a Christian rosary; his godmother urges him not to let a priest bless it, and early on in Ralph's adventures, a priest tries to talk him into giving up the rosary of the Well in exchange for an ordinary Christian rosary, a trade that Ralph refuses.

As he travels, Ralph encounters a young woman named Ursula, who leaves her home for reasons of her own about the same time Ralph does, and he then ends up entangled in the struggle between the Champions of the Dry Tree and the Burg of the Four Friths—an allegory, though a subtle one, of the socialist politics to which Morris devoted many years of his life. He falls in love with the sorceress who leads the Champions and then witnesses her death. Grieving, Ralph then joins a merchant caravan going east and meets several old friends. All the while, rumors and hints about the Well at the World's End whisper around him until he decides to seek it even at the cost of his life.

The caravan reaches the city of Goldburg and turns back, but Ralph travels onward, for he knows that the Well lies further east, and he has also learned that Ursula has come that way and is also seeking the Well. Along the way he is captured and enslaved by Gandolf, the tyrant of Utterbol, but he succeeds in making his escape and meets Ursula in the woods. They flee together to the Sage of Swevenham, a friendly wizard who hides them from the soldiers of Utterbol, initiates Ralph and Ursula into the secrets of the route to the Well, and guides them through the first stage of their journey there.

One of the things that makes this journey so rich for the reader is that the route the characters take leads them through time as well as through space. Morris drew up the imaginary geography of his tale to a very precise scheme. When the characters go north or south, they stay within a given time; when they travel east, they go back through time, and when they go west, they go forward. As Ralph travels from rural Upmeads to the bleak industrial city called the Burg of the Four Friths, he remains in his own time, which is Victorian England under a thin veneer of medieval decor. At the Burg, though, he turns east, just as Ursula, in her parallel journey, goes further south to the fortress of the Champions of the Dry Tree before her fateful eastward turn. From there they go eastward by castles and cities that represent the Renaissance and the Middle Ages, and then through rugged mountain ways that stand for the European Dark Ages. They reach cities that represent the Muslim world and finally come to Utterbol, the realm of the tyrant Gandolf, who stands for the Roman Catholic Church. This is clear from the names: the castle of the Popes outside the gates of Rome, as most people knew in Morris's time and some remember today, is named Castel Gandolfo. As for "Utterbol," it's a neat contraction of the off-color English phrase "utter bollocks," which offers a good hint of what Morris thought about mainstream Christian theology.

From there, the route leads to the Sage of Swevenham and through wilderness paths to the Gate of the Mountains. There, a mighty image of a man in ancient armor holding a sword shows the way onward. Morris knew William

Blake's writings inside and out, and his younger friend William Butler Yeats—the same poet who advised Jessie Weston on the symbolism of the tarot deck—helped edit a complete edition of Blake's writings. It hardly comes as a surprise, then, that Morris put the Titan Albion in the form of Arthur back in the trackless realms before the beginning of recorded history, or that he portrayed the figure of Arthur as the marker that shows the right way. *Follow this clue*, he all but shouted to his readers. Seek the legend of Arthur, and that will show you which route to take.

Beyond the Rock of the Fighting Man, that route leads deeper into time: through wild lands and a year's waiting to the Land of the Innocent Folk, who represent primitive humanity, and then back beyond our species to the origins of life itself. On their journey, Ralph and Ursula go past the terrible Dry Tree, which represents life in the purely material, Darwinian sense, and they finally come to a great headland above the shores of the sea of eternity, for the Well at the World's End stands at the world's beginning. There, after drinking the waters of the Well from a golden chalice and receiving its blessing of abundant life, Ralph and Ursula return the way they came, to find that the world has already begun to change as a result of their journey. When they reach their own time, the Burg of the Four Friths has been overthrown, and Ralph, Ursula, and the Sage are able to gather up an army to save Ralph's home at Upmeads from the last soldiers of the Burg and bring peace and plenty to the land.

What makes this story important to our theme is that Morris built his mighty fantasy around ideas and imagery that we have already discussed in this book. Given Morris's background and interests, this is hardly surprising. *The Well at the World's End* is more than just a fantasy novel—it is, among other things, a summing-up of Morris's long and busy life, and those who study his biography will have no trouble finding the major twists and turns of that life in Ralph's adventures. Still, the Grail legend is at the heart of the tale, and that legend seems to have been greatly on his mind in the last year of his life, as he finished the manuscript of the novel and saw it through the publishing process.

The parallels are astonishingly exact. Compare *The Well at the World's End* to the Grail ritual as outlined by Jessie Weston and the parallels are impossible to miss. To begin with, the Well at the World's End is symbolically a Grail;

there is even a golden cup waiting for those who come to partake of the waters of the Well, and the association of the Grail, a golden cup or bowl, and a well was set out long before Morris's time in the pages of the *Elucidation*. Ralph is a brash young idiot like Perceval, who leaves home just as thoughtlessly as Perceval does and gets in just as many scrapes, and the theme of the Perceval legend—"a brave man slowly wise," in Wolfram von Eschenbach's taut phrasing—is also the theme of Ralph's adventure.[136] Ursula is far and away the smarter and more capable of the two, until Ralph finally catches up to her level. The challenge she has to overcome in order to reach the Well is not cluelessness, but despair.

The Well to Morris was also exactly what the Grail was to Weston: the source and symbol of Life. The Well and the route to it, according to the novel, were established in ancient times by peoples who worshipped the gods of earth, and the rites of the Well are not compatible with Christian orthodoxy; the same is of course true of the Grail in Weston's view. Furthermore, the location of the Well has an uncanny similarity with the location of the ruined temple in Weston's story of that name, cited in the previous chapter. At the end of his book, just in case anyone missed the point he was trying to make, Morris has a character mention that the rosary that leads Ralph to the Well was obtained by his godmother in the city of Sarras, the Grail city of the later versions of the legend.

Megalithic sites also play a fascinating if enigmatic role throughout the story. One of the first places Ralph encounters when he leaves home, and one of the last places he stops before he returns, is Bear Castle, an ancient causewayed enclosure at the top of a hill. Stones bearing the emblem of a sword crossing a three-leafed oak branch show Ralph and Ursula the way to the Well, and the headland of the Well is marked by a stone raised in ancient times. Did Morris recognize the link between the Grail legend and the megalithic age? The evidence I have been able to find so far does not provide an answer to that question, but Morris was a passionate student of British antiquities of all kinds, and he may have intuitively grasped the link between the legends and the old stones and earthworks of Britain.

---

136. Von Eschenbach, *Parzival*, 5.

Woven into the fabric of *The Well at the World's End*, furthermore, is a series of scenes that resemble the stages of an initiation ritual, down to the fine details. Those of my readers who know their way around traditional initiation rituals will recognize those details at once. The initiation through which Ralph and Ursula pass has its ceremonies, its secret lore, and its stages. Candidates for the initiation don special garments: white linen robes cut like the albs worn by Anglican or Catholic priests, with red silk cord belts and gold-colored silk bands at wrists, hem, and collar. As they receive the initiation, Ralph and Ursula are expected to memorize a catechism concerning its symbolism and meaning, just as candidates for initiation do in the degrees of Freemasonry.

Finally, compare the plot of the third book of *The Well at the World's End* to Jessie Weston's essay "The Ruined Temple" and the common structure is clear. In Weston's story, the first challenge the traveler faces is the fear of death while facing the corpse and the broken sword in the Chapel Perilous. In *The Well at the World's End*, the first challenge Ralph faces, once he leaves behind his other concerns and embarks on the quest of the Well in earnest, is that he is captured and enslaved by the tyrant Gandolf of Utterbol and must overcome the fear of death to escape Gandolf's servants. The traveler and Ralph both overcome the challenge and pass on to receive hospitality—the traveler from the Fisher King, Ralph from Ursula, and then the two of them together from the Sage of Swevenham.

The next stage in Weston's story is the temptation by the maidens, a scene that, as already noted, she clearly borrowed from Wagner's opera *Parsifal*. Morris had a far more enthusiastic attitude toward sexuality than Weston, and Ralph's encounter with sexual desire thus has a different resolution: he marries Ursula in the presence of the Innocent Folk. The confrontation with sexuality nonetheless occurs in the same place in both stories. It is after this that the traveler in Weston's story and Ralph and Ursula in Morris's novel can proceed to the final encounter with the source of life.

This takes place on a narrow peninsula or headland beside the sea, where ancient peoples set up stones in a bygone time. The encounter is symbolized by an outpouring of liquid—a stream of blood in the Grail legend, a great stream of water in *The Well at the World's End*—which is related to a cup of precious metal and gives renewed life and strength to those who attain it. Weston's traveler experiences the ceremony in a dream and does not remember it when he wakes up. Ralph and Ursula, by contrast, are fully awake when they taste the waters of the Well and remember it for the rest of their lives—but the experiences themselves are close enough to show the connection.

That connection cannot be found in the medieval Grail legends, by the way. The ceremony of the Grail appears in the medieval romances in fragments and scattered hints, never in a single connected narrative. Even the *Elucidation* only gives half the ritual as Weston and Morris present it. The most likely explanation for the shared details is that Weston and Morris are talking about the same ritual—and that, in turn, suggests that Morris was a member of what I have called the Company of the Grail.

He may have been more than that. When Ralph and Ursula reach the land of the Innocent Folk, they learn that no one has come that way on the quest for the Well for a very long time. Translate that out of the symbolic language of the story and it becomes hard not to see this as an indication that the ceremony of the Grail had become defunct sometime in the centuries before Morris's time, and he played a role in reviving it. What little evidence we have concerning dates indicates that the ritual was being performed by 1920, long after Morris's death. My hypothesis—and it is only a hypothesis at this point—is that Morris, who set so many other things in motion during his career, was responsible for starting the process by which the ceremony of the Grail was revived and celebrated again.

A close look at the biography of William Morris helps put this possibility in context. After years of less-focused activities on the leftward end of British radicalism, he joined the Social Democratic Federation—the leading radical party of the time—in 1883, and plunged into socialist politics with his normal fervor, writing books and pamphlets, lecturing, and taking part in endless meetings. By 1888, however, he was burned out by the constant bickering of his fellow socialists and the failure of the movement to accomplish much of anything. His friend Wilfrid Scawen Blunt commented the next year: "Morris was at that time in a mood of reaction from his socialistic fervor. [...] We had both of us sacrificed much socially to our principles, and our principles had failed to justify themselves by results, and we were both driven back on earlier loves, art, poetry, romance."[137]

As the socialist movement faltered, however, a different movement was beginning to find its feet in Britain. In 1887 Helena Petrovna Blavatsky, head of the Theosophical Society and the most influential occultist in the world, settled in London and began to gather students around herself. In that same year, William Wynn Westcott and Samuel Mathers founded the Hermetic Order of the Golden Dawn, which became the most creative and prestigious magical order of the era. Over the two decades that followed, London became a bubbling cauldron of occult societies and exotic spiritual movements, the kind of cultural setting in which the ceremony of the Grail would have found an instant welcome.

Much of that welcome, strange as it might seem from a modern standpoint, came from within the same socialist circles that Morris had frequented. The doctrinaire atheism and materialism of later twentieth century Marxist socialism was only one of many options in the more freewheeling socialist scene of late Victorian Britain, and there was a substantial overlap between occultism and socialism, precisely during the years between Morris's withdrawal from political activism in 1888 and his death in 1896. That made it easy for people to slip from one of these to another. It was by means of this overlap, for example, that Annie Besant, one of the leading lights of the British socialist and labor union scene in the 1880s and a close friend of William Morris, joined the Theosophical Society in 1889 and rose to become its leader, and William Butler Yeats, another friend of Morris and also a Theosophist for some years, became a socialist for a time—though he eventually went to the other end of the political spectrum.

One of the constant features of Morris's biography is that his friends routinely found themselves drawn along unexpected byways by his passionate enthusiasms. Whatever was hidden behind *The Well at the World's End*, however, did not leave any visible trace among Morris's friends and acquaintances. Morris may not have done anything with the Grail ceremony other than use it as the central symbolic framework for his greatest novel. Alternatively, he may have organized a small group of friends to perform the ceremony in secret.

---

137. Henderson, *William Morris*, 317.

Whether that group continued to perform the ritual after his death, or whether it went in abeyance until Mead founded the Quest Society thirteen years later, is a question that only further research can answer.

Another question that remains open for the time being is where Morris found the secret of the Grail ceremony. His passion for all things medieval took him all over Britain, France, and Belgium, with occasional forays as far afield as Iceland. Wherever he went, he visited old churches, explored libraries and archives, and shopped at antiquarian bookstores. His network of friends extended all over Britain and included many other passionate students of medieval lore. It's possible that he could have found a manuscript from Jacobite times in a bookstall in Paris, and it is just as possible that he might have gotten an unexpected packet in the mail from a friend who had stumbled across an old document in Carlisle—or found himself in possession of the ritual in some other way. Unless documentary evidence turns up, we may never know.

One clue, however, waits to be followed up by researchers with easy access to northern Britain. The headland that Jessie Weston described in "The Ruined Temple" and the peninsula that William Morris described in *The Well at the World's End* are recognizably the same landform, and I know of no evidence suggesting that Weston copied Morris's description—or that she knew about *The Well at the World's End* at all. Weston's headland faces the ocean in the west, while Morris's peninsula juts out into the ocean to the east; one or the other of them—or just possibly both!—has changed the direction, perhaps for symbolic reasons, perhaps to conceal the location of the ruined temple of the Grail. The most likely explanation for the similarities is that both descriptions are based on an actual location, probably, although not certainly, in northern England or southern Scotland. If that location can be found, much that is now obscure about the ceremony of the Grail may become clear.

Whatever William Morris did or didn't do with the Grail ceremony he wove into his great fantasy novel, its track runs very thin from 1896, when Morris published *The Well at the World's End*, to 1909, when G. R. S. Mead founded the Quest Society. There were reasons for that, woven into the shape of popular occultism in Britain during those years, and a glance over the history of that time will help clarify what happened.

From 1887 until 1909, the Theosophical Society dominated the public conversation about occultism in Britain to an extent that is hard to imagine today. Most people in Britain who were interested in occultism in any way belonged to it, if only to get easy access to the Society's large and well-stocked libraries and to have ample opportunities for networking with other occultists. From 1887 to 1903, similarly, the Hermetic Order of the Golden Dawn had an equally dominant role in the more secretive ceremonial end of the British occult scene. Nor were these two groups separate in any real sense; most of the first generation of Golden Dawn adepts were also active in the Theosophical Society, and some—including William Butler Yeats and Golden Dawn founder William Wynn Westcott—were members of the Esoteric Section, the inner circle of Theosophy.

The predominance of these organizations had a potent influence on the forms of occult symbolism and practice that were popular in Britain at that time. Blavatsky claimed that her teachings had been inspired by the sacred teachings of the mysterious East, passed on to her by superhuman masters who lived in the Himalayas. While the Theosophical Society remained central to public occultism in Britain, traditions from India and other Asian countries held center stage and those from the Mediterranean countries and Europe were generally neglected. The Golden Dawn, for its part, drew most of its symbolism from ancient Egypt on the one hand and from the Christian Cabala of the Renaissance on the other. While it dominated the ceremonial magic scene in Britain, traditions relating to European Paganism or Gnostic heresy received little attention by comparison.

A series of lurid political conflicts between 1900 and 1903, however, tore the Golden Dawn apart into squabbling fragments, and the heyday of Theosophy ended in an equally explosive but more prolonged series of schisms that began with Mead's departure from the T. S. in 1909. In response, many occultists in Britain began to turn their attention elsewhere. Mead and Isabel Cooper-Oakley were ahead of the game here with their early interest in the Gnostics. Another straw in the wind was Lewis Spence's *The Mysteries of Britain*, originally published in 1905, which argued that British Celtic traditions were just as valid as a source of spiritual insight as anything imported from India or Tibet. Spence was a rising star in the occult scene at that time, and where he led, others followed.

It was after the rupture in the Theosophical Society, however, that occult groups and magical lodges focused squarely on European Pagan traditions began to appear in the British occult scenes. Some of these emerged from the unlikely but effective fusion of Golden Dawn teachings with the Druid Revival, a movement of nature spirituality inspired by ancient Celtic traditions, which had been quietly active in Britain, Europe, and North America since the eighteenth century. Hybrid Druid/Golden Dawn organizations such as the Cabbalistic Order of Druids, the Ancient Order of Druid Hermetists, and the Nuada and Merlin Temples of the Golden Dawn flourished during the decades that followed and explored various combinations of ceremonial magic with Celtic symbolism and nature religion.[138] Other groups explored less formal modes of magical working and nature spirituality and thus laid the foundation for the rise of Wicca in the second half of the twentieth century.

It was in the midst of this revival of interest in European Paganism and British traditions that the Company of the Grail came together to celebrate the ritual that inspired the Grail romances seven centuries previously. To judge by the degree to which it managed to keep its activities secret, it was never a large organization, and it may never have been much more than a circle composed of Mead's close friends and associates. Nor does it seem to have endured for long. Of its known members, Isabel Cooper-Oakley died in 1914, Jessie Weston died in 1924, and G. R. S. Mead died in 1933, having retired from active involvement in occultism and closed down the Quest Society two years before then.

There may simply have been no one prepared to step into Mead's shoes and keep the Quest Society and the Company of the Grail active. Yet there was another factor at work. Just as in earlier times, the Company of the Grail had its opponents. As before, they came from among those who put their faith in mainstream Christianity in place of the ancient Mysteries and the path of Gnosis.

---

138. I have discussed the history of these Druid/Golden Dawn fusion groups in the foreword to my book *The Celtic Golden Dawn*.

THE HIDING OF
THE HALLOWS

The history of the Grail legend from its first appearance straight through to the present is shot through with a constant tension between two basic themes. The first of them is the one we have explored in the previous chapters: a vision of the Grail as a relic of the ancient Mysteries and an emblem of the Gnostic path, embodying a spiritual tradition at odds with the established churches of the Western world. The second, opposing theme is a vision of the Grail as a symbol of ordinary mainstream Christianity, barricaded against any contact with Pagan Mysteries or Gnostic heresies. This tension is not accidental. It emerges out of an ongoing conflict between those people who feel the call to the higher awareness that the Mysteries communicated and the Gnostics taught and those people who are content to remain within the circle of established doctrine and would rather believe than know.

It's important in this light to remember that this latter group, those who belong to the religious mainstream, are just as serious in their faith as the epoptai of the Mysteries or the initiates of the Gnosis. They believe with all their hearts that theirs is the way that leads to salvation and anyone who strays from their version of the truth will fry in Hell for all eternity. Their response to a resurgence of the alternative perspectives discussed in this book is motivated by a conviction that such perspectives are snares of Satan that will invariably lead souls to damnation. That conviction has led a great many devout Christians down through the centuries to seek to Christianize the Grail—to strip the legend of its links to archaic spiritual teachings and forgotten technologies, and to turn it instead into yet another way that souls can be led to Christ.

That response explains, better than any other factor, the strange history of the Grail romances discussed in the first chapter of this book. The reason that all the early Grail romances spoke of fearful secrets and contained hints of Gnostic mysteries, while the later ones discarded the secret teachings and ceremonies in favor of conventional Christian religion and morality, was that Christian writers in the thirteenth century recognized the link between the Grail and heresy and set out to drown out the voices of dissidence with a version of the legend more congenial to orthodoxy. That was why in these later versions of the legend, Perceval, the brave man slowly wise, was replaced by Galahad the plaster saint, and why the ceremony of the Grail was replaced by the ordinary Christian Mass.

In some cases the sources of the later, Christianized versions of the Grail legend can be traced directly to specific Christian monasteries. Thus it was at Glastonbury Abbey, according to many scholars, that the *Perlesvaus* took its final shape. Others such as the *Queste del Seynte Graal* (*Quest of the Holy Grail*), the most influential of the Galahad-centered versions of the story, are less easy to trace back to their sources. Yet the basic pattern remains clear. As the Cathars flourished, the original Grail romances with their secrets and their ceremony spread far and wide. Once the Cathars fell beneath the swords of the Albigensian Crusade, those were replaced by more orthodox versions stripped of their esoteric content.

The same pattern, as we have seen, appears to have taken place in the eighteenth century during the heyday of the early Masonic hauts grades. If the speculation discussed earlier in this book is correct, the Masonic degree of Rose Croix of Heredom came into being in exactly the same way as the *Perlesvaus* and the *Queste*, manufactured by industrious Catholic intellectuals in imitation of an older original, but with all the heretical elements removed and replaced with details more congenial to the orthodox. The Jesuit college of Clermont played the role here that Glastonbury Abbey played in the origins of the *Perlesvaus*.

In a sense, the same thing happened once again in the early twentieth century. By that time Christian churches had lost a great deal of their political power, and so Weston, Mead, and the other members of the group I have called the Company of the Grail did not have to worry about being hauled before the Inquisition or becoming the victims of a new crusade. By that time, too, Christian churches had many more pressing threats to face, and the revival of the Grail ceremony in Britain was on a small enough scale that in all probability neither the Pope, nor the Archbishop of Canterbury, nor any other high-ranking Christian leader heard about it at all.

Nonetheless, there were devout Christians who were prepared to take up the old struggle against the Grail of the ancient Mysteries and the old Gnosis and to try to force the Grail legend into the Procrustean bed of orthodox Christianity. The most important of these figures was the most influential Christian occultist of the early twentieth century, the redoubtable Arthur Edward Waite.

Waite reached his position as a prime defender of the Christian interpretation of the Grail the hard way. He was born in Brooklyn, New York, in 1857, the illegitimate son of an American sea captain and an Englishwoman. When he was two years old his father died, and his mother returned with him and his newborn sister to Britain, but she was shunned by her family because her children were born out of wedlock. She then converted to the Roman Catholic Church and raised her children in that faith. Waite received only a limited education and went to work as a clerk at the age of fifteen, but he was a voracious reader with a passion for learning and an interest in occultism, and he decided to become a writer. His first published work, a poem titled "An Ode to Astronomy," saw print in 1877. His first book, a translation of writings by French occultist Éliphas Lévi, was published in 1886, and he never looked back.

After the death of his sister in 1874, he left the Catholic Church but remained a devout and relatively orthodox Christian, and his many works on occultism all tried to find ways to reinterpret occult teachings in terms of Christian theology. Whether he was writing about alchemy, Freemasonry, the Rosicrucians, or the Grail, he was always looking for ways in which they could be interpreted as a way to Christ.

Waite, in fact, was a devout mystical Christian. To say that is not to dismiss what he had to say about the Grail legends. Rather, it places him in the context of a specific orientation toward those legends—the same orientation at work in the Middle Ages, when the struggle between Christian orthodoxy and something far stranger left its enduring marks on the Grail legends themselves. For Waite, as for the authors of Grail legends such as the *Perlesvaus* and the *Queste*, the valid meaning of the Grail legend could only be found within the accepted teachings of the established Christian churches, and any path that led away from those teachings led straight to eternal damnation and so had to be barricaded shut. Raising those barricades was thus a central theme of his two books on the Grail.

His first book on the subject was titled *The Hidden Church of the Holy Grail*, and it carried out its mission by playing what might uncharitably be called a bait-and-switch on its readers. In his time, there were plenty of writers and scholars who speculated about a hidden church within Christianity passing on some form of Gnostic initiation from ancient times. Waite dangled that possibility in front of the reader most of the way through his book, then revealed that the hidden church he had in mind had the same theology and traditions as the mainstream churches—it simply took them even more seriously.

His second and more influential book on the subject, *The Holy Grail*, took a different approach. It was subtitled *The Galahad Quest in the Arthurian Literature*, as though the Galahad stories were the only ones that counted and the older versions that centered on Perceval and Gawain didn't exist or didn't matter. He insisted on treating elements that only appear in the Galahad legend as central themes of the legend—the idea that the Grail disappeared once Galahad had found it is one example. His judgment of the merit of each of the Grail texts rested primarily on how well its author kept to the straight and narrow road of Christian theology, and he had nothing good to say about those Grail stories that strayed from that path. Some of his harshest criticisms were accordingly aimed at Jessie Weston's ritual theory and at the broader suggestion that the Grail legends might be descended from a ritual of initiation from some tradition outside the narrow bounds of Christian orthodoxy.[139]

---

139. Waite, *The Holy Grail*, 423–43.

Central to his argument against the ritual theory is the claim that the initiation of the Grail contains features that no initiation ritual known to him ever had. Plod through his labored prose and you will find four such features cited. The first is that the successful Grail seeker becomes the keeper of the Grail, taking the place of the Fisher King. The second is that the Grail seeker must ask a question, and is turned away at his first approach because he does not do so. The third is that the candidate for initiation comes to heal and save a holy place that is in desperate condition. Because no ritual of initiation Waite knew of included those features, he insists, the Grail legend could not have been based on an initiation. Furthermore, he insisted that the Grail legend always ends with the removal of the Grail to some distant place, if not to Heaven itself instead of remaining on earth to be the center of the Mystery ritual.[140]

The problem with these claims is that Waite was quite simply lying. His own writings and life history show that he was aware of other initiations that had exactly those features he insisted did not exist in initiatory ritual. With regard to his first point, as a Freemason and the author of a large and detailed encyclopedia of Freemasonry, he knew perfectly well that several rituals in Freemasonry include a symbolic enthronement of the candidate as King Solomon or as some other monarch. His scholarship was spotty enough that he may not have known that the ancient Greek Mysteries included a stage in which the initiates were crowned like monarchs, but he certainly knew that this happens in Masonic rites.[141]

With regard to his second and third points, it is in fact quite common in initiation rituals for a candidate to be turned away at first for failing to do something he has never been told to do, then allowed to return a second time to get it right and receive the initiation. Waite himself passed through at least two such rituals: the ritual of the Mark Mason degree in Freemasonry and the Adeptus Minor ritual in the Golden Dawn. It is also quite common in initiation rituals for a candidate to go symbolically to the rescue of a holy place in ruins or otherwise-desperate straits. Waite passed through at least one such ritual—the ritual of the Holy Royal Arch in Freemasonry—and he was certainly aware of at least one other, the ritual of Knight Rose Croix of Heredom. He knew, in

---

140. Waite, *The Holy Grail*, 438–39.

141. Sallust, *On the Gods and the World*, 22.

other words, that the features he cited had close parallels in surviving initiation rituals, and he did his level best to hide that fact.

His final point fails to prove anything for the simple reason that only the late Christian versions of the Grail legend include the idea that the Grail has been removed from its place to some distant land, or to heaven. The older versions of the legend—those that, in theory, would be closest to the original ritual—do not have that feature at all. He knew this, furthermore, since his books on the Grail refer in detail to the early romances that do not contain the disappearance of the Grail: the romances, furthermore, that Weston made central to her own analysis of the legend. Yet he erased these in his discussion.

The theological issues involved in the Grail legends offer the best explanation for these troubling evasions. To Waite, as for the Christian authors of the *Perlesvaus* and the *Queste*, the most important issue in the entire debate was the defense of Christian orthodoxy against a resurgent heresy that combined what he must have seen as the worst elements of Paganism and Gnosticism. With the salvation of souls at stake, scholarly accuracy had to take a back seat to the propagation of the One True Faith—and more specifically, in Waite's time as in the thirteenth century, the effort to wrench the Grail legend out of the hands of heretics and put it to work to lead souls to Christ.

His entire discussion of the ritual theory, and his exploration of the Grail legend in general, centers on that theological imperative. Waite insists, for example, that Jessie Weston must have been hoodwinked by unscrupulous occultists who had fabricated a Grail order and its attendant ritual. He offered no evidence for this claim.[142] Nor, of course, did he consider the possibility that the ritual in question might have been reassembled from surviving fragments of a tradition and revived by a group of people who founded an order for the purpose. The irony rises to a fever pitch when he denounces groups that operate outside of Freemasonry "under the style and title of The Rosy Cross"— something he knew a great deal about, since he himself operated two orders of exactly that description, the Independent Rectified Order of the Golden Dawn

---

142. Waite, *The Holy Grail*, 431–32.

and the Fellowship of the Rosy Cross, using rituals he had borrowed from the Golden Dawn and reworked to fit his ideas about Christian theology.[143]

◇

Despite these difficulties with his argument, Waite's claims were widely accepted in the end of the early twentieth century occult community sympathetic to mainstream Christianity. He found a vocal supporter in Charles Williams, another Christian mystic and a powerful and popular writer who was an initiate of Waite's Fellowship of the Rosy Cross and who wrote two volumes of widely acclaimed Arthurian poems, *Taliessin through Logres* and *The Region of the Summer Stars*, all of them focused with laser intensity on the Christian interpretation of the Arthurian legends. Williams's prose essays on the legends of Arthur, published after his death by his friend C. S. Lewis as *Arthurian Torso*, were not as influential as Waite's writings on the subject, but they have the same biases: for Williams, the Galahad version of the legend was the correct one, and he dismisses the Perceval versions out of hand.

With Williams and C. S. Lewis we come within range of another far more influential author whose connections to the Grail legend are rarely recognized today. This is J. R. R. Tolkien, the author of *The Lord of the Rings*. Tolkien's biography is weirdly parallel to Waite's. Like Waite, he lost his father early in childhood, his mother brought him and a sibling back to Britain, and she then converted to Roman Catholicism. Unlike Waite, Tolkien remained a devout Catholic all his life. He was also a better writer and a far more gifted scholar than Waite, with an extraordinary talent for languages that won him entrance to Oxford, followed by a successful academic career as a philologist. It was in his off hours that he wrote the stories that redefined fantasy fiction.

As a scholar, Tolkien's specialty was the Germanic family of languages. In his academic writings he also plunged deep into the same explorations of mythology that helped Jessie Weston find her way to the Grail ritual. He was a passionate fan of the same Norse sagas that helped inspire William Morris—

---

143. Waite, *The Holy Grail*, 432. These rituals have been published. They compare to the original Golden Dawn rituals very much as the later Galahad romances compare to the original Gnostic Grail legends. See Waite, *Inner and Outer Order Initiations of the Holy Order of the Golden Dawn*.

he originally learned Old Norse, in fact, so he could read the sagas in their original language. His studies in archaic European myth and legend took him into nearly every corner of the ancient lore discussed in the second part of this book, and much of that lore can be found in the pages of *The Lord of the Rings*; from the sequence of ages of the world through the traditions of mound burial to the treasure of sovereignty, most of the themes discussed above can be found in the pages of Tolkien's grand fantasy.

Yet in every case, these themes have been reshaped to suit the imagination of a deeply devout and politically conservative Catholic intellectual. The spirits living within the mounds in his trilogy, for example, are not the phantoms of the honored dead but the dread Barrow-wights, from whom the heroes of the story must escape early on in their adventures. The most dramatic reshaping, however, is the treasure of sovereignty itself. I have not been able to determine whether Tolkien read Wagner's essay "The Wibelungs," but he was certainly familiar with the concepts Wagner discussed, and his version of the treasure takes the same Germanic legends Wagner used and casts them in a harsh new light.

The One Ring, Tolkien's version of the treasure of sovereignty, can best be described as the anti-Grail. It is not a talisman of life. Quite the contrary, those who possess the Ring do not die but receive no new life, and the kingdom of the One Ring's maker, the Dark Lord Sauron, is as devastated a Waste Land as anything in the Grail legends. Since the Ring is an anti-Grail, the plot of Tolkien's trilogy stands the Grail quest on its head: the quest of Frodo Baggins and his friends is the first quest in literature where the goal is not to find something, but to get rid of it once and for all. It is one of Tolkien's brilliant touches that Frodo, who begins the story filling the role of the Grail Knight, ends it playing the part of the Fisher King, burdened with a wound that will not heal. Nor is there any healing for him in the story. His only hope is to go west to the Elven-lands across the sea—and in Tolkien's generation, the phrase "to go west" was a common euphemism meaning "to die."

None of this was accidental. As the published volumes of his drafts and papers show, Tolkien was an extraordinarily careful writer fully aware of the mythic background of the words and images he used, and he was also very well read in earlier fantasy fiction. That shows in the way that his novel sets out to challenge the basic ideas of Morris's *The Well at the World's End*. The opposition between the two men and their imaginative visions was inevitable, for

Morris and Tolkien were on opposite sides of the political and religious spectrum. Morris was a socialist who had no time for Christianity; Tolkien was a staunch conservative and a lifelong Catholic. It is far from rare for writers with views this divergent to include their disagreements in their stories, and Tolkien unquestionably did so.

You can see the conflict most clearly in Tolkien's deliberate references to Morris's *The Well at the World's End*. One of the characters in Morris's book, for example, has a horse named Silverfax, while one of the characters in Tolkien's trilogy has a horse named Shadowfax. The most important of these references, of course, is Tolkien's wise and benevolent wizard Gandalf, whose name is one letter removed from Morris's cruel and cowardly villain Gandolf.

A dwarf named Gandalf appears in a list of dwarves in the Old Norse poem *Voluspa*, in the same passage that provided Tolkien with the names of all the dwarves who appear in his children's novel *The Hobbit*.[144] Doubtless, this was one source of inspiration for the name. Tolkien was notoriously fond of puns, however, and it must have tickled his fancy to find a Norse name so close to that of Morris's villain. Nor would he have missed for a moment the implications of Morris's choice of the name, with its deliberate dig at the Catholic Church. Unlike Morris, Tolkien disliked allegories, so it would be a mistake to suggest that he meant Gandalf as nothing more than an emblem of Catholicism. The opposition between the two characters is striking, however, and would have been even more so in the days when most readers of fantasy fiction read Morris's novels.

Nowadays, of course, very few people read Morris and nearly everyone with a taste for fantasy reads Tolkien. The reasons behind that difference are complex. Partly, it is simply a matter of their respective generations. As a nineteenth-century writer, Morris loved the ornate style and formal vocabulary of Victorian fiction, which went out of style a few decades after his death. Tolkien, by contrast, embraced the more straightforward style that had become fashionable in his time, and his story was therefore much easier for twentieth-century readers to enjoy. There may have been other, subtler factors involved, but those can be left for historians of literary taste to consider.

---

144. Carter, *Tolkien*, 153–55.

◇

The point relevant to our exploration is that Tolkien's viewpoint was the one that won out in another, more important sense. The year that the first volume of his trilogy was published, 1954, was also the year that Gerald Gardner's *The Meaning of Witchcraft* first saw print. This latter book was the first public announcement of the "old religion" of Wicca.

The rise of Wicca and the Neopagan movement in general marked a far more drastic break with older esoteric traditions than most people realize today. Following Gardner's lead, Neopagans lost interest in medieval heresies and historically documented Pagan traditions such as the ancient Mysteries and focused instead on goddess-centered beliefs and practices that they claimed, despite a noticeable lack of evidence, had descended in secret from much further back in time. Ironically, Tolkien's trilogy, with its deep roots in political conservatism and traditional Catholicism, was practically required reading in the British and North American countercultures that embraced the Neopagan movement. In the early days of the Neopagan scene, certainly, Tolkien's aesthetic was on display all over the scene, to an extent that sometimes made Neopagan events look like Tolkien fan conventions.

The Neopagan movement had its own complex history, which has been described in useful detail in Ronald Hutton's *The Triumph of the Moon* and other sources. In terms of the history traced in this book, however, what matters about it is that it marked the end of the road for an entire world of Western occultism. Though the Theosophical Society was a waning force by the end of the 1920s, many other organizations, traditions, and movements in the broader world of British occultism kept working along the same general lines that Weston, Mead, Cooper-Oakley, and others had pursued in their time, building on the heritage that had descended from the medieval Gnostics and, through them, from the classical world and before.

As the twentieth century passed its midpoint, all that faded away. I have written elsewhere about the way that most of the organizations that fused the Golden Dawn and Druid Revival traditions guttered out after the Second World War.[145] That was only one part of a much more general twilight of older occult

---

145. In the introduction to Greer, *The Celtic Golden Dawn*.

traditions at that time. During those years, the last Golden Dawn temples in Britain and the United States closed their doors and scores of other magical lodges and occult schools shut down for lack of younger people interested in joining. It was a melancholy era in the history of Western occultism.

To be fair, the rise of Neopaganism was an effect of the changes that brought about that era, not its cause. In the wake of the Second World War, for a galaxy of reasons, it became common for people in Western societies to reject their own cultural heritage and turn instead to borrowings from other cultures, to newly minted visions of the distant past, or to idealized notions of an imagined future. The Neopagan dream of an age before history when Goddess-worshipping wise women taught the ways of harmony with nature appealed powerfully to the hopes and fears of the late twentieth century— more powerfully, certainly, than the older occult traditions of the West, with their sometimes fussy philosophies and their tendency to embrace the ethics and values of an earlier era.

All this happened, furthermore, at a time when magic, occultism, and alternative spirituality were being squeezed out of the cultural mainstream. In the early twentieth century, William Butler Yeats could be publicly known as a practitioner of magic without facing any significant pushback from his audience, and he went on to win the Nobel Prize in literature. By the end of the same century, public figures with similar interests could count on being assailed from one side by religious fundamentalists who insisted they were devil worshippers, and from the other by rationalist atheists who insisted that they were lying or crazy.

The resulting social pressures made life difficult for occultists who weren't interested in dropping out of the mainstream entirely and joining the Neopagan subculture. It also drove a wedge between the realms of scholarship in which Jessie Weston and G. R. S. Mead had labored, on the one hand, and the occult scene on the other. That led, among other things, to the erasure of Weston and Mead from the history of scholarship. Both had been widely accepted as authorities by academics in their own time, but after the Second World War that changed abruptly. Mead's pioneering work in the history of Gnosticism was ignored by later writers, and Weston's ritual theory—and in fact all her many contributions to the study of the Arthurian legends—dropped out of sight. No one wanted to discuss writers who had such obvious connections to the subject of occultism.

One of the many ironies of the era that resulted is that interest in the Arthurian legends, including those concerning the Grail, reached levels unprecedented since the Middle Ages. Novels, movies, musicals, television programs, and plenty of other media variations on Arthurian themes flooded the marketplace and racked up impressive receipts. When practitioners of magic and occultism turned to the same source for raw material, however, they either embraced the orthodox Christian interpretation of the legend or reinterpreted it in terms of the Neopagan version of history, which erased the traditions Jessie Weston studied and replaced them with a variety of newly minted ideologies. It's indicative that two of the most popular occult books on the Grail tradition in the late twentieth century, John Matthews and Marian Green's *The Grail Seeker's Companion* and Shadwynn's *The Crafted Cup*, both reinterpreted the Grail legend in strictly Neopagan terms—and even more revealing that the latter book drew much of its Arthurian lore not from the medieval romances but from Marion Zimmer Bradley's novel *The Mists of Avalon*, a thoroughly Neopagan rewrite of Arthurian legend.

The effects of this broad change in social attitudes on the subject of our exploration can be summed up easily enough. Whether or not the ceremony of the Grail was still being performed after the closing of the Quest Society in 1931, it apparently did not continue after the Second World War or the rise of the Neopagan movement that followed. Certainly I have been able to find no trace of it in the records of the postwar British occult scene. Ross Nichols, one of the most influential figures in that scene, included some important elements of the tradition in his visionary poem cycle "Cosmic Legend," and in the accompanying essay, he called for the establishment of a cycle of public rituals to help modern humanity reconnect with the environment and the cycles of nature. If he had known of the ceremony of the Grail, it is hard to imagine him leaving it neglected, but he chose instead to become active in the Druid Revival tradition and became the founder of the Order of Bards Ovates and Druids (OBOD), the largest Druid order in the world today.[146] His published writings and unpublished papers are rich in occult teachings of many kinds,

---

146. See Nichols, *The Book of Druidry*, for a summary of Druid Revival teachings in Nichols' time.

but references to the ceremony of the Grail that Mead and Weston worked with are absent.[147]

One scrap of evidence suggests, however, that knowledge of the ritual may have crossed the Atlantic in the 1920s. Among the many works of American occultist Manly P. Hall is a thick volume entitled *Lectures on Ancient Philosophy*, published in 1929 as a companion to his lavishly illustrated volume *The Secret Teachings of All Ages*. Like many of Hall's early books, this one includes a discussion of the ancient Mysteries, and in it he provides a diagram and a colorful description of the rituals of the Mystery initiations.[148] Hall was prodigiously learned in ancient Greek mystical traditions, and he had at his disposal all the material we discussed in an earlier chapter about the rites of Eleusis and of Attis and the Great Mother. He could very easily have presented a ritual based on these.

This is not what he did, however. Instead, he outlines a ritual of a type familiar to anyone who has followed the argument of this book. It takes place in four chambers: first, a chamber in darkness, full of the symbolism of death; next, a chamber draped in red in which the candidate for initiation is tested; third, a chamber in dim light, where he is tested again; and finally, a chamber in brilliant light, where the candidate receives the secrets of the mystery. Of the two chambers in the middle, the first is clearly modeled on the depiction of Hell in the degree of Rose Croix of Heredom, while the second has the candidate encounter a group of men seated like the Fisher King and his courtiers at the banquet of the Grail. It looks very much as though someone—possibly Hall, possibly someone else—tried to piece together a ritual that includes the second chamber of both the Grail ceremony and the Rose Croix rite.

In 1929, when Hall wrote this book, he was not yet a Freemason; he was not made a Mason until 1954, and he was initiated into the Scottish Rite in the following year. Thus, it is unlikely that he knew the details of the Rose Croix of Heredom degree twenty-six years in advance. He was a passionate collector of old manuscripts and could have obtained access to that degree by this means,

---

147. I am indebted to Philip Carr-Gomm, then Chosen Chief of OBOD, for the opportunity to examine Nichols' unpublished papers in 2003.

148. Hall, *Lectures on Ancient Philosophy*, 360, 371–74.

but I have not been able to find anything in the published lists of his manuscript collection that includes the ritual in question.

There is another possibility, of course. Hall wrote a book on the Grail legend, and in it he covered much of the story we have traced so far.[149] He was familiar with the details of Isabel Cooper-Oakley's research, and in fact cites her book on medieval mystical traditions in his study of the Grail. He was also familiar with Arthur Edward Waite's writings on the Grail and dismisses them out of hand. Hall's own discussion of the Grail legend is, like so much of his work, curiously evasive; it reads as though he knew far more than he was willing to say. During the 1920s and 1930s, he traveled to Britain and Europe repeatedly. It is at least possible that he knew about the group I have called the Company of the Grail—and it is by no means out of the question that he became a member of it.

Whether or not this is the case will have to be determined by future research. As it stands, Hall's apparent knowledge of the ritual we have been studying, or of a ritual derived from it, is yet another tantalizing hint that might, or might not, point to surviving knowledge of the ceremony of the Grail.

I began searching for the ceremony of the Grail decades ago in the hope that it might lead to more information about the lost secret of the Knights Templar and the earliest Freemasons, the temple technology I discussed at length in my book *The Secret of the Temple*. Over the years since that time, the quest has taken on a life of its own. If the ceremony of the Grail survives, it is worth recovering and performing again, whether or not the secrets that made the fields flourish are still included in the text of the ritual.

Ross Nichols, in the essay cited previously, warned that the breach between humanity and the environment would become a source of serious trouble unless it could be healed, and he proposed that ritual was among the means that could be used to further that act of healing. His warning is even more relevant now than it was in his time. In today's world, racked with the ecological consequences of technology run amok and of a careless consumerism that places momentary enjoyments ahead of the survival of humanity and the

---

149. See Hall, *Orders of the Quest*.

global biosphere, the Waste Land of the old Grail romances seems more like a prophecy than a legend. Anything that can help individuals shake themselves out of the trance of mindless consumption and recognize the need for personal and collective change is a resource we cannot afford to neglect.

I have therefore attempted a tentative reconstruction of the Ceremony of the Grail in the section of this book that follows. Yet it is not impossible that the original can still be located.

The text of the ritual as it was performed in Jessie Weston's time, if it survives at all, is most likely to be found in Britain, in the papers of some member of the Quest Society's inner circle, or in some other collection of documents left behind by the British occult scene of the early twentieth century. The version that inspired the revival of Weston's time, in turn, may still be somewhere in the archives of eighteenth-century literature in Britain or western Europe, quite possibly where William Morris found it in his many travels.

If the astrological symbolism of the Grail legend is to be taken seriously, the court of the Rich Fisherman can again be found now that the age of Pisces is over and the age of Aquarius has arrived. The *Elucidation* tells us that the court was or will be found seven times. Jessie Weston and the other members of the group I have called the Company of the Grail were responsible for one of those successful quests. If this book helps other seekers succeed in the same quest a second time, it will have fulfilled its purpose.

PART FIVE
THE GRAIL CEREMONY

THE CEREMONY OF THE GRAIL: A RECONSTRUCTION

The following ritual is a tentative reconstruction of what the ceremony of the Grail might have been like, in the form that it had during Jessie Weston's involvement in it. I have based it partly on the *Elucidation* and several other early Grail legends, partly on the descriptions in Jessie Weston's "The Ruined Temple" and William Morris's *The Well at the World's End*, partly on late nineteenth and early twentieth century British occult rituals, and partly on the earliest surviving forms of the degree of Rose Croix of Heredom. How close I have come to the original, only those who have access to the ritual itself can say.

Of the Lodge

The lodge proper consists of three chambers. Unless three separate rooms are available for the ritual, the same lodge room will be set up as the first chamber before the ceremony begins and will be changed to represent the second and third chambers at appropriate points as the ceremony proceeds.

The first chamber is draped in black and contains a bier where the King will lie, apparently dead. Two candles in tall candlesticks, one at the head of the bier and the other at the foot, provide the only light. At the four corners of the bier are censers in which bitter incense burns. In front of the bier is a cushion on which the candidate will kneel, and a bell with a deep note, like a church bell, is provided. If possible, the lights in this chamber should be arranged so that they can be turned up gradually, to simulate dawn.

The second chamber is draped in white and is well lit. It contains a table, also draped in white, set for a feast, and several chairs. Soft instrumental music of a medieval type is provided. Bread and wine are ready to be brought in. So are the items of the Grail procession: the spear, the Grail, and two candles in candlesticks—these may be the two candles and candlesticks that were used in the first chamber.

The third chamber is draped in red and gold, and is brightly lit. It contains a throne for the King and seats for all the Companions who are present, arranged in a circle open on the side away from the throne. An extra chair is ready for the King, and later for the candidate. To the right of the throne is a small table with the Grail upon it; to the left, the spear stands upright in a stand. A cushion for kneeling is placed in front of the throne.

An anteroom is located outside the lodge room. This is draped in black and lit by a single dim light. It contains two chairs, one for the Conductor and one for the candidate.

Of the Officers

There are four speaking parts in this ceremony.

The Most Wise King of the Grail represents the Rich Fisherman or Fisher King, and he is clothed and crowned as befits a king, in robes of black trimmed with gold. Over these he wears a cloak of black cloth trimmed with gold, which he will place on the candidate.

The Most Noble Lady of the Grail represents the Grail Bearer, and she wears a gown of white trimmed with gold. She has a loose black cloak with a hood, which is worn over her costume in the First Point.

The Most Worthy Knight of the Grail represents the challenger whom the Grail seeker must overcome, and he is clothed and crowned as a knight, in armor of red and gold. He has a loose black cloak with a hood, which is worn over his costume in the First Point.

The Conductor represents the guide who leads the Grail seeker to the goal, and he wears garments of green trimmed with gold.

At least six members of the Company of the Grail are also needed for nonspeaking roles. They should be dressed in white robes and wear sword belts with swords. They take part in the feast and Grail procession of the Second Point and the Assembly of the Third Point.

Preparation of the Candidate

The candidate is clothed in a white robe trimmed with gold and is girded with a red swoud belt, bearing a scabbard and sword, before being brought into the anteroom by the Conductor. Once the candidate is seated, the Conductor gives the following preliminary address.

CONDUCTOR

Many days have passed since you left the court of King Arthur, having pledged yourself to seek the Grail, and set out in search of the court of the Rich Fisherman. Your journey here has been long and difficult. For seven days you have ridden through a land laid waste, where no tree bears leaves and no water flows. Now as the sun sets and the wind blows chill you behold the first goal of your quest, the Chapel Perilous. You may turn back now if you are unwilling to face the challenge before you. If you choose to proceed, in order to enter the Chapel, you must first take a solemn obligation binding you to secrecy concerning the events of the ceremony you are about to witness. Are you willing to do this?

If the candidate answers yes, the ceremony proceeds. Otherwise the candidate is escorted out of the anteroom and the ritual is at an end.

CONDUCTOR

Since you are willing to proceed, draw your sword and give it to me.

The candidate does so. The Conductor takes it by the hilt and holds it so that the blade is flat and the point is before the candidate's throat.

CONDUCTOR

Place your right hand over your heart and your left hand on the blade of this sword. *(Candidate does so.)* Repeat after me: "I hereby pledge—my sacred honor—to keep secret and inviolate—everything I encounter—and everything I learn—in the ceremony to which—I am about to be admitted." Lower your hands. Take your sword and sheathe it, and be seated and wait beside me with patience.

To Open

All the officers and Companions are seated in a circle, clothed in their proper garments. The King opens the gathering in due form as follows.

KING

Most Worthy Knight, what is our first care when assembled?

KNIGHT

To see that our assembly is properly tiled.[150]

KING

Do your duty then.

The Knight goes to the door and knocks once. He is answered with a single knock from the Conductor, who is in the anteroom.

KNIGHT

Most Wise King, we are properly tiled.

KING

All please rise. *(All stand up.)* Most Noble Lady, what is the hour?

LADY

The hour of sunset, when the sun descends into the western ocean and the weary seeker for the Grail comes to the court of the Rich Fisherman.

KING

Most Worthy Knight, of what is the Grail made?

KNIGHT

The stone named Lapsit Exillas.

---

150. *Tiled* is an old word meaning "covered" or "protected," now used in Masonry to mean "secure."

KING

> Most Noble Lady, what is the meaning of this name?

LADY

> Lapsit Ex Illas: it fell from among them.

KNIGHT

> Lapis Ex Caelis: a stone from heaven.

KING

> Lapis Exilis: the Stone of Exile. *(He extends his arms to both sides in the form of a cross.)* IAO.[151] Such are the words. *(All officers make the Sign of the Grail.[152])*

KING

> In the name of the Holy Gnosis, I declare this gathering open.

The extra chairs are removed.

The First Point

The lights are turned down and the candles and the incense are lit in the first chamber. The King lies on the bier, face up, eyes closed, apparently dead. The Lady and Knight put black hooded cloaks over their costumes. When all is in readiness, the Knight knocks once on the door to the anteroom, and he and the Lady then go stand in places out of sight of the candidate. The Conductor then brings in the candidate and they proceed to the cushion in front of the bier.

CONDUCTOR

> *(in a hushed voice)* You are now within the Chapel Perilous, where you will keep vigil. Once you kneel here, you may not depart this place for peril of your very soul until your vigil is complete. I ask you again: are you willing to proceed? *(If the candidate says yes)* Then kneel on both

---

151. This is pronounced "Ee-Ah-Oh."

152. This is explained later in the ceremony.

your knees.[153] *(The candidate does so, the Conductor assisting if necessary.)* Draw your sword, place the point upon the floor, and hold the hilt in both hands, the blade being in a vertical position. This is the way in which the knights of old kept vigil.

The bell tolls slowly twelve times.

CONDUCTOR

Listen! The bell tolls midnight. I leave you now until dawn.

The Conductor leaves. A minute or so of silence passes, and then sounds of sobbing and weeping are heard, as though people are mourning for the dead king. This continues for several minutes, followed by silence. Then the bell tolls once.

LADY

(after a pause) Never before have you heard the story told truly of which there was once so much noise and outcry, of how and why the rich country of Logres was destroyed, of which there was so much talk in days of yore. The kingdom went to ruin, for they lost the voices of the hills and the damsels that were in them. For this is the great service they once gave, that no one who wandered the roads by night or morning had to go out of his way except to find one of the hills, and then he could ask for nothing in the way of good and pleasing food that he could not have it at once, so long as he asked within reason. All with one accord, fairly and joyously, the damsels served all wayfarers on the roads that come to the wells for food.

A pause. The bell sounds twice.

KNIGHT

(after a pause) King Amangons, the evil and craven-hearted, was the first to break the custom, and after him many others did the same

---

153. If the candidate is physically unable to kneel for a prolonged period, a chair may be used instead.

thing, following the example of their king, whose duty it was to protect the damsels and to maintain and guard them within his peace. He forced himself on one of the damsels and took her virginity to her great sorrow, and stole from her the cup of gold and took it with him, and afterward had himself served with it every day. He richly deserved the fate he suffered. For after that the damsel never served anyone, nor did any other come out of that hill to serve any man who came there asking for food.

A pause. The bell sounds three times.

LADY

(after a pause) The other vassals that were honored by the king, when they saw that their lord raped the damsels whenever he found them pretty, forced themselves on them in the same way and carried off the cups of gold, so that after that the damsels never came from the hills or offered their service. This, my lords, was how the land had its downfall, and the king and everyone else who wronged the damsels all suffered a terrible fate. The kingdom was laid waste so that no tree bore leaves. The meadows and the flowers withered and the waters dried up, nor could anyone find the Court of the Rich Fisherman that had once made the land a glittering glory of gold and silver and all good things.

A pause. The bell sounds four times

KNIGHT

(after a pause) Only when the Court and the Grail are found again will the realm be repopulated so that the waters which had stopped running and the fountains which had stopped flowing, having dried up, will run forth amidst the meadows. Then will the fields be green and bountiful, and the woods clad in leaves the day that the Court will be found. Throughout the country the forests will become so great and thick, so fair and fresh, that every wayfarer journeying through the land will marvel at it.

A pause. The bell sounds five times. Sounds of sobbing and weeping are again heard for several minutes, followed by silence, and then by the tolling of the bell ringing six times to mark the coming of dawn and the end of the vigil.

The lights slowly come on. The Conductor enters.

CONDUCTOR

Seeker of the Grail, you have worthily accomplished your vigil. Arise, sheathe your sword, and come with me, for a feast is to be prepared for your reception.

The candidate does as instructed, and returns with the Conductor to the anteroom.

Second Point

Once the Conductor and candidate have gone to the anteroom, the decorations of the first chamber are removed and replaced by those of the second chamber. The table is set, but the bread and wine are not yet placed on it. The King and several other Companions sit at the table as though ready for the feast. A chair is left vacant for the candidate next to the King's chair. The music begins to play, and the Companions pretend to talk among themselves in quiet voices. Once all is prepared, the Knight goes to the anteroom door, knocks twice, and draws his sword.

The Conductor meanwhile explains to the candidate that certain things will pass by in a procession, and once they have gone out of the room, he/she must ask the King the question "Sire, what do these things mean?" The Conductor has the candidate repeat these words back. Once the Knight knocks at the door, the Conductor brings the candidate into the chamber.

KNIGHT

Conductor, who is this you bring with you?

CONDUCTOR

A worthy seeker of the Grail who has journeyed long by difficult ways in search of the court of the Rich Fisherman.

KNIGHT

Has he/she taken the necessary pledge of secrecy?

CONDUCTOR

> He/she has.

KNIGHT

> Has he/she kept vigil in the Chapel Perilous from midnight until dawn?

CONDUCTOR

> He/she has.

KNIGHT

> Then he/she is permitted to enter and partake of the feast of the Grail.

The Knight sheathes his sword and escorts the candidate to the table.

KNIGHT

> Most Wise King, I present to you a worthy seeker of the Grail who has journeyed long by difficult ways in search of the court of the Rich Fisherman. He/she has taken the necessary pledge of secrecy and has kept vigil in the Chapel Perilous from midnight until dawn.

KING

> Seeker of the Grail, I am pleased to hear of your courage and zeal. Come, sit beside me and partake of the feast of the Grail.

The candidate is seated next to the King. The Knight and several Companions leave the chamber and return with bread and wine, which they serve to the King, the candidate, and the seated Companions. Once bread and wine have been served, the King picks up a piece of bread and raises it in both hands.

KING

> May this bread be blessed by the Infinite One. May it become the bread of Life.

He breaks the bread, gives one piece to the candidate, and eats the other. Once the candidate has eaten, the King spreads his hands, palm down, over his and the candidate's cups of wine.

KING

> May this wine be blessed by the Infinite One. May it become the wine of Gnosis.

He takes his cup and motions to the candidate to do the same. They drink.

KING

> Seeker of the Grail, may the bread of Life and the wine of Gnosis sustain you in your quest now and always.

At this point, the music fades out and the chamber becomes very quiet. In the silence, the Grail procession files into the chamber. First comes the spear, carried point-up by one of the Companions. Then come two Companions carrying candlesticks with lit candles in them, one following the other. Finally the Lady comes bearing the Grail. Once the Grail appears, the King and the other guests rise to their feet, and the King signals the candidate to do the same. The procession goes through the chamber and leaves again, and once it has gone, the King sits down and the guests and the candidate do the same. At this point the candidate must ask the question:

CANDIDATE

> Sire, what do these things mean?

KING

> Seeker of the Grail, it is well for you to ask, though knowledge is not yet. Rejoice! For you have passed the last test that is set before those who seek the Grail. By reason of your asking of the question, the healing of the Waste Land shall begin, and the doors of our innermost mysteries shall be opened to you. You will depart from among us now for a short time, and upon your return, the ceremony of your reception will continue. Most Worthy Knight.

KNIGHT

> (approaches the table) Most Wise King.

KING

> Escort this worthy seeker of the Grail to the anteroom and command
> the Conductor to prepare him/her to be welcomed among the Com-
> pany of the Grail.

*The Knight escorts the candidate to the anteroom and repeats the King's words to the
Conductor there.*

Third Point

*Once the candidate has been returned to the anteroom, the decorations of the second
chamber are removed and replaced by those of the third chamber. The Grail and spear
are set in place, the King is seated on the throne with the Lady seated on his right and
the Knight on his left, so that the Lady is seated beside the Grail and the Knight beside
the spear. The other companions sit to either side. If there are Companions enough,
their chairs form a circle broken only on the side of the chamber facing the anteroom.
Once all is prepared, the Knight goes to the anteroom door and knocks three times. The
Conductor then brings in the Candidate and advances to the cushion before the throne.*

CONDUCTOR

> Most Wise King, I once again present to you this worthy seeker of the
> Grail who has now accomplished his/her quest.

KING

> Seeker of the Grail, before you may receive the secrets of our mystery
> and pass through the First Gate of the Gnosis, it is necessary for you
> to take a solemn obligation of fidelity and fellowship. Know that this
> obligation does not conflict with any duty you owe to your faith, your
> country, your family, or yourself. With this assurance, are you willing
> to take the obligation?

CANDIDATE

> I am.

KING

> (*rising from his throne*) Then you will kneel on both your knees.[154] (*The candidate kneels, the Conductor assisting if necessary.*) Draw your sword and place it in the same position in which you held it during your vigil. (*This is done. The King then places his right hand atop the candidate's hands and the hilt of the sword.*) All rise. (*The Companions rise.*) Repeat after me: "In the presence of the Grail—and of these witnesses—I promise and pledge—that I will ever remain—a faithful guardian—of the secrets confided into my keeping—that I will keep them secret—from every person in the world—except a worthy Companion of the Grail—or within a proper assembly—of the Company of the Grail—I further promise and pledge—that I will be—a true Companion and friend—to all the members of this Company—that I will defend them from harm—uphold their honor—point out their advantage—and guard their secrets—as I would my own—I further promise and pledge—that I will persevere—together with the members of this Company—in the pursuit of Gnosis—and in the quest for the lost wisdom—that will restore the land to fruitfulness—and share my discoveries freely—with all who pursue the same quest—All this I promise and pledge—upon my sacred honor—and may I be cast out forever—from the company of the wise and good—should I violate this—my solemn obligation."

KING

> Receive the blessing of Life, the First Gate of the Gnosis.

King leaves his right hand atop the candidate's hands and places his left hand on the candidate's head. He then silently repeats the words Kalakau, Salasau, Zeesar.[155] *He leaves his hands in place for a moment to allow the blessing to be transmitted, then takes away his hands.*

---

154. Again, if the candidate is physically unable to kneel, a chair may be substituted.

155. The three secret words of the ancient Gnostics, still used by many Gnostic churches today as a form of blessing.

KING

Arise, and be welcome among the Company of the Grail.

ALL PRESENT

(shout) Huzzah! Huzzah! Huzzah!

KING

Most Worthy Knight, you will communicate to our newest member the word of the Grail.

KNIGHT

(advances to stand before the candidate) My Companion, the password of our mystery is *(in a whisper)* Jebelon. *(In an ordinary voice)* Repeat it to me in a whisper. *(The candidate does so.)* This word comes down to us as part of the inheritance of the Knights Templar, who practiced these mysteries before our time. It comes from the Arabic word for "mountain," together with a suffix whose meaning is hidden from you as yet. It is not to be communicated to any person who has not received it in a proper fashion, as you have received it this day. *(Knight returns to stand in front of his chair.)*

KING

Most Noble Lady, you will communicate to our newest member the sign of the Grail.

LADY

(advances to stand before the candidate) My Companion, the sign of our mystery is made as follows. Raise your hands to the level of your face, the elbows being bent and the palms facing each other. Now bring your wrists together so that they touch, and cup your hands and fingers so that the hands resemble the upper part of a chalice and the forearms resemble the stem. This is the Sign of the Grail. Seen from in front, it appears as though your head is in a cup. This refers to those very ancient forms of the Grail legend in which a head in a cup, platter, or cauldron filled the place of the Grail. This sign is only to be made in an

assembly of the Company of the Grail. *(Lady returns to stand in front of her chair.)*

KING

Worthy finder of the Grail, because you have succeeded in your quest and found the Court of the Rich Fisherman, it is fitting that you be robed, crowned, and enthroned as King/Queen of the Grail.

The King, with the help of one or more of the Companions, takes off his cloak and fastens it about the shoulders of the candidate. He then takes off his crown and crowns the candidate with it, leads the candidate to the throne, and seats the candidate in it.

KING

Behold the new King/Queen of the Grail!

ALL PRESENT

(shout) Huzzah! Huzzah! Huzzah!

KING

Know that all the members of the Company of the Grail have been robed, crowned, and enthroned as you have been, and been greeted by the plaudits of their fellows as you have likewise been. For all among us are equal in honor, though not all are equal in the responsibilities they undertake.

Companions, be seated.

All present sit down. The King goes to the extra chair and sits.

KING

Attend now to the words of our Lecturer.

Any of the officers, or any of the Companions, may serve as Lecturer. The Lecturer rises and stands before the candidate.

LECTURER

> King/Queen of the Grail, you were admitted to our fellowship by a form of initiation that dates from the most ancient times and has been practiced in many nations to celebrate the mysteries of Life. That form of initiation is divided into three points. In the first point, you kept vigil in the presence of Death, surrounded by darkness and mourning. This was to remind you that Life is always born from Death, surrounded by Death, and consumed by Death, so that it may rise again triumphant over Death. In that first point you also heard repeated certain portions of that ancient legend of the Grail in which our mysteries were for so many years concealed and embodied.

> In the second point, you were seated at the feast of the Grail as one who had passed the preliminary tests. There you partook of the bread of Life and the wine of Gnosis, beheld the procession of the Grail, and asked the necessary question. The question you asked should always be in your mind when you encounter the legends and the symbols of olden times. Do not pass them by unthinkingly, or accept them at their most obvious value. "What do these things mean?" Let those words ever guide you, like a star in the darkness of the night.

> In the third point, you were brought among the Company of the Grail and there took the solemn obligation of fidelity and friendship. You were acclaimed as a member of the Company of the Grail and you received the word and the Sign of the Grail. You were then robed, crowned, and enthroned as King/Queen of the Grail as all members of our Company have been, and you were acclaimed as such. All this was symbolic of the triumph of Life over Death, and the victory achieved by those who succeed in passing through the First Gate.

The Lecturer returns to his or her place and sits. The King rises.

KING

> Worthy finder of the Grail, rise, and receive the congratulations of your Companions.

All the Companions rise, greet, and congratulate the new member of the Company.

To Close

Before the Closing, the King reclaims his crown and cloak, and he is seated again in the throne. All the Companions, including the new initiate, are seated.

KING

Most Worthy Knight, what is our last care when assembled?

KNIGHT

To see that our assembly is properly tiled.

KING

Do your duty then.

The Knight goes to the door and knocks once. He is answered with a single knock from the Conductor, who is again in the anteroom.

KNIGHT

Most Wise King, we are properly tiled.

KING

All please rise. *(All stand up.)* Most Noble Lady, what is the hour?

LADY

The hour of dawn, when the sun of hope and promise rises in the east to proclaim the eternal victory of Life over Death.

KING

Most Worthy Knight, of what is the Grail made?

KNIGHT

The stone named Lapsit Exillas.

KING

Most Noble Lady, what is the meaning of this name?

LADY

> Lapsit Ex Illas: it fell from among them.

KNIGHT

> Lapis Ex Caelis: a stone from heaven.

KING

> Lapis Exilis: the Stone of Exile. *(He extends his arms to both sides in the form of a cross.)* IAO. Such are the words. *(All make the Sign of the Grail.)*

KING

> In the name of the Holy Gnosis, I declare this gathering closed.

APPENDIX ONE

THE ELUCIDATION

The version of the *Elucidation* that appears here is from a copy of Chrétien de Troyes's *Perceval*, manuscript BN 12576. The translation is mine, based on the medieval French original; I have reviewed the earlier translations by Sebastian Evans and William W. Kibler.

◇

For a noble beginning, here worthily starts a romance of the most delightful story that can be, that is, the story of the Grail, whose secret no man should tell in prose or rhyme, for the story might turn out to be such a thing, when it is all told, that every man might suffer for it even though he had done nothing wrong. So the wise man leaves it alone and simply passes it by, for if Master Blihos does not lie, no man should tell this secret.

Now listen to me, all my friends, and you will hear me tell a story that will be a pleasure to listen to, for in it will be the seven Guardians that rule over the whole world, and all the good stories that have ever been told, as the writing shall set out: what manner of people the seven Guardians are, and how they chose a chief, and whom they chose, for never before have you heard the story told truly of which there was once so much noise and outcry, of how and why the rich country of Logres was destroyed, of which there was so much talk in days of yore.

The kingdom went to ruin, the land was dead and deserted so that it was scarce worth a couple of hazelnuts. For they lost the voices of the hills and the damsels that were in them. For this is the great service they once gave, that no one who wandered the roads by night or morning had to go out of his way except to find one of the hills, and then he could ask for nothing in the way of good and pleasing food that he could not have it at once, so long as he asked within reason. For straightaway, as I understand it, out of the hill would come a damsel—no one could ask for one more fair—bearing in her hand a cup of gold with baked meats, pastries, and bread, while another damsel bore a white napkin and a dish of gold or silver in which was the food that had come for the one who had asked for it. A fair welcome he would find at the hill, and if the food did not please him, they brought him others, and all with one accord, fairly and joyously, the damsels served all wayfarers on the roads that come to the wells for food.

King Amangons, the evil and craven-hearted, was the first to break the custom, and after him many others did the same thing, following the example of their king, whose duty it was to protect the damsels and to maintain and guard them within his peace. He forced himself on one of the damsels and took her virginity to her great sorrow, and stole from her the cup of gold and took it with him, and afterward had himself served with it every day. He richly deserved the fate he suffered. For after that the damsel never served anyone, nor did any other come out of that hill to serve any man who came there asking for food. And all the others did the same.

The other vassals that were honored by the king, when they saw that their lord raped the damsels whenever he found them pretty, forced themselves on them in the same way and carried off the cups of gold, so that after that the damsels never came from the hills or offered their service. This, my lords, was how the land had its downfall, and the king and everyone else who wronged the damsels all suffered a terrible fate. The kingdom was laid waste so that no tree bore leaves. The meadows and the flowers withered and the waters dried up, nor could anyone find the Court of the Rich Fisherman that had once made the land a glittering glory of gold and silver, of ermine and miniver, of rich silk brocades, of food and of fabric, of gyrfalcons and merlins and tiercels and sparrowhawks and peregrine falcons. But once the Court could be found, throughout the country was so much of the riches I have named that I promise you all men marveled at it whether they were rich or poor. After that, as it had once lost everything, so now in the kingdom of Logres was all the richness of the world.

The Peers of the Table Round came in the time of King Arthur. None so good as they have ever been seen since. They were such good knights, so worthy, so strong, so proud, so powerful, and so hardy, that when they had heard the story of the adventures, they immediately wanted to restore the wells. All of them with one will swore an oath to protect the damsels that had been driven out of them and the cups that had been carried away, and to destroy utterly the descendants of those that had wronged them. For these dwelt so close to the wells that the damsels could not go out; and if they could catch any of the maidens, they hanged her or put her to the sword. The knights gave alms and prayed to God that He would restore the wells to their previous condition, and asked that for His honor He would do them the service they asked of Him. But no matter how they searched, they could find nothing. Never a voice could they hear from the wells, nor would any damsel come forth from them.

But thereafter they found so great an adventure that they greatly marveled at it. For in the forest they found damsels as fair as you could ask, and with them knights fully armed upon their chargers, who protected the damsels, and fought against anyone who tried to carry the damsels off. Many a knight they killed, for on account of the damsels, I understand, there was many a battle in the land. For this reason King Arthur could not keep from losing many a good knight, and many a good knight did he gain as well, as the story will tell you.

The knight who was defeated first was named Blihos Bliheris, and Sir Gawain defeated him by means of his great prowess. Gawain sent him to yield himself to King Arthur, and Blihos mounted his horse without tarrying. When he came to the court he surrendered, and though neither King Arthur nor anyone else knew him, he knew such good stories that no one ever grew weary of listening to his words. The people of the court asked him about the damsels that rode through the forest even though it was not yet summer, and they had every right to ask and expect an answer. And he knew how to tell the story so well that they eagerly listened to him, and many a night the damsels and the knights went to find him and listen to him.

He said to them: "You marvel greatly at the damsels that you see going among these great forests, and cannot keep from asking in what country we are born. I will tell you the truth of the matter. We are all descended from the damsels, the most beautiful in the world, that King Amangons raped. Never as long as the world shall last will that wrong be set right. The Peers of the Table Round with their courtesy and honor, with their prowess and valor, have gone forth to restore the wells, of which these men are the squires and knights and nobles. I will tell you the sum of it. They will all journey together, along with the damsels that wander at large through this country by forest and field. They must do this until God shall permit them to find the Court from which shall come the joy by which the land shall be made bright again. To those who seek the Court will befall adventures such as were never before encountered or told in this land." This, which he told and sung to them, was much to their liking, and they were very well pleased.

Soon thereafter the good knights of the court held a great assembly and each made ready to set forth. Boldly then they sought for the Court of the Rich Fisherman, who knew so much about magic that he could change his appearance a hundred times, so that one who sees him in one guise will not know him again when he appeared in another fashion.

Sir Gawain found the Rich Fisherman when Arthur was King, and did indeed come to his Court. You will be told all about the joy that he had there, by which all the kingdom was made better. But before him, the first to find it was a knight of very youthful age, though none more full of courage was to be found in all the world. Then there came to the Table Round the young man I have mentioned, whose prowess surpassed all the knights that ever were or now are in all the countries of the world. He was thought to be of no account at first, yet afterward he was known to be of noble birth, and so thoroughly did he search the land for those that wanted to conquer it, that he found the Court. This is true, and many of you know it. He was Perceval the Welshman. He asked what the Graal served, but did not ask why the Lance bled, when he saw it, nor about the Sword of which one half was taken away and the other lay in the bier over one who lay dead, or about the manner of the great disappearance. But I tell you for certain that he asked about the treasure that was in the hall and the rich cross of silver that came in front of all.

For three hours at a time, three times a day, there was lamentation so great that no man, no matter how brave, could hear it without being stricken with fear. Then they hung four censers on four rich candlesticks that were at the corners of the bier. When they had done the service, straightway the cries continued again, and every man vanished away. The hall, great and wide, remained empty and terrible, and the stream of blood ran from the vessel the held the Lance through the rich channel of silver.

Then the palace filled with folk and knights, and the fairest feast in all the world was made ready. Then the unknown King came forth in all his apparel. From a chamber he came forth robed. He came wearing garments so splendid attire that no one could describe his robe or its ornaments, so passing rich it was, and on his finger had he a splendid ring, and his arms were tightly folded, and upon his head a circlet of gold with stones worth a fortune, and a beautiful belt and buckle. No one could ever find a more handsome man living, and none who saw him could guess that they had seen him earlier the same day dressed as a fisherman.

As soon as the King was seated, then you would see all the knights seated at the other high tables. Then the bread was quickly served and the wine put before them in great cups of gold and silver. After that you would see the Graal come through the chamber door without servant or bearer and serve in a worthy fashion onto dishes of gold that were worth a great fortune. The first serving it put before the King, and then it served all the others around him, and the food it brought to them was no less than a wonder. And then came the great wonder to which no other can be compared.

You will never hear me speak of it, however, for Perceval ought to tell it hereafter in the course of the story, for it is a great mistake and a great shame to tell a good story bit by bit and not the way it ought to go. When the good knight comes who found the Court three times, then you will hear me explain point by point, without making anything up, the truth about the wells, whom they served, of whom these were the knights, and what the Graal served, and I will tell you everything about the Lance that bled, and why the sword was on the bier. I will tell you all and leave nothing out: the lamentation, the vanishing, all of it I will tell those who hear me speak so that they will know after this how the work ought to proceed.

My lords, it is the proven truth that the Court was found seven times in the seven Cloaks of the story. But you do not yet know what this signifies. You must understand, then, that the seven Cloaks are in truth the seven Guardians. Each of these Guardians in his turn will tell you how he found the Court, and this ought not to be told beforehand. Now it is proper for me to name all the seven Guardians, for I would not want to leave out any of them. Rather, I want to name them clearly and speak of them in the order in which they are to be set forth.

The seventh Cloak, which is most pleasant, concerns the Lance with which Longinus smote the side of the King of holy majesty, and the sixth, without question, is the great content of the labor. In the fifth, I shall tell you about the wrath and the loss of Huden. The story of Heaven is the fourth, for no coward was he, the dead knight in the boat that came first to Glamorgan. The next is the third, about the warrior who so frightened Castrars. Pecorin the son of Amangon always carried the scar in his forehead. Now have I named the third to you. The second is not told in verse, according to what good storytellers say. It is the story of the great sorrows, and how Lancelot du Lac came to the place where he lost his virtue. And finally comes the last. Since I have undertaken the task, it is proper for me to tell it, and you shall hear me begin without delay. It is the adventure of the Shield, and there never was a better one.

These are the seven authentic stories that proceed from the Graal. This adventure brought about such joy, that afterward the people repopulated the land after the great destruction. Indeed it was the finding of the Court and the Graal that cause the realm to be repopulated, so that the waters which had stopped running, and the fountains which had stopped flowing, having dried up, ran forth amidst the meadows. Then were the fields green and bountiful, and the woods clad in leaves the day that the Court was found. Throughout the country the forests became so great and thick, so fair and fresh, that every wayfarer journeying through the land marveled at it.

Then came back a people who were full of malice, that is, those who came from the wells but were not cooks. They made castles and cities and towns and strongholds, and built for the damsels the rich Castle of Maidens. They made the Perilous Bridge also, and the great Castle Orguellous. Out of their nobility and lordship they made an order of the Peers of the Rich Household, and in their great pride they set it against the Table Round. It was well known by all the world that each of these knights had his mistress therein, and a splendid life they led. Three hundred sixty-six of them defended the castle, and each of these had twenty knights, of which he was lord; unless I am mistaken, they numbered 7,686. But you should know that they strove in vain, for not one of them may be found in the world any more. They rode through the land and made war upon King Arthur, and the good knights of the court went forth to challenge them, and you should know that when they caught one they did not loosen their grip till they had slain him.

King Arthur wished to go and throw down the castle and destroy it, but everyone that hated him then attacked him at this point and did battle with him, so he had no need to go looking for war. So great were the wars as at this time, that they lasted a good four years, as the story tells us, and so does the man that wrote the book, and so I tell you one by one. He wants you to show everyone what the Graal served, for the service it gave should be shown by a good master, so that the good things that it serves should no longer be hidden, for he will teach it freely to everyone, just as you have heard.

This King Arthur of whom I speak waged war against the folk of his land for four years. But he drew all this to an end, so that there was no no vassal nor neighbour that did not do his will in his land, either freely or by force. This is the proven truth. But you should also know this, that the war turned to their shame and to the honour of the King, as most of you know, for on the very day the Court and the Rich Household were set free, they went hunting in the forest, and those that would rather go hawking followed the good rivers. This is how they behaved. Some only wanted to make love, and others to do other things as they wished. They did nothing but make merry all through the winter until summer came.

ΛPPENDIX TWO
"THE RUINED TEMPLE" BY JESSIE WESTON

"The Ruined Temple" was originally published in *The Quest Magazine* in October 1916. It has been in the public domain for many years, but as far as I know this is its first reprinting.

◇

The traveller looked around him. He was standing on a headland jutting out into the sea. The summit of the cliff as far inland as eye could reach was a wild moorland studded with clumps of gorse and heather, now, in the middle of August, a glory of gold and purple.

At intervals amidst the low clumps of heather stood blocks of grey stone and fallen masonry, scattered, irregular in outline. Yet it was not difficult for a trained eye to discern a certain order and design in their relative positions. Evidently they explained themselves to the observer, for he nodded with keen satisfaction as his eye followed their outline.

"Yes, the building must have been here on the brow of the cliff looking sea-ward. These blocks give the outline approximately—circular evidently. And those monoliths further back mark the approach. Now what was it?—castle—temple?"

His eye fell upon a mound higher, of larger extent, than the surrounding clumps of heather and gorse. It was overgrown with brambles and tall bracken, and the outline was but ill-defined; still there was that about it which betrayed a not altogether fortuitous origin.

He strolled up to it, and began to probe about with his stout walking stick. The soil was shallow. At the depth of perhaps a foot the stick struck on some-thing hard and unyielding.

"Thought as much," he muttered to himself. "There was something here." He walked round, still probing carefully with his stick as he did so. In the midst of the tangle he met with no impenetrable resistance, but at either end, for per-haps a couple of feet, there was evidently stone or masonry. He drove his stick upward through the tangle of growth. At about three feet from the ground he again met a similar obstacle, this time for the depth of a few inches only. Care-fully following this he found that the upper stonework continued at either end somewhat beyond the lower.

"A block of stone on supports of stone or masonry, obviously. Now was it a table or an altar?"

He looked round him keenly. The erection, be it what it might, was placed midway between the heather-encircled blocks of stone. Facing seaward he saw straight in front of him, rising from the tangle of gorse and heather, two corre-sponding monoliths some six feet in height; one still stood erect, the other had sunk sideways to an acute angle. In their original positions they would have framed, for one standing where he stood, a full view of the western sky. At this moment the sun within half an hour of setting was shining full in his face.

He wheeled round. Directly behind him were again monoliths apparently corresponding in height and relative position to the western pair. He paced the distance from the mound to each group. It was practically the same allowing for the irregularities of the overgrowth. He uttered an exclamation of satisfaction.

"Temple evidently! This was the altar; and there were openings east and west for the rising and setting sun. Probably there was one in the roof directly above the altar for the midday. An ordinary dwelling would hardly be so planned. Now who were the people who used it?"

Seating himself on the ground, his back to the altar mound, facing the western outlook, he opened his knapsack and proceeded to make his evening meal of sandwiches and hard-boiled eggs washed down by a bottle of cider. Then lighting his pipe he lay down, hat over his eyes, and proceeded to muse drowsily over the problem.

Who and what had been the people who worshipped in this ruined sanctuary?

The Druids? In that case he would have expected to find trees near at hand. Certainly we knew but little of the details of Druidic Worship. Yet if we bore in mind the important part the oak played in their ritual, would they have been likely to build a temple in so bare and sparsely wooded a district? He had seen no tree worthy of the name in his day's tramp.

If not the Druids, who then? The early Celtic dwellers in these islands? "We know precious little of their beliefs and practices," he muttered to himself. Had there been any other folk? Any settlement? This was a coastline. Suddenly a thought struck him and he sat up. "By Jove! yes, the Phoenicians!" It was not unlikely. This part of the country had once been rich in tin mines. They had fallen out of working long since; but the tradition remained. And his keen eye had noted in certain of the village churches he had explored quaint symbols which he knew to be derived from the old-time community of miners. Clasping his hands around his knees, he looked steadily westward. Yes, there might have been a Phoenician colony here in long-forgotten days. They might have built this temple and celebrated their rites. But what rites?

He drew at his pipe thoughtfully. To think of the Phoenicians was to think of Adonis—that fair youth whose death, burial and resurrection played so marked a role in the solemnities of the Syrian year; whose worship had spread far beyond the bounds of his own land. He was sufficient scholar to be well aware of the importance which the authorities on Comparative Religion had learned of late years to attach to these Nature rituals, traces of which were to be found in all lands. Here in our islands, however, we did not know the name of Adonis. That was true; yet all the essentials of the cult had been traced in fragmentary survivals—our seasonal festivals, folk-dances, mumming plays. "Yes, we had the ritual sure enough," he muttered to himself. But where did it come from? Did it grow up spontaneously in different lands, each folk at a given stage of its development having the same conception of a god, ever youthful, ever dying, ever living, on whose beneficent activities all life, vegetable and animal, depended? Or had there been a borrowing? And if there had been contact, and contact on a practically permanent scale, as must have been the case with a foreign community settled on our shore, could there have been anything else?

It was growing dusk now. The traveller refilled his pipe, lay down on the grass and, his hands clasped behind his head, continued his train of thought. Supposing the Phoenicians had been settled in this part of the country, was not this just the spot they might have chosen for a temple? He thought of the great temple at Byblos, the centre of the Adonis cult on the shore looking westward over the sea across whose waves the unfailing current should bring the god from the Egyptian shore. Yes, this was a likely spot for their rites. But of what character would be the worship? Not merely the popular manifestations of sorrow and joy; they would be but an outer part. And here, in a strange land, with but a small public to take part, they would be shorn of much of their importance. No, in a foreign country such as this had been, the cult, restricted to a limited number of worshippers, must have been more personal than public, more esoteric than exoteric in character.

"Of course," he mused, "there was more in the business than these popular rejoicings and lamentations. It wasn't just the spring god, '*la jeunesse éternelle,*' they were worshipping.[156] The old priests and the inner ring knew better than that. What they were after was the ultimate Source of Life. Wonder how far they got? If they got at anything much beyond the physiological facts? After all we have gone little further. Is there more to know? Admitting the possibility of their having known more, what was it? And how did they get at it?"

The night had closed in, soft, fragrant with the aromatic perfume of gorse and heather. From the beach many feet below came the soothing splash and withdrawal of the small waves breaking with idle reiteration at the foot of the cliff. They seemed to say dreamily: "Listen, we are here; but we are doing nothing, neither harm nor good. We are alive, we are strong; but for the moment our life is slumbering, our strength quiescent. We are resting; rest like us."

Listening to their distant murmur, at ease on his couch of turf and bracken, the man fell asleep.

---

156. *La jeunesse éternelle*: French for "eternal youth."

◇

But was it sleep that fettered him? This strange sensation of sinking downward, downward into an unfathomable depth of darkness? He was powerless to struggle or cry out. His limbs, his senses were borne down by an unutterable sensation of horror...Now he felt firm ground beneath his feet. He was standing upright. But where? In what surroundings? Everything was dark. He dared not move.

Gradually he became conscious of a faint bluish light, or rather of a luminous atmosphere, enabling him dimly to discern his surroundings. He was standing in a small walled space, with columns on either side of him. All was black—floor, walls, the pillar against which he stood, black and cold with a chill that struck to the very depths of his being. Before him, on a black slab raised on a pedestal and approached by steps, lay a still white form behind which burned tapers in tall silver candlesticks, their light seemingly concentrated into two small gleaming points that peered like fiery eyes through the all-pervading haze. Gradually his vision cleared. He grasped what lay before him. It was a dead body, the body of a man, stiff, rigid, with the unmistakable hue of dissolution creeping over it. He had seen dead men before, many times. He had fought as volunteer through a fierce campaign, had seen friend and foe fall around him; yet never had he felt such horror as now lay upon him.

This was not a dead man; it was Death itself—Death in its subtle relentless work of disintegration, going on before his eyes, nay within him. That was the horror. There was something in the place itself, in the environment, which was slowly, relentlessly laying hold of the very springs of his being.

Slowly, slowly, as the grey shadows were creeping over the dead body, so the bitter cold was creeping upward, upward to his heart and brain. He felt his limbs failing and laid his hand for support on the pillar beside him. It was cold, with a chill that struck him to the very heart. Yet he could still think dimly. Through the slowly enveloping cold, the awful horror of approaching dissolution, he felt there was something on which he could lay hold, some weapon of defence against this insidious foe. With a tremendous effort be recalled his thoughts from the contemplation of the horror that beset him and bent his energies inward.

Ah! he had it now, the talisman! This that threatened him, threatened the outward form only, not the I, the Principle of Life itself; that lay deeper, beyond the touch of physical death.

He understood now. Life, true Life, was indestructible. Once called into existence it was and would continue to be. Death, physical death, could lay hold on the body only, the temporary vesture with which Life had clothed itself. Here and now it was still in his power to deny Death that prey.

"I live!" The words were uttered at first feebly, then with gaining strength at each reiterated affirmation; till at last his voice rang in a triumphant shout through the vault.

The atmosphere was growing clearer. The strange blue haze was changing colour, becoming suffused with a rosy hue. Over the limbs of the dead man a faint flush was creeping. Was it the flush of returning life? Now the walls around him seemed to fall away; the chapel-vault was widening to a hall. There was light, voices. With a sensation of unutterable relief he knew he was no longer alone. There were men round him in strange garb, with outstretched hands and friendly faces. He gathered he was being welcomed as one long-looked-for and expected, one who had dared and overcome a great danger and reached an appointed goal.

He was entering another hall now, brilliantly lighted, full of folk. One came to meet him in whom he instinctively recognised the host, a tall benign figure, regal, hierarchical, one who might well be both priest and king. He could not tell what words were spoken. It was strange; he seemed to hear no words, and yet to know what was said. He realized that he had passed triumphantly the first stage of a test, a stage beset with grave and terrible danger. He was at a halting place, a moment of rest and refreshment. There was still more to be achieved. He was conscious of a great lassitude, yet of an underlying tension.

He was seated by his host now at a table. Platters of silver, cups of precious metal, were before them. Up and down the hall moved youths bearing great pitchers from which they poured wine into the cups, filling them to the brim. He set the cup to his lips. The draught ran glowing through his veins, filling him with new vigour. But he was hungry and would fain eat. Where was the food? Why did it delay?

He looked up and met his host's eyes bent on him, calmly, kindly, as one measuring alike his strength and his understanding. Silently he waited. Suddenly there was a stir in the hall. He saw nothing, he heard nothing; yet the atmosphere was vibrant with a force that all seemed to feel. Old men straightened their bent shoulders and sat upright; pallid faces became flushed and rosy; eyes were keen and bright. What had happened? Something had passed through the hall—something that had left behind it an invigorating potency. And behold, the table was no longer bare. Before each man the platter was heaped with viands, strange meats and fruits such as he had never seen, of an odour, a fragrance, enticing to the senses.

He looked at his host and felt rather than heard himself put the question: "What passed but now?"

He felt also his host's reply, given with a gladness of response: "Thou hast done well to ask, though knowledge is not yet. Eat of the Food of Life!" And he ate, feeling his youth renewed within him.

All languor and weariness had left him now; mind and body were refreshed. All disappointment, all sense of disillusion had vanished like a cloud. He was as one who midway through a long and weary journey should find himself suddenly re-endowed with the vigour and energy, the sense of joyful anticipation, with which he set out upon his course. He ate and drank, and his heart grew light within him.

$$\diamondsuit$$

Suddenly he became conscious that he was alone. Host and fellow guests had vanished. How or whither he could not tell. He had not seen them pass. The sound of music was in his ears, the scent of flowers was in the air. Now a group of fair maidens surrounded him. He was disrobed by deft hands and led to a couch heaped with soft cushions and silken coverings. He lay down, conscious of a languor that was hardly weariness; for his pulses throbbed with the vigour of youth and through his veins ran the fiery impulse of desire.

His eyes took in the beauty of the attendant maidens—their shining eyes and perfumed hair, their white limbs scarcely veiled by the thin gauze of their robes. He was young and they were fair—and willing. He had but to make his choice.

"See," they whispered, "We await thy will. Time passes. Youth endures but for a short space. Choose now among us. Youth and maiden, we were made the one for the other. We, we are the Source of Life. Without us Life would cease to be."

He listened and his senses gave assent to their pleading. Yet even as he did so he was conscious of a questioning within him—of a dim groping after a deeper-lying truth. Before his mind rose the vision of the black chapel and the lifeless body. The horror of his experience was again upon him. What had he learnt then? Surely that beyond and beneath the mystery of physical life lay another and a deeper mystery! Slowly it dawned upon him that, though clothed in so different a form, the test confronting him was the same. It was the temptation to rest content with the life of the body—its beginning, its end; to stop short in the quest for the hidden Source of Life itself; to mistake the proximate for the ultimate. He scarce knew what he felt, what were the motives prompting him; but dimly he apprehended that to take what was offered now would be a practical renunciation of the ground already won, a denial of the experience gained. It would be to accept the lower, to reject the higher, solution of the problem. As he had faced the test of bodily dissolution by an affirmation of the indestructibility of Life, so now, before the insistent and insidious claim of the supremacy of bodily Life, he gave utterance to the growing conviction within him: " I live indeed by the Flesh; yet not by the Flesh alone."

And as his mind seized this conviction and his lips affirmed his belief, the music grew fainter, the faces and forms of the maidens receded into the distance…He was once more alone.

It was broad daylight now; and again he was one of many. He was clad in white and stood with others in an ordered ring, within the walls of a circular building. Before and behind him, through open doorways, the light and air streamed in, a fresh pungent air laden with the salt tang of the sea, and an aromatic perfume that in some strange way seemed familiar to his senses. In the centre of the vaulted roof was an opening through which the rays of the sun were striking obliquely. He foresaw that very shortly, at midday, the full glory of the light would pour downward…On what?

Below this central opening stood a flat stone slab raised on four supporting blocks of masonry. On this, exactly under the opening, stood a vessel, a silver cup in which a spear stood upright. Ceaselessly, from the point of the spear, a thin stream of blood trickled slowly downward into the vessel below.

Behind the altar, facing eastward, stood his host. If before he had seemed to combine in himself the attributes of priest and king, now he was all priest, as in gorgeous broidered robes with filleted hair he stood with folded hands and uplifted eyes awaiting the revelation.

It came slowly, gradually. The point of the spear caught the sunlight, caught and held it. The light spread downward, downward. Now the weapon had changed into a quivering shaft of flame. It was as if the light, flowing downward, were not merely caught and held, but returned upon itself in an upward aspiration. Steadily the illumination grew. The liquid within the cup, suffused with light, swelled upward, a rosy stream on either side of the central flame, overflowing, pouring downward. It was no longer cup and spear, but a glowing Fiery Heart.

"Behold the Flesh transformed by Spirit."

He felt rather than heard the words, all his being intent upon the revelation before him.

Gradually he became aware that the Heart was no mere form, but a quivering, pulsing, centre of Life. Around it the glory grew and spread—a soft rosy glow, quickened as with the beating of countless wings. A ceaseless tremor as of Life pouring downward, soaring upward, spreading outward, till he felt himself touched with the quickening rays, drawn in toward the glowing centre. He thrilled with a strange poignant bliss, so keen that it was almost agony. Life was pouring into him in every vein, his pulses throbbing with an excess of Life. He was drawing closer, closer, to the very Fount of Life itself. In a very ecstasy of Being it was as if he ceased to be.

With a start the traveller sat upright. It was morning. The sun had risen above the horizon. Below, the wavelets already touched with its beams were breaking idly on the sand. A lark sang shrilly above his head.

He looked round him smiling; then rose to his feet. He was conscious of a strange feeling of refreshment; youth seemed to have returned. Dimly he knew he had passed through some great experience; but what? He could not remember. Had he had a dream? A vision?

He paused, musing. Had he not somewhere read of the practice of Incubation? Of the virtues of the Temple-sleep? These were Temple ruins, he was sure. Was there something in the tradition after all?

With a whimsical smile on his lips, he began digging with his stick under a block of stone which lay close to where he had slept. With an effort, using the stick as a lever, he raised it to an upright position. "Beth-El!" he murmured softly, raising his hat as he turned away.

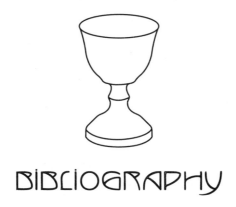

BIBLIOGRAPHY

Ashe, Geoffrey. *Camelot and the Vision of Albion*. London: Heinemann, 1971.

———. *Mythology of the British Isles*. North Pomfret, VT: Trafalgar Square, 1992.

Barber, Richard W. *The Holy Grail: Imagination and Belief*. Cambridge, MA: Harvard University Press, 2004.

Beaumont, Matthew. "Socialism and Occultism at the *Fin de Siècle*: Elective Affinities." *Victorian Review* 36, no. 1 (Spring 2010): 217–32. https://doi.org/10.1353/vcr.2010.0048.

Birge, Darice Elizabeth. "Sacred Groves in the Ancient Greek World." PhD diss., University of California, Berkeley, 1982.

Blacker, Carmen. *The Catalpa Bow: A Study of Shamanistic Practices in Japan*. London: Allen and Unwin, 1986.

Bower, Herbert M. *The Elevation & Procession of the Ceri at Gubbio: An Account of the Ceremonies*. London: David Nutt, 1897.

Bradley, Ian C. *William Morris and His World*. New York: Charles Scribner's Sons, 1978.

Burke, John, and Kaj Halberg. *Seed of Knowledge, Stone of Plenty: Understanding the Lost Technology of the Ancient Megalith-Builders*. San Francisco: Council Oak Books, 2005.

Burkert, Walter. *Greek Religion*. Translated by John Raffan. Cambridge, MA: Harvard University Press, 1985.

Burl, Aubrey. *Prehistoric Avebury*. New Haven, CT: Yale University Press, 1979.

Carey, John. *Ireland and the Grail*. Aberystwyth, Wales: Celtic Studies Publications, 2007.

Carter, Lin. *Tolkien: A Look Behind the Lord of the Rings*. New York: Ballantine, 1969.

Cooper-Oakley, Isabel. *Traces of a Hidden Tradition in Masonry and Medieval Mysticism*. London: Theosophical Publishing House, 1900.

Croteau, Jeffrey, Alan E. Foulds, and Aimee E. Newell. *The 1783 Francken Manuscript*. Lexington, MA: Supreme Council of the Ancient and Accepted Scottish Rite, 2017.

da Silva, Sara Graça, and Jamshid J. Tehrani. "Comparative Phylogenetic Analyses Uncover the Ancient Roots of Indo-European Folktales." *Royal Society Open Science* 3 no. 1 (January 2016): 1–11. http://dx.doi.org/10.1098/rsos.150645.

Davies, Stevan L. *The Gospel of Thomas and Christian Wisdom*. New York: The Seabury Press, 1983.

de Hoyos, Arturo, and Alain Bernheim, eds. *Freemasonry's Royal Secret: The Jamaican "Francken Manuscript" of the High Degrees*. Washington, DC: Scottish Rite Research Society, 2014.

———, and S. Brent Morris, eds. *The Most Secret Mysteries of the High Degrees of Masonry Unveiled*. Washington, DC: Scottish Rite Research Society, 2012.

de Santillana, Giorgio, and Hertha von Dechend. *Hamlet's Mill: An Essay Investigating the Origins of Human Knowledge and Its Transmission through Myth*. Boston: Gambit, 1969.

Drummond, John G. "Mystery Cults in Roman Britain." Master's thesis, University of Southampton, 2013.

Eisler, Robert. *Orpheus the Fisher: Comparative Studies in Orphic and Early Christian Cult Symbolism.* London: J. M. Watkins, 1921.

Eliot, T. S. *The Waste Land, and Other Poems.* New York: Harvest Books, 1934.

Evans, Sebastian, trans. *The Elucidation.* Ancient Texts. Accessed February 13, 2020. www.ancienttexts.org/library/celtic/ctexts/elucidation.html.

Evans-Wentz, W. Y. *The Fairy-Faith in Celtic Countries.* New York: Citadel, 1966.

Fuchs, M., A. Lang, and G. A. Wagner. "The History of Holocene Soil Erosion in the Phlious Basin, NE Peloponnese, Greece, Based on Optical Dating." *The Holocene* 14, no. 3 (2004): 334–45.

Gaffney, Mark H. *Gnostic Secrets of the Naassenes.* Rochester, VT: Inner Traditions, 2004.

Gargola, Daniel J. *Lands, Laws, and Gods: Magistrates and Ceremony in the Regulation of Public Lands in Republican Rome.* Chapel Hill: University of North Carolina Press, 1995.

Gerald of Wales. *The Journey through Wales and the Description of Wales.* Translated by Lewis Thorpe. London: Penguin, 1978.

Goldin, Owen. "The Ecology of *Critias* and Platonic Metaphysics." In *The Greeks and the Environment,* by Laura Westra and Thomas More Robinson, 73–80. Lanham, MD: Rowman & Littlefield, 1997.

Greer, John Michael. *The Celtic Golden Dawn: An Original & Complete Curriculum of Druidical Study.* Woodbury, MN: Llewellyn Publications, 2013.

———. *The Mysteries of Merlin: Ceremonial Magic for the Druid Path.* Woodbury, MN: Llewellyn Publications, 2020.

———. *The Secret of the Temple: Earth Energies, Sacred Geometry, and the Lost Keys of Freemasonry.* Woodbury, MN: Llewellyn Publications, 2016.

———, and Christopher Warnock, trans. *Picatrix: The Classic Medieval Handbook of Astrological Magic.* Iowa City, IA: Adocentyn Press, 2010.

Hahn, Robert. *Anaximander and the Architects: The Contributions of Egyptian and Greek Architectural Technologies to the Origins of Greek Philosophy*. Albany: State University of New York Press, 2001.

Hall, Manly P. *Lectures on Ancient Philosophy*. New York: TarcherPerigee, 2005.

———. *Orders of the Quest: The Holy Grail*. Los Angeles: Philosophical Research Society, 1996.

Hanson, Victor Davis. *The Other Greeks: The Family Farm and the Agrarian Roots of Western Civilization*. New York: Free Press, 1995.

Hawkins, Gerald S. *Stonehenge Decoded*. New York: Dell, 1965.

Henderson, Philip. *William Morris: His Life, Work, and Friends*. New York: McGraw Hill, 1967.

Hesiod. "Theogony" and "Works and Days." In *Hesiod and Theognis*, translated by Dorothea Wender. New York: Penguin, 1973.

Hughes, J. Donald. *Pan's Travail: Environmental Problems of the Ancient Greeks and Romans*. Baltimore, MD: Johns Hopkins University Press, 1994.

Hutton, Ronald. *The Rise and Fall of Merry England: The Ritual Year 1400–1700*. Oxford: Oxford University Press, 1994.

———. *The Triumph of the Moon: A History of Modern Pagan Witchcraft*. Oxford: Oxford University Press, 1999.

Hyde, Walter Woodburn. *Greek Religion and Its Survivals*. New York: Cooper Square Publishers, 1963.

Kahane, Henry, and Renée Kahane. *The Krater and the Grail: Hermetic Sources of the Parzival*. Urbana: University of Illinois Press, 1965.

Kalogera, Lucy Shepard. "Yeats's Celtic Mysteries." PhD diss., Florida State University, 1977.

Kibler, William W., trans. *The Elucidation*. The Camelot Project. Accessed February 4, 2020. https://d.lib.rochester.edu/camelot/text/elucidation.

Lacy, Norris J., and Geoffrey Ashe. *The Arthurian Handbook*. New York: Garland, 1988.

Laing, Gordon L. *Survivals of Roman Religion*. New York: Cooper Square Publishers, 1963.

Lambert, Timothy James. *The Gnostic Notebook, Volume One: On Memory Systems and Fairy Tales*. Self-published, 2015.

Loomis, Roger Sherman. "Bleheris and the Tristram Story." *Modern Language Notes* 39, no. 6 (June 1924): 319–29.

———."Onomastic Riddles in Malory's 'Book of Arthur and His Knights.'" *Medium Ævum* 25, no. 3 (1956): 181–90. https://doi.org/10.2307/43631130.

Matthews, Caitlin, and John Matthews. *The Lost Book of the Grail*. Rochester, VT: Inner Traditions, 2019.

Matthews, John, and Marian Green. *The Grail Seeker's Companion: A Guide to the Grail Quest in the Aquarian Age*. Wellingborough, UK: Thorsons, 1986.

Meyer, Marvin W., ed. *The Ancient Mysteries: A Sourcebook of Sacred Texts*. Philadelphia: University of Pennsylvania Press, 1987.

Michell, John. *New Light on the Ancient Mystery of Glastonbury*. Glastonbury, UK: Gothic Image Publications, 1997.

Morris, John. *The Age of Arthur: A History of the British Isles from 350 to 650*. New York: Charles Scribner's Sons, 1973.

Morris, William. *The Well at the World's End I & II*. New York: Ballantine Books, 1970.

Murphy, G. Ronald. *Gemstone of Paradise: The Holy Grail in Wolfram's Parzival*. Oxford: Oxford University Press, 2006.

Mylonas, G. E. *Mycenae's Last Century of Greatness*. London: Methuen, 1968.

Nichols, Ross. *The Book of Druidry*. London: Aquarian Press, 1990.

———, and James Kirkup. *The Cosmic Shape*. London: Forge, 1946.

Nitze, William A. "The Fisher King in the Grail Romances." *PMLA* 24, no. 3 (1909): 365–418. https://www.jstor.org/stable/456840.

———. "The Sister's Son and the Conte del Graal." *Modern Philology* 9, no. 2 (January 1912): 291–322. https://www.jstor.org/stable/432438.

Ovid. *Metamorphoses*. Translated by Mary M. Innes. London: Penguin Classics, 1955.

Phillips, Graham. *The Chalice of Magdalene: The Search for the Cup that Held the Blood of Christ*. Rochester, VT: Bear & Co., 2004.

Robb, Graham. *The Debatable Land: The Lost World Between Scotland & England*. New York: W. W. Norton, 2018.

Roberts, Allen E. *The Craft and Its Symbols: Opening the Door to Masonic Symbolism*. Richmond, VA: Macoy Publishing, 1974.

Robinson, John J. *Born in Blood: The Lost Secrets of Freemasonry*. New York: M. Evans & Company, 1989.

Rogers, Guy MacLean. *The Mysteries of Artemis of Ephesos: Cult, Polis, and Change in the Graeco-Roman World*. New Haven, CT: Yale University Press, 2012.

Rouse, Robert, and Cory Rushton. *The Medieval Quest for Arthur*. Stroud, UK: Tempus, 2005.

Sallares, Robert. *The Ecology of the Ancient Greek World*. Ithaca, NY: Cornell University Press, 1991.

Sallust. *On the Gods and the World*. Translated by Thomas Taylor. Los Angeles: Philosophical Research Society, 1976.

Scholem, Gershom. *The Origins of the Kabbalah*. Princeton: Princeton University Press, 1990.

Schuchard, Marsha Keith. *Emanuel Swedenborg, Secret Agent on Earth and in Heaven*. Boston: Brill, 2012.

———. *Restoring the Temple of Vision: Cabalistic Freemasonry and Stuart Culture*. Boston: Brill, 2002.

Shadwynn. *The Crafted Cup: Ritual Mysteries of the Goddess and the Grail*. St. Paul, MN: Llewellyn Publications, 1994.

Skeels, Dell. *The Romance of Perceval in Prose: A Translation of the E. Manuscript of the Didot Perceval Hardcover*. Seattle: University of Washington Press, 1961.

Smyers, Karen A. *The Fox and the Jewel: Shared and Private Meanings in Contemporary Japanese Inari Worship*. Honolulu: University of Hawai'i Press, 1999.

Snodgrass, A. M. *The Dark Age of Greece: An Archaeological Survey of the Eleventh to the Eighth Centuries BC*. Edinburgh: Edinburgh University Press, 1971.

Sonoda, Minoru. "Shinto and the Natural Environment." In *Shinto in History: Ways of the Kami*, edited by John Breen and Mark Teeuwen. Honolulu: University of Hawai'i Press, 2000.

Spence, Lewis. *The Mysteries of Britain: The Secret Rites and Traditions of Ancient Britain Restored*. North Hollywood, CA: Newcastle Publishing Company, 1993.

Stevenson, David. *The Origins of Freemasonry: Scotland's Century, 1590–1710*. Cambridge: Cambridge University Press, 1988.

Stewart, R. J., ed. *The Book of Merlin: Insights from the Merlin Conference*. London: Blandford Press, 1987.

Sullivan, William. *The Secret of the Incas: Myth, Astronomy, and the War Against Time*. New York: Crown, 1997.

Tolstoy, Nikolai. *The Quest for Merlin*. Boston: Little, Brown, 1985.

Turner, P. F. J. *The Real King Arthur: A History of Post-Roman Britannia*. Anchorage, AK: SKS Pub Co., 1993.

von Eschenbach, Wolfram. *Parzival: A Romance of the Middle Ages*. New York: Vintage Books, 1961.

Wagner, Richard. "The Wibelungen: World History as Told in Saga." In *Pilgrimage to Beethoven and Other Essays*, translated by William Ashton Ellis, Lincoln: Nebraska University Press, 1994.

Waite, Arthur Edward. *Inner and Outer Order Initiations of the Holy Order of the Golden Dawn*. Burnaby, BC: Ishtar Publishing, 2005.

———. *The Holy Grail: The Galahad Quest in the Arthurian Literature*. New Hyde Park, NY: University Books, 1961.

Weston, Jessie. *From Ritual to Romance*. Gloucester, MA: Peter Smith, 1983.

———. "Notes on the Grail Romances." *Romania* 43, no. 171 (1914): 403–26. https://www.jstor.org/stable/45044214.

———. *The Legend of Sir Perceval*. 2 vols. London: David Nutt, 1906.

———. *The Quest of the Holy Grail*. London: G. Bell & Sons, 1913.

———. "The Ruined Temple." *The Quest Magazine* (October 1916): 127–39.

Westra, Laura, and Thomas More Robinson. *The Greeks and the Environment* Lanham, MD: Rowman & Littlefield, 1997.

Wood, Michael. *In Search of the Trojan War*. New York: Facts on File, 1985.

Yates, Frances A. *The Rosicrucian Enlightenment*. London: Routledge & Kegan Paul, 1972.

Yeats, W. B. *A Vision and Related Writings*. Edited by A. Norman Jeffares. London: Arena, 1990.

INDEX

To Write to the Author

If you wish to contact the author or would like more information about this book, please write to the author in care of Llewellyn Worldwide Ltd. and we will forward your request. Both the author and publisher appreciate hearing from you and learning of your enjoyment of this book and how it has helped you. Llewellyn Worldwide Ltd. cannot guarantee that every letter written to the author can be answered, but all will be forwarded. Please write to:

John Michael Greer
⁒ Llewellyn Worldwide
2143 Wooddale Drive
Woodbury, MN 55125-2989
Please enclose a self-addressed stamped envelope for reply,
or $1.00 to cover costs. If outside the U.S.A., enclose
an international postal reply coupon.

Many of Llewellyn's authors have websites with additional
information and resources. For more information,
please visit our website at http://www.llewellyn.com.